WHAT YOU SHOULD KNOW ABOUT THE BIBLE

A Practical Guide to Bible Basics

By Stanford Herlick

Library Of Congress Catalog
Card Number 85-82137

ISBN 0-9616026-0-0

Published by FBF Publications
P.O. Box 3296 • San Bernardino, CA 92413
(714) 864-0865

Acknowledgements

To my wife, Carolyn, without whose devoted encouragement this book would not have been possible. She has dedicated many hours to proofreading and checking scriptural references back against the Bible.

To our daughter, Mary Catherine, and our daughter-in-law, Bonnie Trusler, for their commitment to typing many drafts and the final manuscript. To our good friend, Diane Kellingsworth, for her diligence in the preparation of maps and charts. And to longtime friend and associate, John Morthland, whose editorial and technical expertise has transformed a manuscript into a book.

73357

TABLE OF CONTENTS

MAPS

CHARTS

TOPICAL TABLE OF CONTENTS

Page

CHAPTER ONE

INTRODUCTION

One of the most frequent comments I hear when the subject of the Bible comes up is, "I'd sure like to get into the Bible, but every time I start reading, I get confused; so, I just put it back on the shelf." People have asked me why the books of the Bible are placed where they are, and an acquaintance wanted to know if the King James version was the original Bible. I believe that these are all valid comments or questions, for they indicate an interest in the all-time best seller of books and a willingness and desire to know more about it. It has been said that any question about the Bible is a good question, because a correct answer may remove a barrier to the asker's further consideration of the scripture. So, if you have questions about the Bible, you are not alone, and this book is intended for you.

The Bible, consisting of the Old and New Testaments, is without doubt the most influential book ever published. It has had a profound effect throughout the world as the foundation for personal and national freedom. The power behind the contents of this book is evidenced by the fact that it is feared by the leaders of dictatorial governments, and copies must be smuggled into their countries for the millions of people desiring access to a Bible. The reason for the attitude of oppressive governments is pointed up by what the famous journalist Horace Greeley said almost a century ago: "It is impossible to enslave mentally or socially a Bible-reading people. The principles of the Bible are the groundwork of human freedom."

The Bible has been translated into every major language, and the work of translating it into all languages is an ongoing process by Bible societies such as Wycliffe Translators and the American Bible Society. In the western free world, just about every household owns one or more Bibles. The World Book Encyclopedia reports that millions of copies are sold each year and that the Bible or portions of it may be found in every part of the world. Widespread distribution of the Bible was made possible by the invention of the movable-type printing press in 1440. The inventor Gutenberg printed many Bibles which are collectors' items today. Since then, millions of copies have been printed. The American Bible Society has distributed about a billion copies in the last hundred years and has printed over 15 million copies of the "Good News" version. Many other organizations also distribute copies of the Bible, including the Gideon Society, Brother Andrew (communist countries), and Chaplain Ray (prisons). A large variety of books on biblical subjects is also available.

WHAT YOU SHOULD KNOW ABOUT THE BIBLE stems from outlines and other material which I have put together for lectures and class studies about the foundational facts, history, and basic principles of the Bible. It has been my experience that many people are interested in this type of information, even people who do not profess any religion. Many study the Bible because of its importance as the most carefully preserved of ancient literature and its unique role in human history and thought. An interesting sidelight to the presentation of basic information included in this book has been the number of people who have said that it has renewed their interest in reading and studying the Bible.

Basic Primer. This book is not intended as a Bible handbook or other type of commentary based upon a verse-by-verse format; nor is it intended as a theological or doctrinal treatise about interpretation. This book has one purpose — to supply information about the Bible, its makeup, its expressed principles, and its history. It is hoped that as a "basic primer" it will serve as a "launching pad" for the reader's more comprehensive study utilizing the Bible and other in-depth study materials. The approach here is strictly non-denominational and non-doctrinal.

The Need for an Overview. There are those who say that it is difficult to read the Bible because of contradictions and inconsistencies. However, if one has a grasp of the main principles and lines of thought which run through both the Old and New Testaments, he or she will be able to see that it is just the reverse. The Bible has withstood the test of time and criticism because of its continuity and consistency. Therefore, the format of this effort is designed to present an overview of these aspects of the Bible. It is also designed to convey a maximum amount of information in as few words as possible so that the reader may read it rapidly and gain a comprehension of the biblical "big picture." In Chapter Two we discuss the makeup of the Bible, the categories of books, the history of their writing and translation. Chapter Three reviews basic lines of thought in the Old Testament as a preparation for reading Chapter Four which is a brief synopsis of the historical and prophetic books and Chapter Five discussing the wisdom and poetry books. Chapter Six deals with the historical developments during the 400 so-called "silent years" between the Old and New Testaments which aid our consideration of some aspects of the New Testament. Chapter Seven covers the main principles found in the New Testament as a base for reading Chapter Eight, a synopsis-digest of the four Gospels; Chapter Nine, a review of the book of Acts; and Chapter Ten reviewing the Epistles and book of Revelation.

Basic Considerations. The Bible is a library of books about God and the relationship between him and his human family on the planet Earth. The Bible reveals God as the all-powerful, all-knowing creator and sustainer of all things; that every man, woman, and child is made in God's image and likeness. It outlines God's covenants and promises which set out the principle of mankind's freedom of choice. In the Bible one finds passages dealing realistically with the conflict between good and evil including that which is in each individual. A general truism is found to the effect that the spirit is willing but the flesh is weak. God promises that he will visit his people in the flesh through a virgin woman in order to reconcile all people to himself, to abolish sin through his own son's death, and return in the spirit to dwell within his children. The Bible sets out principles and guidelines for human conduct and people's interaction with each other. These principles are calculated to assure an anxiety-free life on earth and in the hereafter in harmony and right-standing with God. These revelations are set out in the Bible in 66 books of varying types and lengths written over a time span of about 1500 years. One of the most helpful of basic facts assisting the Bible reader to realize how the biblical message is presented is that the books of the Bible are grouped in categories in both the Old and New Testaments. Therefore, the starting point for "getting a handle" on the Bible is knowing these categories and how they relate to each other. This is not too difficult when one sees the purpose of the groupings and how the Bible developed over the centuries. (See Chapter TWO.)

What the Bible Is According to the Bible. One cannot read the Bible without soon discovering that it claims to be the word of God. God speaks. He speaks out directly; he speaks through angels; he speaks through prophets. God directs Moses to write his words, and he directs the prophets to be his spokesmen. His words are spoken by Jesus Christ of Nazareth and recorded by the gospel writers. The epistle writers convey God's messages of instruction and encouragement. The apostle Peter sums up the Bible's view of itself when he says, "[F]or the prophecy came not at any time by the will of man, but holy men of God spoke as they were moved by the Holy Spirit."(2 Peter, Chapter 1, verse 21)

The apostle Paul in writing to his aide, Timothy, defines the nature and purpose of scripture in these words: "[F]rom childhood you have known the sacred writings which are able to give you the wisdom that leads to salvation through faith which is in Christ Jesus. All scripture is inspired by God and profitable for teaching, for reproof, for correction, for training in righteousness."(2 Timothy, Chapter 3, verses 15 and 16)

In the four Gospels of the New Testament, Jesus verifies the validity of the Old Testament, including the principles, covenants, and prophecies which it sets forth.(Matthew, Chapter 5, verses 17-20; Chapter 7, verse 12)   He says that what he does and says is by authority and will of our heavenly Father; that he is the Messiah whom the prophet Moses wrote about.(John, Chapter 5, verses 19-47)   He also makes it clear that his gospel message will be preserved; that it will be preached to the whole world.(Matthew, Chapter 24, verses 14, 35)   Jesus gives the apostles authority to carry on in his name and to take his message to the people.(Matthew, Chapter 28, verse 19)   He tells them that the Holy Spirit will bring to their remembrance everything which he has told them.(John, Chapter 14, verse 26)   The apostle Paul lets it be known that he did not receive the good news of peace and grace (which he explains in 14 epistles) through any man but through a revelation from Jesus Christ.(Galatians, Chapter 1, verses 3, 12)   Thus it is that every part of the Bible attests to its own origin as the word of God.

Why Should We Read the Bible? Why are you interested in reading the Bible? Whatever reason you may have for reading it is a good reason. What a person receives from the Bible quite often is governed by the point of view, the problem, or the question motivating the reader at the time. For example, are you a believer or a nonbeliever? Are you interested in it because it is ancient literature? Are you merely curious about what it says? Do you believe that the Bible is the word of God, or do you regard it merely as the ideas of men? Regardless of the particular circumstance causing you to read the Bible, you will feel its challenge, for one must come to grips with what it claims for itself and the fact that it demands a response. You may respond by acceptance or rejection, but you will form some kind of response to the views and principles which it sets forth. Perhaps the biggest challenge to our minds is that the Bible speaks in the spiritual realm, and we are not always ready to "shift gears" and leave our materialistic frame of reference to contemplate the idea that we are spiritual beings with a future in a totally spiritual setting.

Spirituality. Our English word "spirit" comes from the Latin word **spiritus** which means "wind" or "breath." In the Greek language, the word is **pneuma** and in Hebrew, **ruah.** The World Book Dictionary says that "spirit" refers to that aspect of every human which is not material. It is equated with "soul" or "personality." Webster's Dictionary defines "spirit" as "the breath of life" or "life-giving force," connecting it with mind and emotions. These definitions show a universal awareness of our spiritual nature which, I venture to say, we recognize or suspect whether or not we deem ourselves to be very "spiritual." A starting point for gaining a sharper conception of our nonmaterial makeup is to reflect upon the variety of well-known human characteristics. Consider, for example, such attributes as personality, thought, ideas, reason, belief, intellect, emotion, and intuition; also, love, hate, wisdom, character, right and wrong, anxiety, humility, pride, compassion, peace, joy, and happiness. None of these elements is physical; yet each one is very real. There are, of course, many more than these, and it might be both interesting and revealing if you would make a list of those qualities, attributes, and capabilities which apply to you. Others you might also consider are talent, creativity, language, insight, and mystique. These aspects of our being are invisible, but we know that they exist, and we have words in our language describing them. They give us clues to understanding our personal identities which are not confined to the limits of a three-dimensional world. If these attributes are in another dimension, that is, a nonphysical, perhaps fourth, dimension, is not our real identity in the same dimension, which we may refer to as the spiritual dimension? Every civilization has had a concept of this realm as evidenced by a belief that a person lives on after the demise of the physical body. The person in this continuum is referred to as a "spirit" or "soul." One is no less spirit while in this earthly plane while experiencing the mysterious coalescence of spirit and body. Someone has said that a human is spirit, has a soul, and lives in a body. A realization of this status, whether consciously or subconsciously, moves mankind to seek a supreme being who has power and authority over the universe and who through his love and concern communicates with and helps his people.

The Search. The search for the meaning of life and the reasons for existence is continual. The questions, "Who am I" and "Why was I born," send millions of people to the psychiatrist's couch. In psychiatry, the individual in a motivational sense is said to be the instinctive "id" which is directed by the "ego" with ultimate control in the "super-ego." The theory is that conflicts between these personal entities cause fear and anxiety or neurosis. Another word used in medical parlance to describe the non-material human aspects is "psychē" which generally is defined as (1) the human soul or spirit; or, (2) the mind. Whatever name is used, there is universal recognition of an existence or identity beyond that which we perceive only with our bodily senses, beyond that which science is able to deal with on an experimental basis. Human inner conflict is the greatest human problem, epitomizing the struggle between good and evil which we see not only on an individual basis but also on a worldwide scale. As an eminent psychiatrist put it not long ago in a television interview, "The greatest problem confronting our profession is the mystery of the element of violence in mankind."

Biblical Answers. The Bible addresses itself to all these questions and claims to have the answers. That people readily seek these answers from the Bible is pointed up by the continual worldwide demand for it. The reason for this demand for the Bible over other writings, philosophic or religious, may be illustrated by a composite of what several people have expressed to me: "Before studying the Bible, I searched for spiritual truth in books on philosophy and various religions. I found that some had more questions than answers, and none of them was able to give or claimed to give the whole picture except the Bible. The Bible has more answers than questions and presents the truths of life and my relationship with God in terms which I can understand." As pointed out in many secular encyclopedias, it is a historical fact that since its completion in the first century A.D. the Bible has been the premier influence on society and culture. Our ideas of freedom, personal worth, individual rights, and social justice, along with the impetus to put these ideas into democratic action, stem from the teachings found in both the Old and New Testaments.

Today there seems to be a growing acceptance of the concept of a supreme God who created and sustains all things. Many in the scientific community postulate God's existence through both logic and belief, much as the philosophers, Plato and Aristotle, did centuries ago. They reasoned that given a universe which has obviously been created, there must be a creator, a prime mover. Plato referred to the creator as the "demiurge." Aristotle used the term, "uncaused cause." In more recent times, Einstein and the renowned mathematician, Godel, shared the same view, using such terms as "God" or "The God," "The One," "The Mind," "The Absolute." (See "Science '82," October, p. 60.) The Bible attests to the fact of creation of the universe, including Earth, mankind, and all other living things by an omnipotent and caring God. It is only logical that having created human beings in his own image and likeness that he would want to communicate with them. The Bible reveals the many ways in which God has accomplished his communications with us. The Bible has withstood the test of time and trial. It continues to be the one reliable source of truth, strength, and consolation. One has only to hear the testimonies of those who have studied and meditated upon its message to realize the effect, often miraculous, which it can have in people's lives.

So in the interest of understanding how the Bible reveals these truths and gives the answers, let's move on to a consideration of what the Bible is and what it tells us.

CHAPTER TWO

BOOKS OF THE BIBLE AND THEIR AUTHORS

General Makeup of the Bible. The Bible is not just a book. It is actually a library of 66 books which were written during a total time span of about 1500 years by 40 human writers who, the Bible attests, were inspired by God to do so. The word "bible" comes from a Greek word meaning "book." In the early Christian period, scripture was referred to as "the book," thus, "Bible." All of the human writers were Hebrews, including those who wrote the New Testament. The Bible has two basic divisions: the Old Testament (39 books) and the New Testament (27 books). The Old Testament was written during the period from about 1450 B.C. to about 425 B.C. The original text of the Old Testament was written in the Hebrew language except for a few passages in Aramaic. In about 250 B.C., Jewish people in North Africa desired a version of the scripture in the Greek language, and 72 Jewish scholars produced the Septuagint (referring to the 72 scholars). The Septuagint is sometimes referred to by the Roman numeral for 70, namely, LXX. Both the Hebrew and Greek versions of the Old Testament were available during the time of Christ and the early Christian period. The New Testament books were written between about A.D. 47 and 95. New Testament writers wrote in **koinē** Greek, that is, the everyday form of Greek which was the common commercial language in the ancient Near East at the time. Chart A shows a time-line representation of the periods of scripture writing. It also shows the "silent period" between the testaments which extended from about 425 B.C. to the birth of Christ and which is also called the intertestamental period.

The Apocrypha. There is a group of books which were written between about 200 B.C. and the time of Christ's birth. These are important from a historical point of view but are not considered as inspired writings and thus are not included in most Protestant versions of the Bible. The Roman Catholic Church does consider most of them to be scripture and includes these in its version of the Bible. These intertestamental (between the testaments) writings are called "Apocrypha," a word which means roughly things which are "hidden" or "outside." These books were not included in the Hebrew text, but some of them were included in the Septuagint, i.e., the early translation of the Old Testament into

Chart A
PERIODS OF WRITING SCRIPTURE

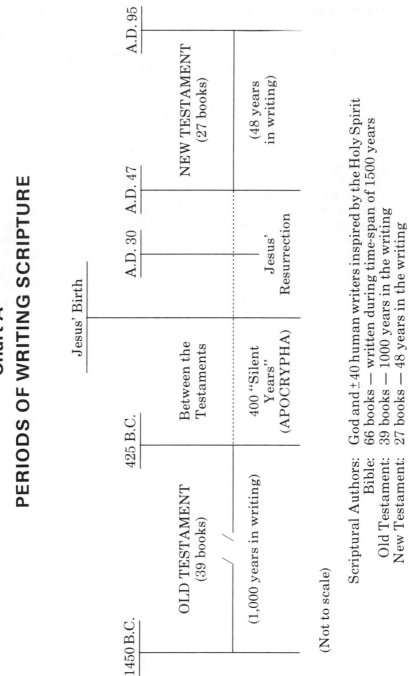

1450 B.C.

OLD TESTAMENT
(39 books)

(1,000 years in writing)

425 B.C.

Between the
Testaments

400 "Silent
Years"
(APOCRYPHA)

Jesus' Birth

A.D. 30

Jesus'
Resurrection

A.D. 47

A.D. 95

NEW TESTAMENT
(27 books)

(48 years
in writing)

(Not to scale)

Scriptural Authors: God and ±40 human writers inspired by the Holy Spirit
            Bible: 66 books — written during time-span of 1500 years
   Old Testament: 39 books — 1000 years in the writing
   New Testament: 27 books — 48 years in the writing

the Greek language. There is also a group of writings known as
New Testament Apocrypha which did not attain the same stature
as the Old Testament Apocrypha and were never seriously
considered by the early Christians. Books on the Apocrypha are
available in bookstores. (See Chapter SIX for an outline of OT
Apocrypha.)

Chapters and Verses. Numbered chapters and verses were
not a part of the Bible until the 16th century A.D. While some
work on a numbering system had been begun earlier by both
Jewish and Christian theologians, a printer in Paris named
Robert Stephens published the first version with chapter and
verse numbers in the 1550's. The first English Bible having these
divisions was the Geneva Bible published in 1580. This system is
helpful in referring to verses of scripture. In writing such
references, a type of shorthand has been developed utilizing
abbreviations for book names, along with the chapter and verse
numbers. For instance, Genesis, chapter 1, would be "Gen. 1."
Two or more chapters will be shown in this way: "Gen. 37 - 50."
Verses within a chapter are shown by the chapter number
followed by a colon and the verse number or numbers. Thus,
Genesis, chapter 1, verse 1, is written "Gen. 1:1," Genesis, chapter
2, verses 5 through 7, becomes "Gen. 2:5-7."

Other examples:

    Isa. 1 = Isaiah, chapter 1

    Ex. 12 - 20 = Exodus, chapters 12 through 20

    Jer. 31:31 = Jeremiah, chapter 31, verse 31

    Matt. 28:16-20 = Matthew, chapter 28, verses 16 through 20

    Acts 16:3 - 20:4 = Acts, chapter 16, verse 3 through chapter 20,
                verse 4

The Old Testament. The 39 books of the Old Testament are
grouped according to three main categories: (1) history; (2)
wisdom and poetry; (3) books of the writing prophets. The first 17
books, Genesis through Esther, are history books. The first five of
these — Genesis, Exodus, Leviticus, Numbers, and Deuteronomy
— are called the Torah (meaning "The Law" in Hebrew) and are
also referred to as the Pentateuch (meaning "five books" in
Greek). In the second category are five books of wisdom and
poetry, Job through Song of Solomon. In the third category are 17
books of the writing prophets, Isaiah through Malachi. His-
torically, the wisdom and poetry books and the prophecy books
were written within the same overall time frame as the history
books. Also, the 17 prophecy books were written during the last
400 years of the history depicted in the history books. The

categories are by their major thrust; that is, the historical books are chiefly history, and the prophecy books are mainly prophecy. However, there are prophecy and poetry in the history books and historical significance in the other books. Chart B lists the Old Testament books in the order in which they appear in the Bible, along with the approximate dates of their writing. Lines have been drawn under Esther and Song of Solomon in order to show the three main categories. You may designate these categories in the Old Testament table of contents in your own Bible by drawing in these lines.

Chart B
OLD TESTAMENT BOOKS

Book	Abbr.	Human Writer	Approx. Date (B.C.)	Book	Abbr.	Human Writer	Approx. Date (B.C.)
[1.] HISTORY (17 Books)				[3.] PROPHECY (17 Books)			
Genesis	Gen.	Moses	(1450	Isaiah	Isa.	Isaiah	700
Exodus	Ex.	Moses	(	Jeremiah	Jer.	Jeremiah	586
Leviticus	Lev.	Moses	(to	Lamentations	Lam.	Jeremiah	586
Numbers	Nu.	Moses	(	Ezekiel	Ezek.	Ezekiel	570
Deuteronomy	Dt.	Moses	(1410	Daniel	Dan.	Daniel	530
Joshua	Josh.	Joshua	1390	Hosea	Hos.	Hosea	725
Judges	Judg.	Unknown	1050	Joel	Joel	Joel	600
Ruth	Ruth	Unknown	1000	Amos	Amos	Amos	750
1 Samuel	1 Sam.	Samuel	1000	Obadiah	Obad.	Obadiah	587
2 Samuel	2 Sam.	Unknown	950	Jonah	Jonah	Jonah	745
1 Kings	1 Ki.	Unknown	550	Micah	Micah	Micah	700
2 Kings	2 Ki.	Unknown	550	Nahum	Nah.	Nahum	612
1 Chronicles	1 Chron.	Ezra	450	Habakkuk	Hab.	Habakkuk	612
2 Chronicles	2 Chron.	Ezra	450	Zephaniah	Zeph.	Zephaniah	626
Ezra	Ezra	Ezra	450	Haggai	Hag.	Haggai	520
Nehemiah	Neh.	Nehemiah	425	Zechariah	Zech.	Zechariah	520
Esther	Esther	Unknown	425	Malachi	Mal.	Malachi	425
[2.] WISDOM & POETRY (5 Books)				*One Psalm was written by			
Job	Job	Unknown	900	Moses c. 1450-1410 B.C. (Ps. 90)			
Psalms*	Ps.	David & Others	Davidic 1000 Others 1000 - 500				
Proverbs	Prov.	Solomon & Others	950 - 500				
Ecclesiastes	Eccl.	Solomon	950				
Song of Solomon	S of S	Solomon	950				

Next, Chart C, a time-line chart, sets out the books of the Old Testament according to approximate dates of writing in each of the three main categories. One sees that all of the Old Testament books were written during the same 1,000-year period; that from about 1450 B.C. to about 425 B.C. books in all categories were being written. For example, while scribes were writing historical books, others including David and Solomon were writing Psalms and Proverbs. While Kings, Chronicles, Ezra, and Nehemiah were being prepared, the writing prophets were penning their messages. The date 425 B.C. denotes the writing of the final three books, Nehemiah, Esther, and Malachi.

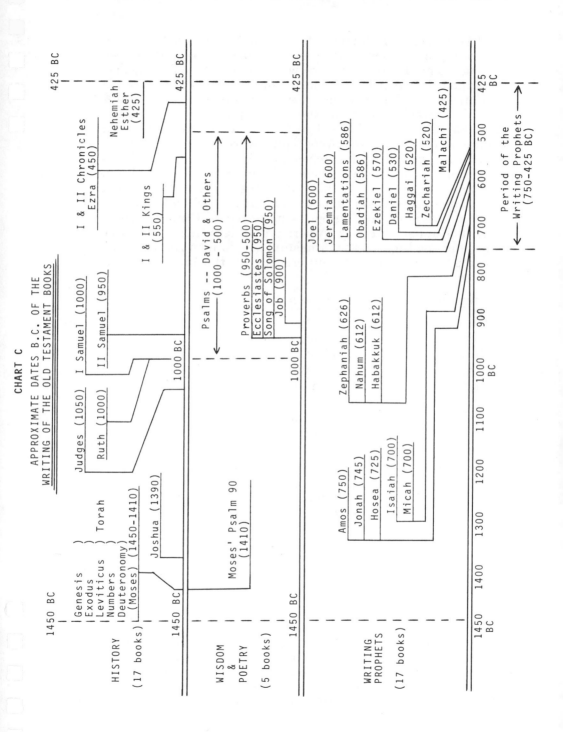

CHART C

APPROXIMATE DATES B.C. OF THE
WRITING OF THE OLD TESTAMENT BOOKS

1450 BC   425 BC

HISTORY
(17 books)

Genesis   )
Exodus   )
Leviticus) Torah
Numbers   )
Deuteronomy)
(Moses) (1450-1410)

Joshua (1390)

Judges (1050)   I Samuel (1000)

Ruth (1000)   II Samuel (950)

I & II Kings (550)

I & II Chronicles
Ezra (450)

Nehemiah
Esther (425)

1450 BC   1000 BC   425 BC

WISDOM
&
POETRY
(5 books)

Moses' Psalm 90 (1410)

Psalms -- David & Others (1000 - 500)

Proverbs (950-500)
Ecclesiastes (950)
Song of Solomon (950)
Job (900)

1450 BC   1000 BC   425 BC

WRITING
PROPHETS
(17 books)

Amos (750)
Jonah (745)
Hosea (725)
Isaiah (700)
Micah (700)

Zephaniah (626)
Nahum (612)
Habakkuk (612)

Joel (600)
Jeremiah (600)
Lamentations (586)
Obadiah (586)
Ezekiel (570)
Daniel (530)
Haggai (520)
Zechariah (520)
Malachi (425)

Period of the
Writing Prophets
(750-425 BC)

1450
BC   1400   1300   1200   1100   1000   900   800   700   600   500   425
                                          BC   BC

13

Old Testament in Catholic Bible. The early Christians used the Septuagint version extensively, because it was in the Greek language. The Jewish scholars who did the translating also rearranged the order of the books from the traditional Jewish groupings of the Law (Torah), the Prophets, and the Writings. They also attached some of the Apocrypha. Thus, when the Christian Bible was finalized in the early centuries, the Old Testament order and the Apocrypha were adopted from the Septuagint. The Latin Vulgate version of A.D. 400 followed this same format as did the later Douay-Rheims English translation. The book names were also taken from the Septuagint. Some of these names are different or have spellings different from the Protestant versions in English. A more recent Catholic translation in English, the New American Bible, utilizes the same names and spellings as the Protestant versions in English. The following chart shows the differences in the older Catholic versions:

Protestant	Catholic
1 Samuel	1 Kings
2 Samuel	2 Kings
1 Kings	3 Kings
2 Kings	4 Kings
1 Chronicles	1 Paralipomenon*
2 Chronicles	2 Paralipomenon*
Ezra	1 Esdras
Nehemiah	2 Esdras
Song of Solomon (Song of Songs)	Canticle of Canticles**
Hosea	Osee
Obadiah	Abdias
Zephaniah	Sophanias
Haggai	Aggeus

*means "things omitted" — here from the books of Kings, thus supplementary to Kings
**"canticle" means "song"

New Testament Books. Our next chart shows the 27 books of the New Testament, human writers, and approximate dates of writing. By the year A.D. 100 or about 70 years after Jesus' death, resurrection, and ascension, the New Testament was complete. It is apparent that the New Testament books are also arranged according to categories. The first category is comprised of the four

Chart D
NEW TESTAMENT BOOKS

Book (Abbr.)	Writer	Approx. Date	Book (Abbr.)	Writer	Approx. Date
Gospels:					
Matthew (Matt.)	Matthew	A.D. 60	1 Timothy (1 Tim.)	Paul	A.D. 62
Mark (Mk.)	Mark	A.D. 55	2 Timothy (2 Tim.)	Paul	A.D. 63
Luke (Lk.)	Luke	A.D. 60	Titus (Tit.)	Paul	A.D. 62
John (Jn.)	John	A.D. 85	Philemon (Philem.)	Paul	A.D. 60
History:			Hebrews (Heb.)	Paul	A.D. 60
Acts	Luke	A.D. 64			
Paul's Epistles:			**General Epistles:**		
Romans (Rom.)	Paul	A.D. 55	James (Jas.)	James	A.D. 47
1 Corinthians (1 Cor.)	Paul	A.D. 54	1 Peter (1 Pet.)	Peter	A.D. 63
2 Corinthians (2 Cor.)	Paul	A.D. 55	2 Peter (2 Pet.)	Peter	A.D. 64
Galatians (Gal.)	Paul	A.D. 49	1 John (1 Jn.)	John	A.D. 85
Ephesians (Eph.)	Paul	A.D. 60	2 John (2 Jn.)	John	A.D. 85
Philippians (Phil.)	Paul	A.D. 61	3 John (3 Jn.)	John	A.D. 85
Colossians (Col.)	Paul	A.D. 60	Jude	Jude	A.D. 65
1 Thessalonians (1 Thess.)	Paul	A.D. 50	**Apocalypse:** Revelation (Rev.)	John	A.D. 95
2 Thessalonians (2 Thess.)	Paul	A.D. 50			

Gospels. The Gospels tell of the birth, life, ministry, and death of Jesus Christ. In them one finds the discourses or teachings of Jesus, as well as narrative, that is, the happenings, miracles, and healings. Acts, the fifth book of the New Testament, is a history of the first century Christians. It describes the action of the apostles and other disciples from the time of the ascension of Christ to about A.D. 64. Acts is followed by 21 Epistles, letters written to Christians by the apostles Paul, Peter, and John, and two important letters written by Jesus' half-brothers, James and Jude. Paul wrote 14, Peter, two, and John, three. Scholars disagree as to who wrote the Letter to the Hebrews. Early tradition ascribes it to Paul. Chapter 13 in style and content suggests Paul. Therefore, in this effort, we show the writer of Hebrews as Paul. The final book of the New Testament is Revelation written by the apostle John relating his vision on the isle of Patmos. For the most part, with the notable exception of John's books, the New Testament books were written during the period covered by the book of Acts. The names for these books are the same in the Protestant and Catholic versions.

Preservation of Scripture. In Romans 3:1-2, Paul says that the chief advantage or profit which the Jewish people have had is having been entrusted with the "oracles" (words) of God. The Israelites always had a "loyal remnant" who watched over and made copies of the Old Testament books. Likewise, the Christians have been guardians of both Old and New Testament documents. In times of persecution the originals were lost so that we are indebted to the scribes who so carefully made and maintained copies of the various books. Jewish scribes developed a system of copying to assure accuracy which the later Christian copyists were able to use. The oldest copies of the Old Testament in Hebrew are the Dead Sea Scrolls found in 1947. They date from about 200-100 B.C. The oldest document of the New Testament is the Rylands Fragment, a part of a copy of John's Gospel, dated at A.D. 135. There are about 5,000 copies of the New Testament or parts of it written in Greek dating from about A.D. 200 to 1100. In addition there are the writings of the early "Church Fathers" discussing the New Testament books. These writings date from about A.D. 95 to 500. Ancient Bible documents are kept in various libraries throughout the world, including the Vatican Library in Rome. The Dead Sea Scrolls are in the Shrine of the Book in Jerusalem, where scholars continue to study them.

Translations of the Bible. As mentioned before, the Old Testament was translated from Hebrew to Greek in about 250 B.C., resulting in the Septuagint version. During the early

centuries of the Christian church, the scriptures continued to be
in the Greek language. In about A.D. 150 there were also the Old
Latin and Syriac versions. In A.D. 400 a western scholar, Jerome,
produced a translation in the Latin of the marketplace, and for
this reason it has been called the Vulgate. Jerome established his
headquarters for research in Jerusalem so that he could learn
Hebrew and thus translate the Old Testament from its original
language. The Vulgate became the official Bible of the western or
Roman Catholic church. In more modern times the Bible has been
translated into all the major languages and numerous other
languages. It was translated into French and Italian in the 12th
and 13th centuries. Shortly thereafter versions in German and
English began to appear. Luther translated the Bible into
German in 1534. Versions of note in the English language are the
following:

   Wycliffe's Bible, 1382
   Tyndale's Bible, 1525
   Coverdale's Bible, 1535
   Matthew Bible, 1537
   Great English Bible, 1540
   Geneva English Bible, 1560
   Bishops' Bible, 1568
   Catholic, Douay-Rheims English Bible, 1609
   King James (Authorized) Version, 1611
   Catholic, Confraternity English Bible, 1952

Among other versions available today in English are:
   Scofield Reference Bible, 1969 (KJV)
   New American Standard Bible, 1972 (NASB)
   Jerusalem Bible (Catholic)
   The Chain Bible (KJV Study Bible)
   The Phillips Bible
   Good News Bible
   The New American Bible (Catholic)
   New English Bible (NEB)
   New International Version (NIV)
   Revised Standard Version (RSV)
   The Amplified Bible (Ampl.)
   The Living Bible
   The New King James Version
   The Open Bible (Study Bible in either KJV or NASB versions)

A question frequently asked is, "What is the best version to
read?" A reply often given is, "The one you are reading now." I
would say that all of the English translations available are good.
I use mainly the Open Bible versions of the King James and the

New American Standard because of the headnotes and study materials included. For double-checking word meanings, I have found the **Interlinear Greek-English New Testament** by George Berry to very helpful.

Dates, History, and Archeology. The Bible does not give calendar dates for the events described. Occurrences are set out in relation to reigns of kings or to the times of certain people or to particular places and events, such as religious feasts. We correlate these events to our modern, western calendar-dating by virtue of information available from nonbiblical, historical, and archeological sources. Given the dates of certain events, we can establish dates for the same or contemporaneous events described in the Bible. Various time periods in the Bible can then give us approximate dates for other biblical activities.

Old Testament Dating. There are many examples of correlation between historical events from secular sources and biblical accounts. For example, the Bible states that the Egyptian pharaoh Shishak attacked Jerusalem during the reign of Solomon's son, Rehoboam.(1 Ki. 14:25-28; 2 Chron. 12:2-12) Archeologists have discovered Shishak's own account of this campaign, dating it at about 910 B.C. Ancient Assyrian records refer to Israel as the "House of Omri" (a king of the northern kingdom), and these records also list other kings of Israel, namely, Ahab and Jehu. These records are assigned to a period between 869 and 815 B.C.(1 Ki. 16:21-34; 2 Ki. 10:30) One Assyrian obelisk dated at 841 B.C. shows Jehu bowing before Shalmaneser III and bearing tribute of silver and gold. The Bible tells of the military campaigns of the Assyrian kings — Tiglath-Pileser, Shalmaneser V, Sargon, and Sennacherib — and how they eventually conquered Israel and forced the Judean king, Hezekiah, to pay tribute.(2 Ki. 16 - 18; Isa. 20:1)   The annals of these Assyrian kings show how they controlled Israel from about 743 B.C., placed Hoshea on the Israeli throne, then completely destroyed the kingdom in 722/721 B.C. Sennacherib recorded how he had Hezekiah in a cage like a bird in about 686 B.C. Babylonian records describe the fall of Jerusalem and Judah to Nebuchadnezzar in 587/586 B.C.(2 Ki. 24 - 25; 2 Chron. 32 - 36) The dates of the reigns of Persian kings — Cyrus, Darius, Xerxes, and Artaxerxes mentioned in Isaiah, 2 Chronicles, Daniel, Ezra, Nehemiah, and Esther — are well-known in secular history, i.e., 539-423 B.C. Working back from this information according to the passage of time indicated by the Bible, the departure of Abraham and Sarah from Ur of the Chaldees (Gen. 11:31) computes to about 2100 B.C. The unearthing of this ancient city by archeologists has revealed its establishment in about 3000 B.C. The crossing of the Red Sea by Moses and the children of Israel works out to about 1450 B.C.

New Testament Dating. As to the New Testament, dates are known from nonbiblical sources for the reigns of Herod I (Lk. 1:5; Matt. 2:1; 37-4 B.C.), Augustus Caesar (Lk. 2:1; 30 B.C. - A.D. 14), Tiberius (Lk. 3:1; A.D. 14-37), and Claudius.(Acts 11:28, 18:2; A.D. 41-54) Other known dates include those for the Roman procurators of Judea, specifically, Pontius Pilate (Matt. 27:2; A.D. 26-36), Felix (Acts 23 - 24; A.D. 52-59), and Porcius Festus.(Acts 25 - 26; A.D. 59-62) The death of Herod Agrippa I described in Acts 12 is known to have occurred in A.D. 44.

The foregoing are but a few of the historical and archeological facts giving an insight to the time of the biblical accounts. For those interested in more information on this subject and corroborative nonbiblical discoveries, let me suggest further reading in **The Bible and Archeology** by J. A. Thompson; **A Survey of Israel's History** by Leon Wood; **New Testament History** by F. F. Bruce.

The Calendar Problem. The Julian calendar was used throughout the Roman empire from 46 B.C. to about A.D. 500 when Pope Gregory decided that time should be counted from the date of Christ's birth. He set a monk named Dionysius Exiguus to work on this project. Dionysius came up with a very accurate calendar, called the Gregorian calendar, which is the one used today in western countries. But there is one problem. Dionysius miscalculated the year of Jesus' birth by six years due to a miscounting of the date from the Julian calendar. Thus, by the Gregorian calendar, Jesus was born in about 6 B.C. during the reign of Herod I who died in 4 B.C.

Human Writers of the Bible. Since our approach here is to outline what the Bible says, we are interested in what it says about authorship. For example, the Bible says that Moses wrote his book and turned it over to the priests and Levites.(Dt. 31:24-26) Joshua wrote his book.(Josh. 24:26) Isaiah says that he was commissioned by God to prophesy to the people.(Isa. 6:1-13) In the New Testament the epistle writers identify themselves. Where a book does not state who the writer was, early Hebrew and Christian traditions often supply names.

Certifying the Bible. One question people often ask is, "Who certifies these particular 66 books as being the Bible?" Some ask whether the King James version is the "real" or "official" Bible against which others are to be compared. We have seen how the

Bible was written over a long period of time in Hebrew and Greek. Unfortunately, the originals of these books are not available, and we must rely upon copies. The Hebrew text called the Masoretic text (for the Jewish scholars known as Masoretes) is considered the most accurate and is the one used by translators of modern English versions of the Old Testament. For comparison there is also the Septuagint and Jerome's Latin translation of about A.D. 400. The Dead Sea Scrolls provide another source, and while the work of cataloging and studying them is still in progress, thus far, they confirm the accuracy of the Masoretic text. The New Testament contains references to or quotations from most of the Old Testament books. Jesus and the apostles attested to their validity. The 27 books of the New Testament are the ones accepted by the early Christians as inspired scripture. Important in the determination of these books are the writings of the previously mentioned early "Church Fathers" from about A.D. 95 to A.D. 500 discussing the 27 books. In A.D. 393 to 397, at the Councils of Hippo and Carthage, church leaders declared these books to be the only canonical books of the New Testament. In the 1500's the reformers — Luther, Calvin, and others — discussed the relative merits of some of the books, but their translations included them all. Early English translations included the same 66 books of the Bible, and as noted before, the apocryphal books were set out separately. In 1603 James I became King of England. He desired that there be a translation of the Bible in contemporary English for use by the Church of England and by the people, to be published without the doctrinal marginal notes which some of the previous translations featured. Fifty-four Bible scholars skilled in the ancient languages were appointed to complete the work. (Attrition reduced their number to 47.) The commission worked by committees utilizing Hebrew texts (including the Masoretic) and Greek texts, along with the previous English versions. In 1609, while the commission was still at work, the Catholic Douay-Rheims English translation was completed. The King James commission finished its work in 1611 with the publication of the "Authorized Version" which in the United States is called the "King James Version" or KJV. Between 1611 and the present, additional ancient New Testament manuscripts in Greek have come to light, and scholars translating for more modern versions have had the benefit of these later discoveries. A comparison with the KJV shows that it is remarkably accurate. It can be, and has been in certain editions, updated merely by using modern words for some 17th century words which have become archaic. Today the KJV is still the most popular of the many English translations available. One reason for this is its unique, beautiful, and impressive form and style.

Canonicity of the Bible. Determination of those books comprising the Bible, that is, considered to be holy scripture, comes under the heading of "canonicity." You may have already encountered this word along with the words "canon" and "canonical." The word "canon" means a standard, a measure, or criterion for use as a guide or comparison. This word comes from a Greek word meaning "reed" or "rod," as a measuring rod. The books of the Bible are considered canonical as measuring up to certain tests or criteria. These criteria as reported by Bible scholars and church theologians are:

Old Testament
1. Attestation as holy scripture by Jesus Christ and apostles.
2. Consistency of message regarding God's redemptive plan for mankind and God's attributes.
3. Statements regarding appointment of human writers as God's spokesmen.
4. Israelite and Jewish history and tradition.
5. Determination and preservation of scripture by Israelite and Jewish leaders, as well as by the Christian church.
6. The writings of rabbis, other Jewish scholars, the early "Church Fathers" and other Christian scholars.
7. Corroboration by the Apocrypha.
8. Historical and archeological corroboration.

New Testament
1. Authorship by an apostle or by one intimately associated with an apostle.
2. Consistency of the sermons in the book of Acts and the messages in the Epistles and Revelation with the teachings of Jesus Christ in the Gospels.
3. The nature of the principles contained in the NT message.
4. Acceptance, use, and preservation by early Christians; writings of the early "Church Fathers" and writings of Christian scholars.
5. Consistency with and use of OT by Jesus and NT writers.
6. Corroboration by early Christian era apocryphal writings.
7. Church decrees of Council of Hippo and Council of Carthage (A.D. 393-397).
8. Continuous acceptance by Christians to the present time.
9. Historical and archeological corroboration.

Of course, there is a sense in which each Bible reader resolves the question of canonicity for himself or herself. This involves the reader's faith and belief in the Bible as God's word and how it speaks to him or her.

Inspiration of the Bible. This term refers to the Bible's claim to be the inspired word of God. Key passages are 2 Tim. 3:15-16; 2 Pet. 1:21 and the others discussed previously in Chapter ONE. We should also mention John 17:17 in which Jesus praying to the Father says, "Sanctify them through your truth; your word is truth." The principle of the inspiration of the Bible is that the human writers of its books recorded God's word as moved by him through his Holy Spirit.(2 Pet. 1:21)

CHAPTER THREE

INTRODUCTION TO THE OLD TESTAMENT

The Basic Problem and the Redemptive Plan. In this chapter we underscore the basic principles set out in the 39 books of the Old Testament, principles which furnish the backdrop for the action and the message in both testaments. The book of Genesis introduces God as the supreme being who created and sustains all things including earth and its inhabitants. Mankind has been fashioned in God's image and likeness and has been given the task of populating and caring for the earth and all living things. Humans are permitted the freedom to make choices, but they separate themselves from God by choosing to know both good and evil, taking heed of the purveyor of evil— satan. God makes a judgment or decree placing the human race on probation, so to speak, subject to certain terms and conditions. He continues to provide for his creatures, but humans must labor to obtain those things necessary to sustain life. They must conquer the perverse nature which they have taken on and control their propensity to miss the mark with God, that is, their tendency to sin. Also, God is resolute in his desire to have fellowship with his human family, for they have been made in his image and likeness, and they do know good as well as evil. He therefore provides a way for them to regain full right-standing with him and also to live in peace, harmony, and good health.(Gen. 1-4)   In the Old Testament, God reveals this plan of redemption and salvation through word and deed. His teachings and instructions are transmitted to the populace through people of faith who are chosen to deliver and record his messages. Implicit in God's plan is the continuation of the freedom of men, women, and children to make choices. He wants people to come to him freely, voluntarily, knowledgeably, and wholeheartedly.

Progressive Revelation. Thus, the Bible deals with God's plan to bring humanity back to the pre-fall state, back into full communion, cleansed of the negative aspects of our beings, enjoying the fullest blessings he has to bestow, living a peaceful life on earth realizing that our identities are spiritual, as he is, and preparing for an eternal blessedness in another dimension. This plan is made known in the Bible through what is called "progressive revelation." God reveals himself more and more, and his promises, his provisions for us, get progressively better and more precise. The promises are revealed in his covenants or contracts with us. These covenants have terms and conditions. If we do thus and so, then God will do this. If we don't do thus and so, we are left to our own devices and the vagaries of the world. God's plan is revealed in six main covenants, all set forth in the Old Testament. The last covenant is the New Covenant which is fulfilled when the Messiah (anointed one) is sent to be God's direct representative who will lead all mankind (both Jew and Gentile) back into righteousness, that is, a right relationship with God. It is in relation to this covenant-base that all the human activity takes place in the Old Testament. People sometimes wonder what is to be made of all of the human failure depicted in account after account in the historical books. Even the great heroes of the Old Testament show their "clay feet" time after time. The human activity shows mankind's limited response to the covenant promises and requirements. It also gives good example through the heroes of faith and a "loyal remnant." [NOTE: In the New Testament, we find a discussion of the Old Testament heroes of faith in Heb. 11; a review of Israel's limited response and God's continuing concern for his covenant-people in Rom. 9-11; and an admonition to avoid their mistakes in 1 Cor. 10:6-11.]

The Mystery of Evil. The interaction between God and humans in the Old Testament also reveals what God is like, that is, it shows what are referred to as the attributes of God. It shows his love for his creatures, his patience with them, and his willingness to forgive and forget if they give him honor and make a bona fide effort to walk in his ways. Also, God is good, and he wages a continuing, albeit mysterious, battle with evil (satan) in the spiritual realm (just as humans fight the battle of the "flesh," the "old man" that is a part of each of us, as Paul so clearly describes in Rom. 7, which seems to compel us to do those things which our consciences tell us are wrong). God is a jealous God and classifies the worship of idols and other material objects as evil and pointless. Paganism and its idol-worship are to be eliminated. (For additional discussion about satan, see the topic "Satan" in Chapter SEVEN.)

God's Attributes

God of Love and Justice. It has been said that the Old Testament shows a God of wrath, the New Testament a God of love. However, God is no less a God of love in the Old as he is in the New; and, likewise, he is no less a God of justice in the New than he is in the Old.(Heb. 12:1-29) According to both testaments, God never changes.(Mal. 3:6; Jas. 1:17; Heb. 13:8) In the New

Testament we see a new dimension, a new and more personal manifestation of love, along with a clearer definition of love's spiritual nature and the spiritual oneness with God which is possible. A key factor to consider in assessing the two testaments is the difference in the state of paganism and its effect upon the Jewish people in the two time frames. First, in giving the law to Moses, idolatry and the making of images were prohibited. God wanted to stamp out idolatry, and the children of Israel were to be his vanguard to accomplish the task.(See: Dt. 32; 33:29) It is important to realize that when the Lord ordered the Israelites to eradicate the local groups in Canaan, or to forsake foreign wives as in Ezra and Nehemiah, every one of the pagans involved could have escaped that judgment by forsaking paganism and by worshiping the one true God. Also, any person could bring himself or herself within the terms of the covenants made known through the Israelites. Under the law of the stranger or sojourner, anyone could become an Israelite (later, a Jew). But the Israelites themselves fell prey to paganism, worshiping idols at the "high places," engaging in the wild parties in "the groves," keeping small statues of pagan gods in their houses, and even passing children through the fire of the pagan god Molech.(2 Ki. 21:3-7) Another problem was the taking of "foreign wives" who continued their pagan worship in Israel and Judah. This problem was pretty well eliminated after the Jews returned from captivity in Babylon. The big issue in Judea when Jesus came on the scene was not paganism among the Jews but a different form of idolatry — the adherence to legalistic interpretations of scripture which ignored the law of love set out in the covenants, the Mosaic code, and the words of the prophets. As we show later on, in Jesus' day, the top people in the Jewish religious establishment were corrupt, lovers of money and position, and the lay groups who tried to live by the law were lost in trivialities and exclusivism.

Names for God. The attributes of God are revealed both by what he does and by what he says, for example, the act of creation and provision for his creatures and his words as recorded in scripture.(See Psalms 23, 91, 103, 104) In the New Testament Paul says that all are without excuse, for if you don't know God from scripture, you know him from what has been created. (See: Rom. 1:19-20) Hebrew writers of the Old Testament often incorporated an attribute in a name for God. The root word for "god" throughout the ancient Near East was "el." This word in combination with descriptive terms results in the names used. "El" also shows up in people's names, such as, Samu-el (name of God) or Micha-el (who is like God). Another word for God, which is exclusively Hebrew, is "Yaweh" which in English is rendered

"Jehovah." The ancient Hebrew alphabet did not have any vowels, and "Yaweh" was written "YHWH." The meaning is "I am that I am." When Moses was commissioned to lead the children of Israel out of Egypt, he asked God to tell him his name so that he could answer the Israelites if they asked who sent him. God said "YHWH," that is, "I am that I am." Moses was to say that "I am" had sent him to them.(Ex. 3:14)   Centuries later, when Jesus told the scribes and Pharisees, "Before Abraham was, I am," they took up stones to throw at him, because they realized that he was claiming to be God. YHWH was considered the covenant-name of God and was so holy to the Israelites that they would not pronounce it. When reading scripture aloud, they substituted "adonai" which means "lord."

Attributes of God in Old Testament

Attribute	Hebrew Name
Creator	Elohim
Loving, Merciful God	Jehovah-Hesed (Yaweh-Hesed)
Father	Ab (familiar form: Abba)
Healer	Jehovah-Ropheka (Yaweh-Ropheka)
Provider	Jehovah-Jireh (Yaweh-Jireh)
All-powerful	El Shaddai
Supreme	El Elyon
Everlasting	El Olam
God of peace	Jehovah-Shalom (Yaweh-Shalom)
Lord of Heavenly Hosts	Jehovah-Sabaoth (Yaweh-Sabaoth) also Elohim Sabaoth
Leader, Protector, Shepherd	Jehovah-Nissi (Yaweh-Nissi), also El Roi or Yaweh-Roi
Covenant God "I am"	Yaweh (Jehovah) also El-elohe-Israel
Righteous God	Jehovah-Tsidkenu (Yaweh-Tsidkenu)
Judge	Shaphat
Redeemer	Gaol
Savior	Yasha
Shield	Magen
Deliverer	Palat
Foundation, "Rock"	Sur

The Six Covenants

1. **Adamic Covenant.** God permits Adam and Eve to eat freely the fruit of any tree in the Garden of Eden except the tree of the knowledge of good and evil.(Gen. 2:16-17)   However, they disobey this order and succumb to the serpent's temptation. They eat of the forbidden fruit, thereby gaining a knowledge of good and evil, injecting themselves into an ongoing struggle between God and satan (i.e., the serpent; Rev. 12:9), and taking upon themselves the characteristics of this struggle between the goodness of God and the evil of satan. According to scripture, satan is a spiritual being with limited power who rebels against God and seeks to obtain equality with him.(See: Isa. 14:12-13; Ezek. 28:13-19; Jude 6)   For their disobedience (called "The Fall"), Adam and Eve are expelled from Eden under a decree that their lives will be filled with sorrow. God tells Adam that he must now work outside the garden tilling the soil which is cursed and overrun with thorns and thistles. Eve is told that she will have many children but will also have sorrow when they are born.(Gen. 3:16-19)   From dust they were formed, and to dust they will return.(Gen. 3:19)   There will be enmity between their descendants and satan. One of their descendants will defeat satan (bruise or crush the serpent's head) although satan will wound his adversary (bruise his heel).(Gen. 3:15)   As Cain is told, sin "lies at the door, and his desire is" to control the individual. One must gain control over him.(Gen. 4:7)   As the number of children and grandchildren of Adam and Eve increases, they begin to "call upon the name of the Lord."(Gen. 4:26)   Thus, God has made provision for humans to redeem themselves by doing well, gaining control over sin, and calling upon the name of the Lord. Eventual and complete victory over satan through a descendant of Adam and Eve is assured.

2. **Noahic Covenant.** After the ark lands on Mount Ararat, God makes a covenant with Noah and his descendants that the ground will continue to give forth a harvest; the seasons will not cease; Noah and his family are blessed and will be fruitful and multiply and replenish the earth. God will not again destroy all mankind with a flood. The rainbow will be the sign of the everlasting covenant.(Gen. 8:21 - 9:16)

3. **Abrahamic Covenant.** In about 2100 B.C. God makes a covenant with Abram and his wife Sarai (later changing their names to Abraham and Sarah) to the effect that they will become the founders of a great nation through a son to be born to them even though they are senior citizens. Abraham's name will be great, and in him all families of the earth will be blessed.(Gen.

12:1-3) Abraham and Sarah will be the father and mother of many nations. The covenant will apply to their son as well. Circumcision of all males will be the sign of the covenant. The land of Canaan will be given to them as a possession forever (Gen. 17:8-27), although their descendants will live in a strange land for 400 years before this happens.(Gen. 15:13-16) This covenant is confirmed with their son, Isaac, and Isaac's son, Jacob.(Gen. 26:4; 28:13-15) Jacob's name is changed to Israel by an angel of the Lord, because Jacob is considered as a prince having power with God.(Gen. 32:28) The terms and conditions of this covenant are to be carried out by the tribes of Israel, that is, the descendants of Jacob's sons — Judah, Benjamin, Levi, Joseph, Reuben, Simeon, Issachar, Zebulun, Dan, Naphtali, Gad, and Asher.(Gen. 48 - 49; Ex. 1:1-7)

4. **Mosaic Covenant.** In furtherance of the Abrahamic covenant, God calls out Moses in about 1450 B.C. to lead the Israelites out of Egypt. God makes a covenant with Moses and the Israelites that this is the time when they are to occupy the promised land. This covenant includes a code of laws beginning with the Ten Commandments; instructions for building a tabernacle and the Ark of the Covenant; instruction on how to worship God and to obtain forgiveness of sin. The words of God are to be put down in writing and preserved within the Ark of the Covenant. The terms and conditions of this covenant are in Exodus, Leviticus, Numbers, and Deuteronomy. The heart of the covenant is found in Dt. 28 - 30. If the Israelites keep the commandments and the law with heart and soul, they will be blessed both spiritually and materially. They shall become a nation above other nations. The covenant applies to them and to others not with them. But if the covenant is ignored, they will suffer dire consequences including dispersion to and captivity in other lands. If this should happen, provision is made for repentance, restoration of their relationship with God, and reestablishment of their nation.

5. **Davidic Covenant.** Some 400 years later God makes a covenant with David, the king-prophet-poet of Israel. God will make Israel secure. A temple is to be built for the Lord, but it will be David's son who will build it. David's throne and kingdom, and his son's, will be established forever.(2 Sam. 7:10-16) This covenant is confirmed with David's son, Solomon, after he is king of Israel. In speaking to Solomon, God also includes a warning that if the Israelites do not follow the law as written and if they serve other gods, the negative clauses in the Mosaic covenant will be enforced.(I Kings 9:3-9)

6. **The New Covenant.** The Psalms and the writing prophets record God's desire for a right heart-attitude in worship as preferable to sacrifices and offerings made simply because prescribed by the Mosaic code. The people are called to magnify the name of the Lord, to repent, to be sorrowful for their sins, to seek God's forgiveness which he will give because of his loving-kindness.(Ps. 40; Isa. 1:11-18)   He will make an everlasting and merciful covenant applicable to everyone (Hos. 1:10; 2:23; Isa. 55:3-5; 61:8); a covenant of peace and safety.(Ezek. 34:25)   In about 600 B.C. Jeremiah reports God's intention to put the new covenant into operation for a Jewish nation chastened and cleansed by their captivity in Babylon. This new covenant will not be according to the covenant made through Moses, which they broke. Under this new covenant, God will put his law in their inward parts. No one will have to teach others to know the Lord, for all shall know him. He will forgive their iniquity and remember their sin no more.(Jer. 31:31-34; see also Ezek. 36:33) About the same time as Jeremiah's prophecy, Joel prophesies that the day will come when God will pour out his spirit on all mankind; that whoever calls upon the name of the Lord shall be delivered.(Joel 2:28-32)   The people will be given a new heart and a new spirit.(Ezek. 36:26-27)   [NOTE: In the New Testament Jesus says that his is the blood of the new covenant.(Lk. 22:20)   In Hebrews 8 - 10 it is said that Jesus is the fulfillment of the new covenant set forth by Jeremiah and that Jesus is the mediator of its terms. In Acts 2:16-21 Peter declares the fulfillment of Joel's Prophecy.]

The Messiah. The new covenant presages a new beginning —the ultimate in God's relationship with his covenant-people. He will be their God, and they will be his people. There will be peace in the land, and the great prophet like unto Moses will lead mankind into all the right paths.(Dt. 18:15-18)   This prophet is the Messiah.(Dan. 9:25)   David and other psalmists speak of him (Ps. 2; 8:5; 16:10; 45; 72; 110; 118:22-26), and the words of the prophets are specific: he will be born of a virgin (Isa. 7:14) in Bethlehem.(Micah 5:2)   He will be of David's line (Isa. 11:1-5, 10; Jer. 23:5), and, as God's son, he will also be "the mighty God, everlasting Father, prince of peace" (Isa. 9:6; Dan. 9:25), and "son of man."(Dan. 7:13)   He will be a humble king who will come riding upon a "colt, the foal of an ass," bringing salvation to the people.(Zech. 9:9)   Being prince, shepherd (Ezek. 34:23-24), and servant, yet righteous judge (Isa. 11:1-5; 52:13-15), he will be rejected (Isa. 53:3) and sold for 30 pieces of silver.(Zech. 11:12)   He will be slain, bearing the sins of many and being counted among wrongdoers.(Isa. 53:12)   But he will rise again and make intercession for the transgressors.(Isa. 53:10-12) [NOTE: The Hebrew word "mashiach" which is rendered "messiah" in English and the Greek word "christos" from which comes the word "Christ" both have the same meaning, namely, "anointed one." In the New Testament Jesus says that he is the Messiah proclaimed in the Old Testament (Lk. 22:67-70), and fulfillment of these prophecies is declared.(Lk. 4:17-21) There are other Old Testament prophecies about the Messiah; according to some, there are as many as 300. The Open Bible lists 38.]

The Covenants and the Gentiles

A Servant-Nation. Isaiah pointed out to his people that they were chosen to be a servant of God and to be a light to the Gentiles.(Isa. 49:3, 6) [A Gentile is anyone who is not Jewish, that is, not a descendant of Jacob (Israel).] So Israel was a nation formed through divine action to provide a cohesive community of people who were entrusted with God's truth embodied in the covenants and laws. They were his writers and protectors of the written word, i.e., scripture. Before Abraham and Sarah there were no Hebrews, Israelites, or Jews. In fact, Abraham paid honor and tithe to a non-Hebrew priest of the most high God named Melchizedek.(Gen. 14:17-20) Moses' father-in-law was a Midianite priest who worshiped the God of Israel.(Ex. 2:16-21; 18:12) The law given to Moses contained provisions for accepting strangers and sojourners among them.(Ex. 12:11-48) Except for Passover, a Gentile could worship at the tabernacle and offer sacrifices and attend sacrificial feasts.(Ex. 12:48; Dt. 16:11) If a Gentile man were circumcised he could observe the Passover.(Ex. 12:48)

God's Love for All. The law declares God's love for everyone, both Israelite and Gentile. The stranger and sojourner among the children of Israel are loved by God, and the Israelites must love them also.(Dt. 10:18-19) They are to be protected against injustice and violence (Ex. 23:9) and provided for in the same manner as are widows and orphans.(Dt. 10:18; 26:12-13; Lev. 19:10) Two prominent Gentiles who became Israelites were Rahab (Josh. 6:23) and Ruth (Ruth 1:16-17), both of whom were ancestresses of David and Jesus' foster father, Joseph.(Matt. 1:5-16) The task of Israel was to be a light to the nations, not only through preservation of God's word, but also through the witness of their actions in conformance to the word (Gen. 12:1-3; 49:10-12; Dt. 4:6) so that all nations would know and worship the one true God.(Ps. 32:12; 72:11; 148:11) Having failed to do so under the old covenant which included the laws, the new covenant was promised through the prophets both to bring Israel (Judah) back to God and to provide a means to bring his message to the whole world.(Hos. 1:10; 2:23; Isa. 52:15; 55:5; 66:19-24; Jer. 33:9)   As we have seen, Joel's prophecy about the pouring out of the Holy Spirit includes the declaration that whoever calls upon the name of the Lord will be delivered.(Joel 2:32)   Israel's last Old Testament prophet, Malachi, predicted that God's name will be great among the Gentiles and that they will worship him.(Mal. 1:11)

Worship Under the Old Covenant

The Tabernacle. Before the giving of the law under the Mosaic covenant, worship of God often included sacrifice of an animal on an altar made of rock and earth and dedicated to God by the worshiper. (See: Gen. 8:20; 12:7-8; 33:20) As expressed in Ps. 40:1-8, God looks to the faith of the person and his or her obedience to God's direction more than to sacrifice. Abraham's faith was counted to him for righteousness, God looking to the intent of his heart and soul.(Gen. 15:6)   In the Mosaic law, to provide a framework for regular worship, God ordained that the Israelites would provide him with an abode for his earthly manifestation — the tabernacle. Detailed plans were given for a large tent with two rooms. The first room contained commemorative items, a stand for showbread, a golden candlestick, and an altar of incense. The second room was the Holy of Holies. In it were the Ark of the Covenant, a gold-covered chest containing the law, a pot of manna, and later the rod of Aaron.(Ex. 16:33; Nu. 17:10; Heb. 9:2-4)   The lid of the ark was called the mercy seat and was engraved with two figures representing angelic beings called cherubim. The Holy of Holies was separated from the other room by a heavy curtain called the veil. Only the high priest could enter the Holy of Holies and then only once per year on the day of atonement.(Lev. 16:1-28)   The tabernacle was surrounded by a fence composed of curtains supported by a wooden frame, forming a courtyard around the tabernacle. In front of the tabernacle in the courtyard were placed an altar for making animal sacrifices and a laver (a washstand) for use by the priests in performing the required washings.(Ex. 35 - 40)   The tabernacle served as the central point for worship until replaced by a permanent temple built under Solomon's direction.(1 Ki. 6)

Priests and Levites. Moses' brother Aaron was the first high priest, and his sons were also priests. Future priests must be descendants of Aaron, and the high priest is to be selected from their ranks and appointed for life.(Ex. 28:1, 43)   Centuries later, the high priesthood was limited to descendants of Aaron through the line of Zadok, a high priest during David's reign.(Ezek. 44:13-

15; 1 Chron. 6:3-8)   Moses and Aaron were Levites, that is, of the tribe of Levi. All Levites were bound to serve at the tabernacle and were assigned the task of dismantling it and carrying it as the children of Israel marched around in the wilderness.(Nu. 3:1-49)

Sabbath and Feast Days. In addition to the Sabbath, the day of rest and worship every seventh day, the law prescribes many feasts and observances throughout the year. Probably the most important is the day of atonement ceremony when the high priest is to enter the Holy of Holies and offer sacrifice and repentance to God for the forgiveness of the sins of all the people (Yom Kippur). Two goats are to be used. One is to be sacrificed; the high priest is to lay hands on the other, symbolically transferring the people's sins to the goat, called the scapegoat. This goat is to be released to carry the sins away.(Lev. 16:1-28)   Another important observance is the Feast of Tabernacles (also called Booths or Ingathering) held in thanksgiving for the harvest. The people stay in booths or huts made with branches and leaves to remind them of their manner of life in the wilderness. This festival amounts to a seven-day retreat. It is a time for praising God, rejoicing, and hearing the reading of the law.(Nu. 28:12; Dt. 16:13-15; 31:9-13)   The Passover and Feast of Unleavened Bread commemorate the passing of the angel of death over the Israelites' homes in Egypt, the sparing of the lives of their firstborn, and the escape to the promised land.(Ex. 12:11-51)   The Feast of Weeks (Pentecost), or Firstfruits, celebrates the beginning of Harvesttime.(Lev. 23:17; generally, see Nu. 28 - 29)   The Mosaic law also provides for a "Year of Jubilee" every 50 years. This special year for proclaiming liberty begins with the day of atonement observance. During this year the ground is to lie fallow. It is a time when property and bondservants may be redeemed, and special efforts are to be made to help the poor.(Lev. 25:8-55)

Teaching Scriptures. The priests and Levites are also to teach the Torah to the people.(Lev. 10:8-10; Dt. 33:8-10) Joshua was admonished by the Lord to meditate on the book of the law day and night. He inscribed the law on stones and read it to the Israelites and the strangers among them.(Josh. 1:8; 8:30-35)   In the final analysis, however, it is the duty of the parents to teach their children the law at every opportunity and to write it on the doorposts of their houses and upon their gates. Observance of the law is their righteousness.(Dt. 6:6-9, 20-25)

Other Laws; the Golden Rule

Love Thy Neighbor. Just about every phase of life is covered in the Mosaic code. There are laws relating to property, crimes, diet, health and healing, morality, marriage, divorce, master and servant, and other interpersonal relationships. The code has been recognized as remarkable for the breadth of its coverage and specifically for its public health ordinances which stress isolation of diseased people, avoidance of touching cadavers, cleanliness, and placing sanitation facilities outside the camp. As Jesus is later to point out, the Golden Rule is set out in the law. It is embodied in the laws regarding the unfortunate and the stranger and laws prohibiting harm, theft, and even coveting. But there are two which Jesus said were supreme. On them hang all the law and the prophets: (1) Love the Lord your God with all your heart, soul and might (Dt. 6:5), and (2) Love your neighbor as yourself.(Lev. 19:18; Matt. 22:37-40)

God and the Individual in the Old Testament

God's Love and Concern. The Old Testament, particularly in the wisdom and poetry books, describes God's love and concern for the individual and his or her welfare.(Ps. 17:7; 36:7; 104:24) God is everywhere, always present (Ps. 139) and ready to help, at both the spiritual (Ps. 31:5) and material levels (Job 42:12; Ps. 92:12-15) those who call upon him in faith.(Ps. 11:1, 31:14; Hab. 2:4)   He forgives iniquities and heals diseases.(Ps. 103:3; Ex. 15:26)   Through the prophets Elijah and Elisha, he demonstrates his healing power.(1 Ki. 17:22; 2 Ki. 4:35; 5:14)   He knows each person from his or her formation in the womb and each one's innermost thoughts.(Ps. 22:9-10; 139)   The result of doing things God's way is joy, happiness, and prosperity.(Ps. 4:7)   David says, "Happy are the people whose God is the Lord."(Ps. 144:15) Those who delight in the Lord and his commandments will enjoy peace of mind and prosperity (Ps. 112); whereas the unrighteous flee when no one is pursuing.(Prov. 28:1)   He hears the humble (Ps. 10:17-18), redeems the lost (Ps. 78:22-35), is a refuge for the oppressed (Ps. 9:9), gives peace and rest to the weary (Ps. 4:8; 29:11; 36:7) so that one's soul may dwell at ease.(Ps. 25:13)   The Lord is a hiding place, putting those who love him under his wings.(Ps. 32:7; 36:7)

Communication with God. What does God expect a person to do to qualify for all these blessings? As we have seen, in giving the commandments, he has said that he shows mercy on those who love him.(Ex. 20:6)   He is desirous of communication and fellowship with his children (Ps. 16:7-11; 18-6; 23; Dan. 9:21-23); he takes pleasure in his people.(Ps. 149:4)   This relationship is not a passive thing. God says that he is a jealous God and expects his people's full attention.(Ex. 20:5)   As he said to Judah, "You shall be my people, and I shall be your God." The relationship he has in mind is like that of husband and wife (Jer. 31:32) with endearing affection.(Song of Solomon)   God wants our recognition that he is the creator and sustainer of all things.(Job 38-41)   He wants us to repent of our sins, ask for forgiveness, and thank him for it when given.(Job 42:1-6; Ps. 51)   He is more interested in a right heart-attitude than he is in a person's sacrifices or offerings for the altar.(Ps. 40:4-6; 51:13-15)   Since the ways of the world are a trap and a snare leading to possible disaster, one should not lean to his or her own view as taught by the world but should trust in the Lord.(Ex. 34:12) When the Lord loves, he corrects as does a loving father.(Prov. 3:5-12)   Trusting in the Lord involves meditation upon him and his word (Ps. 1:2; 104:34), staying close to him in prayer.(Ps. 3:4-5; 5:2; 18:3,6; Dan. 9:21-23)   A person who does this will find favor with God (Prov. 3:4) and resultant wisdom and happiness.(Prov. 3:13)   Such a one will praise God joyfully in song, music, and dance, and God will receive it with gladness.(Ps. 149, 150)

The Human Spirit; Spiritual Unity. This relationship of God-to-person and person-to-God has a special unity. Each person is a spiritual being (Gen. 2:7) made in God's image.(Gen. 1:26; 9:6)   Thus, the human spirit proceeds from God.(Job 27:3; 33:4)   This nature as spirit transcends the physical and intellectual world (Eccl. 12), and God's spirit within gives true wisdom and understanding.(Job 32:8; Pr. 2:6; Ex. 28:3)   It is this spiritual quality in every person which compels him or her to seek God, to have a spiritual realization of that unity.(Isa. 26:9; Ps. 63:1)   This entails concentration and purpose, for each one must rule his or her own spirit.(Pr. 25:28)   God recognizes the efforts of the spirit who seeks him and provides both spiritual and material blessings in the earthly sphere.(Pr. 3:1-10; Ps. 23:1; Dt. 28:1-9)   Full unity is realized when each one returns to the creator in a purely spiritual dimension.(Eccl. 12:7)   There is also a sense in which people can experience spiritual unity among themselves. Dt. 13:6 describes the "friend who is as your own soul." First Sam. 18:1 says that the friendship of David and Jonathan was so strong that "the soul of Jonathan was knit with the soul of David."

The Holy Spirit. The Bible stresses the principle that a person seeking truth, wisdom, and unity with God is not left entirely to his or her own devices, for God recognizes the seeker and provides help through the imparting of an extra measure of his spirit — the

Holy Spirit. The Old Testament shows the working of the Holy Spirit and indicates his availability to the faithful, but the idea of the outpouring of the Holy Spirit and his unifying work in the world is stressed as a future blessing in connection with the New Covenant and its implementation as more precisely seen in the New Testament. However, there are numerous references in the Old Testament to the "spirit of God" and his special anointing. The Bible says that God's spirit fell upon Moses (Nu. 11:17); Joseph (Gen. 41:38); the judges Othniel and Samson (Judg. 3:10; 14:6); Saul and David (1 Sam. 10:6; 16:13); Elijah and Elisha.(2 Ki. 2:9, 15) Through the reception of the Holy Spirit one becomes as a new person with a new heart.(1 Sam. 10:6, 9) David prayed that God would not remove his Holy Spirit from him; that God would renew his spirit and rescue his soul.(Ps. 51:10-12; 143:11) There are also indications that any seeker might open himself or herself to the reception of the Holy Spirit. For example, in Proverbs, wisdom personified says, "Turn you at my reproof; behold, I will pour out my spirit unto you; I will make known my words unto you."(Prov. 1:23) When Moses was ordaining the 70 elders, the Holy Spirit not only fell upon them but also upon two men in the camp. When asked about this, Moses replied, "Would God that all the Lord's people were prophets and that the Lord would put his spirit upon them."(Nu. 11:29) As mentioned, the scripture reveals the culmination of Moses' desire as an integral part of the New Covenant.(Joel 2:28; Isa. 32:15; 44:3)

Prayer. According to the dictionary, "prayer" is the act of communicating with deity by way of request, petition, supplication, praise, and worship. "Prayer" is also used to indicate the message itself. In the Old Testament we see prayers addressed to God on both an individual and representative basis, the priests offering sacrifices and prayers for the people in atonement for their sins. God regarded these sacrifices and prayers as a "sweet savor."(Gen. 8:21; Ex. 29:18) But as previously noted, God let it be known that sacrifice and offering without a right heart-attitude were not acceptable, and that true sacrifice is "a broken spirit; a broken and contrite heart," that is, having sincere regret for one's sins.(Ps. 51:17) The Bible says that shortly after the "fall," people began to "call upon the name of the Lord."(Gen. 4:26) Enoch "walked with God."(Gen. 5:24) Noah built an altar and sacrificed to God.(Gen. 8:20-21) Abraham interceded for any righteous people in Sodom.(Gen. 18:22-33) Moses spoke to God on behalf of his people (Ex. 32:31) and admonished the people to turn to the Lord and cleave to him.(Dt. 30:10,20) Other notable prayers in the Old Testament include those of Daniel (Dan. 6:10-11; 9:3-19); Ezra (Ezra 9:5-10; 10:1) and Nehe-

miah.(Neh. 1:4-11)   Voluntary fasting in connection with prayer
is evident in the Old Testament.(Nu. 6:2-4; Dan. 9:3; Neh. 1:4; 2
Sam. 12:16) The importance of prayer is emphasized in the
wisdom and poetry books. Job's book tells of his healing and
prosperity after his prayer for his friends.(Job 42:10)   The
Psalms are prayers of praise, worship, and supplication, seeking
the Lord and expressing trust in him (Ps. 34:4; 63:1; 25:2; 31:1) as
provider (23:1) and protector.(23:4; 91)   Prayer includes singing
heartfelt praises to God (9:1; 75:9); offering him blessings
(145:21); giving thanks (136:1-3); seeking his mercy.(52:8; 35:1;
51:1) Prayer involves humility and confession of sins (10:17;
32:5); pouring out and lifting up one's soul to God.(42:4; 86:4) The
Lord hears righteous prayers and regards them as a delight and
pleasant words.(Prov. 15:8, 26, 29) The Lord answers prayer,
giving good gifts (Eccl. 5:19-20) often before people pray or while
they are still speaking.(Isa. 65:24)   In response to prayer God
blesses, protects, and strengthens those who put their trust in
him.(Ps. 18; 27; 86:7-17; Isa. 58:9)

Social Welfare Laws

The Torah contains a number of provisions dealing with the
Israelites' duty to assist the less fortunate. In Dt. 15:11 it says,
"For the poor shall never cease out of the land. Therefore I
command you, saying, you shall open your hand wide to your
brother, to your poor, and to your needy in your land." It was
declared to be a sin not to help the needy; but also, helping
someone brings God's blessings to the helper.(Dt. 15:9-10; 24:20)
The provisions dealing with this duty usually classify a group of
those who may be in need; thus the same duty applies with regard
to the stranger, the sojourner, the widow, the fatherless, and the
poor. Helping the poor honors God.(Prov. 14:31, 17:5, 28:27, 29:14,
31:9. Compare: Matt. 25:35-45)   It is not enough just to provide
material help. The unfortunate are entitled to respect (Lev.
19:15), to freedom from oppression (Ex. 22:22-24), and to
justice.(Ex. 23:6) Special provisions enforced a societal obligation. Every Israelite was obligated to give a tithe to the Lord, that
is, one-tenth of his or her earnings, whether crops, cattle, or
money. This offering was turned over to the priests for use in
supporting the tabernacle and the priests and Levites who took
care of the tabernacle. Every third year the tithe was used for
helping the Levites, the stranger, the fatherless, and the
widow.(Dt. 26:12-13)   And every seventh year a special effort was
to be made in helping the poor.(Dt. 14:22 - 15:11)   Interest could
not be charged for a loan to a poor person.(Ex. 22:25)   When land
lay fallow, the poor were allowed to get whatever food they could
from it.(Ex. 23:11) During harvest the corners and

gleanings must be left for the poor, the widow, the fatherless, and the stranger.(Lev. 19:10; 23:22; Dt. 24:19-21)   As illustrated in the Gospels, any hungry person could enter a field and handpluck (no sickle) enough to appease the hunger.(Dt. 23:25; Lk. 6:1) Reminders of these obligations are included in Proverbs, Psalms, and books of the prophets.(See: Prov. 14:31; Ps. 9:18; 12:5; 82:3-4; Isa. 58:7; Mal. 3:5)

Developments After Moses

The books of the Old Testament after Deuteronomy all revolve about Israel's attempt to function under the principles contained in the first five covenants including the Mosaic code. The 10 centuries of history after Moses show failure after failure at the human level. In response, God raised up prophets to guide the Israelites, to show them the error of their ways and how to return to the fold. As prophesied by Moses, the Israelites want a king instead of judges. God gives them kings, but with a few exceptions they are all evil and give the prophets a bad time. God shows his continuing love for his chosen nation and his patience with them. Three facts stand out from their history: (1) There was a "loyal remnant" composed of some kings, the prophets, some priests, and scribes who maintained scripture and their observance of the law; (2) Israel, and later Judah, had the only "congregation" following a single, wholly good and spiritual God in the midst of a pagan world; and (3) God believes that humanity must have the freedom of choice. He reveals; he presents alternatives; he does not force. He pleads and exhorts his children to make a positive choice for the fulfillment of a right relationship. And he also allows the decision to turn down the covenant promises, but subject to the consequences which follow such a choice. Through the prophets he in effect repeats the message which Moses gave in Dt. 30:19-20:

> . . . I have set before you life and death, blessing and cursing; therefore, choose life, that both you and your descendants may live; that you may love the Lord your God; that you may obey his voice and that you may cleave to him, for he is your life and the length of your days . . .

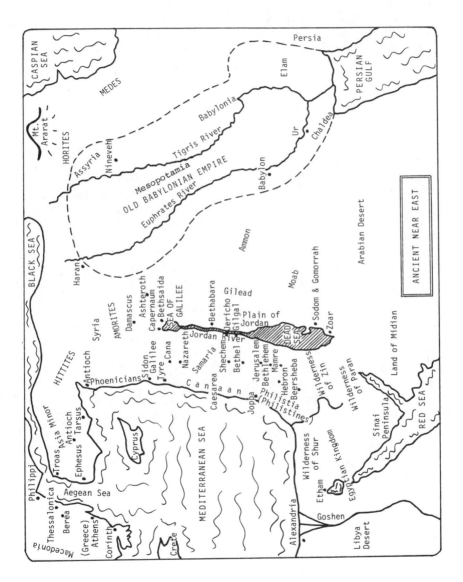

CHAPTER FOUR

OLD TESTAMENT HISTORY AND PROPHETS

This chapter outlines the major events in the 17 historical books and the basic messages contained in the 17 books of the writing prophets. The books of the prophets are discussed in their historical setting since each prophet was addressing people of his own time, as well as prophesying future events.

GENESIS: Creation; Adam and Eve. God creates the universe by virtue of his spiritual dynamic, including heaven and earth, animals, plants, and the first humans, Adam and Eve. God makes Adam and Eve in his own image and likeness and breathes into them the breath of life. They are given dominion over the earth and all animal and plant life. Adam and Eve are to be fruitful, and their offspring will fill the earth. A man will leave his father and mother and join with his wife, the two becoming one flesh.(Gen. 1 - 2) Through the temptation of the serpent (satan, Rev. 12:9), Adam and Eve partake of the forbidden fruit of the tree of knowledge of good and evil, and for this act of disobedience they are expelled from the Garden of Eden. To the serpent God says, "Because you have done this, you are cursed above all cattle and every beast of the field; and on your belly you shall go, and dust shall you eat all the days of your life. I will put enmity between you and the woman and between your seed and her seed; and he will bruise your head, and you will bruise his heel." (**Covenant No. 1**) To Eve God says, "I will greatly multiply your sorrow and your conception; in sorrow you shall bring forth children; and your desire shall be for your husband, and he shall rule over you." To Adam God says, "Because you have hearkened to the voice of your wife and have eaten of the tree, although I commanded you not to eat of it, cursed is the ground because of you; in sorrow shall you eat of it all the days of your life. Thorns and thistles shall it bring forth to you, and you shall eat the plants of the field. In the sweat of your face shall you eat bread until you have returned to the ground, for out of it you were taken. For dust you are, and to dust you shall return."(Gen. 3)

Need To Conquer Sin. Adam and Eve have two sons, Cain and Abel. Cain becomes angry when the Lord recognizes the sacrifice of Abel as more worthy than that which he offered. The Lord asks Cain why he is angry and says, "If you do well, will you not be accepted? And if you do not do well, sin lies at the door. He desires you, and you must rule over him." But Cain, jealous of his brother, slays him. When the Lord confronts him, Cain asks, "Am I my brother's keeper?" God then banishes Cain to a vagabond life. Adam and Eve have many more children, both sons and daughters (Gen. 5:4), including a son named Seth. Then men begin to call upon the name of the Lord.(Gen. 4)

The Generations. Adam lives to the age of 930 years, his son Seth to the age of 912 years. There are numerous generations of descendants between Seth and Noah who have long lives. Notable is Enoch who walks with God and at the age of 365 years is taken up (translated) by God.(Gen. 5:21-24; see also: Heb. 11:5, Jude 14-15) Enoch's son Methusaleh lives to be 969 years old. Methuselah's grandson is Noah, of whom his father, Lamech, says, "This (son) shall comfort us concerning our work and toil of our hands because of the ground which the Lord has cursed." When Noah is 500 years old, his sons, Shem, Ham, and Japheth, are born.(Gen. 5)

Noah, the Ark, and the Flood. After these generations, the human race has become self-satisfied and continuously evil. God is sorry that he created them and decides to eliminate them and to start over. One family has been faithful, that of Seth's descendant, Noah. "Noah was a just man, perfect in his generations. Noah walked with God."(Gen. 6:9) God directs Noah to build a huge boat called the ark, measuring 450 feet in length, 75 feet in width, and 45 feet in height. All living things on the land are to be eradicated by a flood, except Noah and his wife, their sons, Shem, Ham, and Japheth, and their wives, and the animals which they take on board the ark with them. Noah and his family do as directed. Then the flood comes from a rain which lasts 40 days and 40 nights. When the flood ceases, the ark lands on Mount Ararat (in what is now Turkey). God makes a covenant with Noah. He and his family are to be fruitful, multiply, and replenish the earth with the human race. Murder will be a crime punishable by death, because each person is made in God's image. Mankind will have dominion over all animal and plant life. God will not again cause all life to perish by flood. The sign of the covenant is the "bow in the cloud" (**Covenant No. 2**).(Gen. 6 - 9)

Descendants of Noah; Tower of Babel; Confusion of Languages. Time passes. Descendants of the Shem, Ham, and Japheth families multiply and build cities. Prominent among the families is Nimrod, a great hunter and king, and Asshur who

builds Nineveh and other great cities.(Gen. 10) The people
continue to speak one language and are not interested in going to
the various parts of the earth. They decide to build the tower of
Babel as a monument to their own accomplishments. God
confuses their languages, stops the building project, and scatters
them so that they will populate the whole planet.(Gen. 11)

Abraham and Sarah (c. 2100 B.C.). At this point in time God
determines to raise up a people who will be wholly devoted to him
and his principles so that they may be made known to all people.
To this end, God calls out Abram and his wife Sarai to become the
first Hebrews.(See Gen. 14:13)   The call comes about in this way:
Terah, a descendant of Shem, lives with his family in Ur of the
Chaldees, a city on the Euphrates River not far from the city of
Babylon (today southern Iraq). [Excavations reveal that Ur was
a large city at that time.] Terah leaves Ur and travels north to
Haran, a city in northern Canaan (today northern Syria) and
settles there with his son Abram, Abram's wife Sarai, and their
nephew Lot. (Sarai is also Abram's half-sister.(Gen. 20:12)) Death
comes to Terah when he is 205 years of age. God then speaks to
Abram instructing him to move on to another land which will be
shown to him, and he and his family will become a great nation.
Their names will become great, God will bless them, and they will
be a blessing to all families of the earth. Abram and Sarai have
accumulated wealth and many people who work for them. They
and Lot and his family all leave Haran and become tent dwellers
as they move south in Canaan to what is now referred to as
Palestine and Israel. At this time Abram is 75 years of age, and
Sarai is 65.(Gen. 11 - 12)

Egypt to Hebron. Because of drought conditions in Canaan,
they move further south into Egypt. The pharaoh sees that Sarai
is a woman of great beauty and takes her into his house, for
Abram had told her to say that she is his sister rather than his
wife. Pharaoh discovers the deception when the Lord visits
plagues upon Egypt, and after confronting Abram, pharaoh
expels them from the country. They return to Canaan, and some
time later Abram and Lot agree to separate and occupy different
areas, because each one's herds of livestock have grown so large
as to create many problems. Lot has the choice, and he elects to
settle in the eastern area near the cities of Sodom and Gomorrah.
The Lord speaks to Abram and says that his land and that of his
numerous descendants will be the land of Canaan as far as he can
see. Abram and Sarai settle in Mamre in the vicinity of Hebron,
and he builds there an altar dedicated to God.(Gen. 12 - 13)
[Hebron is a city which has been inhabited since about 3000 B.C.
and is located about 25 miles south of Jerusalem.]

Lot Rescued; Melchizedek. Over in the area where Lot has settled, the kings of Sodom and Gomorrah lead a rebellion against a greater king named Chedorlaomer whom they have served. Chedorlaomer and his allies put down the rebellion and carry away all their possessions and many people including Lot. When news of Lot's capture reaches Abram, he with some local help mounts a small army and pursues the invaders. Near Damascus they meet and defeat the enemy and rescue Lot, the other captives, and all their goods. On their return they are met near Salem (later, Jerusalem) by the king of Sodom and the king of Salem. The king of Salem is Melchizedek who is also a priest of the most high God. He brings bread and wine to Abram and blesses him and gives praise to the most high God who has delivered them from their enemies. Abram then gives a tithe (10 percent) of all the goods to Melchizedek. [NOTE: Reference to this level of high priesthood is made in the messianic prophecy of Ps. 110, which in turn is quoted and discussed in the New Testament in Heb. 6:20 - 7:21: "Jesus made a high priest forever after the order of Melchizedek."] The king of Sodom wants to give Abram all the remaining goods, desiring only the return of his people. But Abram turns down the offer, for he has made a vow to God that he will take nothing lest anyone claim that he made Abram rich. The others who helped should receive their proper recompense, however.(Gen. 14)

Covenant Terms; Hagar and Ishmael. God continues the revelation of his covenant with Abram and Sarai (**Covenant No. 3**). God's chosen nation will be descendants of a son to be born to them. They will be as numerous as the stars which Abram can count. Abram believes the Lord, and his faith establishes him in right-standing with God. But before the descendants of Abram form their nation and enter the promised land, they will be strangers in a country that is not theirs for 400 years. Then they will come forth and take possession of their own land which will extend from Egypt to the Euphrates River. Though the covenant has been set, Sarai remains barren. She has the idea that a child of Abram's by her handmaid Hagar would suffice under the covenant. Thus (per ancient custom) she gives Hagar to Abram as a wife. A son, Ishmael, is born to Hagar when Abram is 86 years of age. An angel of the Lord appears to Hagar telling her that Ishmael will be prosperous and have many descendants.(Gen. 15 -16)

The Sign of the Covenant. When Abram is 99 years of age, God continues his covenant instructions. Abram will be the father of many nations, and his name from this time on is

Abraham (father of a multitude). Sarai will be the mother of many nations and kings; thus her name is changed to Sarah (princess). God's covenant with Abraham and Sarah is an everlasting one; God will make his covenant with their descendants, and he will be their God. The sign of the covenant is circumcision of all males in the household. While God has heard Abraham's request for consideration of Ishmael, the covenant applies to their descendants through a son to be named Isaac who will be born to Sarah. Ishmael will be the father of many nations, but the covenant-nation will come through Isaac. Abraham falls over laughing at the idea of a 100-year-old man and a 90-year-old woman becoming parents, but God assures him that it will happen. In conformity with the covenant, Abraham has himself, Ishmael, and all the men of his household circumcised. One day the Lord comes to Abraham, along with two angels, all three appearing as men. They ask for Sarah since she is to bear a son. Sarah is in the tent, and when she hears the part about a son, she laughs to herself. The Lord asks why she laughed. She denies laughing, but the Lord affirms that she did laugh.(Gen. 17 - 18:15)

Judgment on Sodom and Gomorrah. The Lord then confides to Abraham that he has judged Sodom and Gomorrah for the wickedness of the people, and he is going to destroy those cities. Abraham pleads for any righteous people who may be there, and the Lord agrees that if there are 10 he will save the cities for their sakes. But there are not and the decision is firm, and Sodom and Gomorrah are destroyed with fire and brimstone. The two angels warn Lot and his family to get out of Sodom and not even to look back. After some difficulty with the townspeople, they leave. However, Lot's wife looks back and is turned into a pillar of salt. Lot and his two daughters settle in a city called Zoar. The daughters, fearing that they are not desirable to potential husbands, decide not to be left childless. They accomplish their purpose after getting their father drunk with wine. The resulting children are Moab and Benammi, ancestors of the Moabites and Ammonites.(Gen. 18 - 19)

Birth of Isaac. Abraham and his people travel to various parts of Canaan. They go south from Hebron to Gerar where Abraham again represents Sarah as his sister rather than his wife, this time to the ruler of the area. Again God intervenes, and Sarah is sent back to Abraham who is verbally chastised. Through a miraculous conception, Sarah bears Abraham's son, and when he is born, he is named Isaac (meaning laughter). Abraham is 100 years of age and Sarah 90 at this time. After Isaac's birth things do not go well between Sarah and Ishmael.

Sarah sends Hagar and Ishmael away which grieves Abraham. But the Lord assures both Abraham and Hagar that he will watch over her and her son.(Gen. 20 - 21)

Sacrifice of Isaac. After many years the Lord tests Abraham's resolve to carry out the covenant. He speaks to Abraham and directs him to offer his son Isaac as a sacrifice on Mt. Moriah. [NOTE: Mt. Moriah is today within the old city of Jerusalem. It is near the site of the former temple of Israel and is covered by a Moslem Mosque called the Dome of the Rock.] Abraham and Isaac go to Moriah, but when Abraham takes the knife to sacrifice Isaac, an angel of the Lord speaking out of heaven tells him not to harm Isaac. Abraham has passed the test. Looking up, Abraham sees a ram caught in a thicket, and he offers the ram as a burnt offering. Abraham calls the location Jehovah-Jireh (the Lord provides). Then the Lord reconfirms his covenant with Abraham. They return south and continue to live in the area of Beersheba, located about 30 miles south of Hebron.(Gen. 22)

Deaths of Sarah and Abraham. Sarah dies at age 127 years, and Abraham mourns her passing. He purchases a family burial ground near Hebron (Mamre) and Sarah is laid to rest in a cave.(Gen. 23)   After some time, Abraham marries again, and his wife's name is Keturah. They have children, but when these children are grown, Abraham gives them many gifts and sends them east. The bulk of his estate is preserved for Isaac. At age 175 years, Abraham dies "in a good old age and full of years" and is "gathered to his people." Isaac and Ishmael bury their father with Sarah in the family burial ground.(Gen. 25:1-10)

Isaac; Jacob; Israel in Egypt (c. 2000-1800 B.C.). [The remaining chapters of Genesis depict the activities of Isaac and his wife Rebekah, their son Jacob and his family, and their eventual migration into Egypt through the efforts of Jacob and Rachel's son Joseph, all in furtherance of the Abrahamic covenant.] After his mother's death Isaac marries Rebekah, a cousin from the Haran area. Rebekah conceives twins whose movement within her troubles her, and she seeks an answer from the Lord. God lets her know that these children will start two nations and that the older of the two children will serve the younger. The firstborn is named Esau and the second, Jacob. When they reach manhood, Esau sells his birthright to Jacob for a meal of bread and lentils. Isaac favors Esau, but Rebekah wants Jacob to receive the patriarchal blessing. She and Jacob trick Isaac into believing that Jacob is Esau which is possible only because of Isaac's failing eyesight. Isaac blesses Jacob. Esau appeals to his father, but what's done is done, and Isaac tells him to be content serving his brother. However, Esau, vowing to kill Jacob, leaves, aligns himself with Ishmael, and marries one of Ishmael's daughters. Esau becomes the father of the Edomite nation.(Gen. 24 - 27:40; also Gen. 36) [Herod in the New Testament was an Edomite.]

Jacob, Rachel, and Leah; the Covenant Reconfirmed. To escape Esau's wrath, Jacob travels north to Haran to stay with his uncle, Laban. One night he has a vision of angels ascending and descending a ladder which reaches to heaven. God speaks to him, reminding him of the covenant and assuring him that he will be protected wherever he goes. Jacob vows to be resolute in carrying out his part. On reaching the Haran area, he is welcomed by his uncle who has two daughters, Leah and Rachel. Jacob falls in love with Rachel, the younger of the two, and agrees with Laban's requirement that he work for him for seven years after which he may have Rachel as his wife. At the appointed time, however, Laban tricks Jacob and substitutes Leah. He tells Jacob that this is necessary, because the younger should not marry before the older; that he can also marry Rachel if he agrees to work seven more years. Jacob accepts, marries Rachel, and continues in Laban's employ. Fearing barrenness at certain times, Rachel and Leah, following ancient custom, give their handmaids, Bilhah and Zilpah, to Jacob as additional wives. During the ensuing years, Jacob fathers 13 children by his four wives:

Leah: Reuben, Simeon, Levi, Judah, Issachar, Zebulun, Dinah

Rachel: Joseph, Benjamin

Bilhah: Dan, Naphtali

Zilpah: Gad, Asher

Jacob Becomes Israel. Tiring of Laban's changing of his wages several times, Jacob learns how to crossbreed cattle and to trick Laban in the division of them. He takes his share and leaves to return to his father's land. The Lord helps in this, for he has seen Laban's deception. Jacob knows that he will be going through Esau's territory as they move south, so he prepares to give him a gift of many animals. One night while by himself, Jacob meets an angel of the Lord who appears as a man and wrestles with him. Realizing who the man is, Jacob refuses to let go until the angel blesses him. The angel not only blesses Jacob, he also changes Jacob's name to Israel, for Jacob is a prince having power with God and man. When Jacob and Esau meet, the gift is made, and the brothers are reconciled.(Gen. 27:41 - 33)

Jacob Returns to Hebron. Jacob and his family settle in an area about 90 miles north of Hebron. Jacob's elder sons avenge the advantage taken of their sister Dinah by a local prince who wants to marry her. Her brothers decimate the city of Shechem causing Jacob and his family and followers to leave the area to avoid retaliation. The Lord speaks to Jacob instructing him to go to Bethel, about 30 miles to the south, and build an altar to God. Jacob discovers that some of his people have taken up idol-worship and orders them to turn over to him all their idols, rings, and earrings which he then buries. They move on to Bethel where Jacob builds the altar, and God reconfirms Jacob's part in the working out of the Abrahamic covenant. Jacob decides to rejoin his father at Hebron. On the way, at Ephrath (Bethlehem) Rachel gives birth to Benjamin, but she has difficulty and dies. Jacob buries her at Ephrath. Shortly after Jacob's arrival in Hebron, Isaac dies at the age of 180 years.(Gen. 34 - 35) [The traditional location of Rachel's grave is marked by a tomb in Bethlehem; that of Abraham, Isaac, and Rebecca, by a shrine in Hebron.]

Joseph in Egypt. When Jacob's eleventh son, Joseph, is 17 years of age, he displays an ability to interpret dreams. His older brothers are jealous of Joseph for two reasons. He is his father's favorite, because he is of Rachel. And the dreams which he relates show that they will be subordinate to Joseph. They try to get rid of Joseph by abandoning him in a pit, but some Midianites find him and sell him to some Ishmaelites who take him to Egypt and sell him to one Potiphar as a slave. The brothers convince Jacob that Joseph was killed by an animal showing him Joseph's coat which they have dipped in goat's blood. In Egypt Joseph prospers, being the steward in Potiphar's house. But the amorous wife of Potiphar issues a false report about Joseph when he resists her advances, and he ends up in the jail which houses the king's prisoners. He soon becomes the jailer's chief assistant and in effect runs the jail. There he meets two prisoners, the pharaoh's chief butler and baker who were incarcerated for offending their master. Each of them has a dream which Joseph correctly interprets. That of the butler indicates that he will be reinstated, but the baker will not be as fortunate. When the butler is released to resume his duties, Joseph asks him to remember him to the pharaoh so that he can be released. But the butler forgets until two years later when the pharaoh has a dream about fat and lean cattle and seven good ears of corn and seven thin and parched ears. When no one can interpret this dream, the butler remembers Joseph the Hebrew and tells pharaoh about him. Joseph is brought before pharaoh and is asked if he can interpret dreams. Joseph informs the pharaoh that he does not interpret dreams; it is God who provides the answers. The pharaoh's dream of cattle and corn means that there will be seven years of great plenty in the land followed by seven years of famine. He advises the pharaoh to appoint administrators over the harvests and to ration grain so that there will be enough to eat during the long period of drought. Pharaoh says, "Can we find such a one as this, a man in whom the spirit of God is?" He then appoints Joseph as the chief administrator, second only to pharaoh in power in Egypt. Joseph is 30 years of age at this point. He marries Asenath, daughter of an Egyptian priest, and two sons are born of this union, Manasseh and Ephraim.(Gen. 37 - 41)

Years of Plenty; Years of Famine; Jacob's Family in Egypt. After seven years of plenty, the seven years of famine begin in all the ancient Near East. The food which has been stored is made available for a price. Jacob, hearing that food can be bought in Egypt, sends 10 of his sons (all but Benjamin) there to buy food. Joseph recognizes them, but they do not recognize him. Joseph sets up a scheme to test their loyalty to their father and to each other. He charges them with being spies, holds Simeon as a hostage, and sends the others back to Canaan to get Benjamin. On their return to Egypt, Joseph tells them that he will keep Benjamin as a servant and send them back to their land. They plead for their brother and their father, remembering the heartache they caused in their treatment of Joseph. At this, Joseph relents and reveals himself as their long-lost brother, saying that he was sent by God to Egypt to prepare a place to preserve their posterity. After an emotional and tearful reunion of all the brothers, Joseph arranges for the migration of the whole family to Egypt. Word goes to Jacob (Israel), and he prepares to go visit Joseph. In Beersheba he offers a sacrifice to God. The Lord speaks to him telling him to go to Egypt, and he will become a great nation which God will bring out again. Thus, about 1880 B.C., Jacob and his wives and children and their families, a total of 70 people, journey to Egypt. With the pharaoh's permission, they settle in the fertile area of Goshen (also referred to as Ramses) located in the northeastern part of Egypt. There they continue in the business of raising livestock. Jacob lives to the age of 147 years, and on his deathbed he blesses all his children and obtains a promise from Joseph that he will be buried in Canaan with Abraham, Sarah, Isaac, and Rebekah. A special blessing is laid upon Joseph's sons (Manasseh and Ephraim), for Joseph's descendants will have a double portion. Jacob gives a prophecy of the deeds of the 12 tribes of Israel, the descendants of his 12 sons. Upon Jacob's death, Joseph and his brothers take his embalmed body to Hebron and bury him in the family burial ground. When they return to Egypt, the brothers, to make sure of their status, ask Joseph's forgiveness for their evil deeds of years before. Joseph tells them that he is not God. They thought they were doing evil, but God meant it to be for good in order to save many people. Years pass, and when Joseph realizes that death is coming, he tells his people, "God will surely visit you and bring you out of the land into the land which he swore to Abraham, to Isaac, and to Jacob." He asks that his bones be carried with them out of Egypt. Joseph dies at age 110, and his body is embalmed and put in a coffin.(Gen. 41 - 50)

EXODUS: Moses the Prophet (c. 1530-1410 B.C.). After the children of Israel have been in Egypt for close to 350 years, they have multiplied to an extent which alarms a pharaoh "who knew not Joseph." Not only are the Israelites everywhere, but also they are a prosperous and mighty force. Pharaoh puts them into slavery and sets them to building cities, making brick and mortar and working in the fields. The slave masters deal harshly with them, but the harder their lives, the more they multiply. In about 1530 B.C. the pharaoh puts out an edict that newly born male Israelites are to be put to death. When Moses is born to Amram and Jochebed of the tribe of Levi, his mother, to save his life, puts him in a basket which she hides in the bulrushes by the river. There he is found by pharaoh's daughter who raises him as her own child. Moses is 40 years of age when his Hebrew heritage moves him to protect another Hebrew from an attack by an Egyptian. Moses slays the Egyptian and buries his body. But the matter becomes known, and Moses flees to Midian in Palestine to escape pharaoh's wrath. There he marries Zipporah, a daughter of Jethro, a Midianite priest. They have two children, Gershom and Eliezer.(Ex. 1 - 2; 18:3-4)

The Call of Moses; Crossing the Red Sea. Moses at age 80 (c. 1450 B.C.) is called by God from the burning bush to return to Egypt and lead the children of Israel to the promised land. He, the God of Abraham, Isaac, and Jacob, has heard the cries of their children, and he has come to free them from their Egyptian taskmasters. Moses objects that he is not qualified to perform such an assignment. The Lord assures Moses that he will be with them, puts down Moses' protests, and appoints his brother Aaron to assist. Moses asks who shall he say has sent him to be their leader. God answers, "I am that I am." Moses is to say that "I am" (YHWH; i.e., Yaweh or Jehovah, God's covenant name), the God of Abraham, Isaac and Jacob, has sent him. God reiterates the Abrahamic covenant of redemption and promises that the children of Israel will be a special people. Moses returns to Egypt and confronts Pharaoh who refuses to let the Israelites go. God sends 10 plagues upon the Egyptians: blood, frogs, lice, flies, disease on the cattle, boils, hail, locusts, darkness, death of the firstborn. The Passover is instituted to celebrate the passing of the angel of death over the Hebrew dwellings so that only the Egyptians' firstborn are taken. God in a pillar of fire shows the Israelites the way, and Moses leads them across the Red Sea while the waters are held back by a miracle of God. Moses takes Joseph's bones with him. During their 430 years in Egypt the Israelite population has grown from 70 people to about 2,000,000 people (603,550 men able to wage war).(Ex. 3 - 14; Nu. 1:45-56)

In the Wilderness. As they move along in the Palestine wilderness, the Israelites begin to complain about the lack of food and water. They register this complaint many times. God supplies them with water and with food in the form of manna, like coriander seed and tasting like wafers made with honey. God assures the people that if they hearken to his commandments, they will be free of diseases, for he is the Lord who heals. In the wilderness the Israelites with God's help defeat the Amalekites who have been plaguing them. Moses is visited by his father-in-law, Jethro, who brings Moses his wife, Zipporah, and their two sons. During this visit Jethro makes some helpful suggestions to Moses in setting up a system of leaders and judges to take care of many disputes and inquiries which are being brought to him.(Ex. 15 - 18)

The Ten Commandments. In the Sinai region God directs Moses to bring the people to the foot of the mountain so that he can speak to them all. When they are assembled, God's voice comes forth from heaven, and all hear him deliver the Ten Commandments.

1. I am the Lord your God who has brought you out of the land of Egypt, out of the house of bondage. You shall have no other gods before me.
2. You shall not make for yourselves any idol or any likeness of anything that is in heaven above, in the earth beneath, or in the water under the earth. You shall not bow down to them or serve them. For I, the Lord your God, am a jealous God, visiting the iniquity of fathers upon the third and fourth generations of those who hate me; showing mercy on thousands of those who love me and keep my commandments.
3. You shall not take the name of the Lord your God in vain; for the Lord will not hold him guiltless who takes his name in vain.

49

4. Remember the Sabbath day to keep it holy. Six days you shall labor and do all your work. But the seventh day is the Sabbath of the Lord your God. In it you shall not do any work, you, nor your son, nor your daughter, nor your manservant, nor your maidservant, nor your cattle, nor your stranger within your gates. For in six days the Lord made heaven and earth, the sea and all that in them is and rested the seventh day; wherefore, the Lord blessed the Sabbath and made it holy.

5. Honor your father and your mother, that your days may be long on the land which the Lord your God has given you.

6. You shall not murder.

7. You shall not commit adultery.

8. You shall not steal.

9. You shall not bear false witness against your neighbor.

10. You shall not covet your neighbor's house; you shall not covet your neighbor's wife, nor his manservant, nor his maidservant, nor his ox, nor his ass, nor anything that is your neighbor's.

The effect of these words, which are punctuated by thunder, lightning, trumpet sounds, and smoke, is so great that the people ask Moses to bring them the rest of God's message, and they move away from the mountain.(Ex. 19 - 20)   God then gives Moses many laws for guidance of the Israelites. He tells Moses that an angel with full authority will go before them and protect them, but they must not be tempted by the idol-worship of the people already in Canaan, and on the contrary, the Israelites are to overthrow the pagan practices and images. Moses writes down all the laws given by the Lord in the book of the covenant. He builds an altar on which animals are sacrificed as offerings to the Lord. The blood from the animals is sprinkled on the altar, and the book of the covenant is read to the people. They agree to do all that the Lord has said and to be obedient. Moses then sprinkles the people with some of the blood and says, "Behold the blood of the covenant which the Lord has made with you concerning all these words" (**Covenant No. 4**).(Ex. 20 - 24) [NOTE: During the Last Supper Jesus refers to his own blood as the blood of the new covenant.(Lk. 22:20)]

Plans for the Ark of the Covenant and Tabernacle. Moses returns to the mountain and receives from God specific instructions about the construction of the Ark of the Covenant in which to keep all of his testimony and commandments. Also, Moses receives detailed plans for the construction of a tabernacle, a house for God, which is to contain the Ark of the Covenant. It is to be built so that it can be quickly disassembled and moved from place to place. Moses' brother Aaron and his sons are to be the priests who represent the people in worship services at the tabernacle. Special clothing is designated for the priests. The manner of sacrifices is prescribed, including daily sacrifices and a special sacrifice on the annual day of atonement. God reiterates the importance of the Sabbath, then gives Moses two stone tablets on which his words are written.(Ex. 25 - 31; Lev. 16)

Paganism in the Camp. After having been on the mountain for 40 days, Moses returns to the camp with the tablets and finds that in his absence the people have reverted to pagan practices and are worshiping a golden calf. Moses' anger is so great that he breaks the tablets and destroys the calf. Severe punishment is meted out by both Moses and the Lord. Moses prays for God's forgiveness of the people, and God instructs them to adhere to his directions. Moses moves a tent outside the camp where he talks with God who manifests himself as a cloudy pillar. Moses asks to meet him face to face and to see his glory. God replies from the cloud that no man can experience his glory directly and live. But he will do this: he will put Moses in a cleft in the rock, and as he passes by, Moses will be able to get a glimpse of his backside. Moses is told to hew two more stone tablets and to bring them with him to Mount Sinai.(Ex. 32 - 34)

The Covenant Confirmed. Moses remains on the mountain another 40 days, the Lord being with him in the cloud. The covenant is confirmed, and God gives a warning about idolatry. He is a merciful, loving, and forgiving God but also a jealous God; in fact, his name is Jealous. They are to make no images. When they enter the promised land, they are to destroy pagan altars and images. They are to observe the Passover, the feast of unleavened bread, the feast of first fruits, and the feast of ingathering. Moses is told to write down all the words he has spoken as a record of the covenant. On the tablets Moses writes the Ten Commandments. When Moses returns to the camp, his face shines so much that he wears a veil among the people.(Ex. 34)

Building of the Tabernacle. Moses sets the craftsmen to work on the tabernacle which is built to the specifications given by the Lord, the people donating the materials including gold and jewelry. When it is finished, Aaron and his sons are consecrated into the priesthood, the tablets of testimony are put into the Ark of the Covenant, and the furnishings set in place. Then a cloud covers the tent, and the glory of the Lord fills the tabernacle. Thereafter, when the cloud fills the tabernacle, they camp. When the cloud is lifted up, they continue their journey.(Ex. 35 - 40)

LEVITICUS: the Holiness Code. Leviticus is a book of laws given to the Israelites through Moses. Certain laws are also set out in Exodus, Numbers, and Deuteronomy, which are also "action" books, but Leviticus is essentially a compilation of regulations for Israel. In giving these laws, God does not let the children forget who the lawgiver is, for the Lord frequently says to Moses, or to Moses and Aaron together, "Speak to the children of Israel and say to them . . ." The statutes and ordinances cover every phase of human life and relationships. They deal with worship, sacrificial offerings, tithes, and offerings for the support of the tabernacle, the priests, and Levites; also, marriage, divorce, personal cleanliness, public health and quarantine, morality, personal relationships among family members, rules for master and servant, property, including proper use of the land, crime and punishment, and help for the poor, the widow, the orphan, and the stranger. Certain animals are "unclean" and not to be eaten. They are not to eat blood, because "the life of the flesh is in the blood." They are not to eat any food which has been sacrificed to idols. Every fiftieth year is to be a year of jubilee, a period during which there can be, under varying conditions, redemption of bond-servants and land previously sold. Rewards for walking in God's statutes and keeping his commandments will be assured, as well as penalties for any failure to comply.

NUMBERS: the Census and the Journey. Still, in the Sinai region, a census is taken as directed by the Lord. There are 603,550 men capable of going into battle. The Levites are assigned to take care of the tabernacle and to move it during the journeys of the Israelites.(Nu. 1 - 4, 8, 18) Regulations are set for those who take the Nazarite vow of prayer, fasting, and holiness. The tabernacle is dedicated, and each tribe brings an offering.(Nu. 6 - 7) On the anniversary of their departure from Egypt, the Passover is observed. The law is set that the Passover is to be kept on the fourteenth day of the first month each year.(Nu. 9:1-14)

Departure from Sinai. The children of Israel depart from the Sinai region when the cloud over the tabernacle moves and comes to rest in the wilderness of Paran. After they camp, the cloud returns to the tabernacle. The people complain bitterly about their limited diet of manna. Moses asks the Lord to take the burden of this people from him, but the Lord arranges for the appointment of 70 elders upon whom he has placed the same spirit who rests upon Moses. The elders will help Moses administer the Israelites. Then the Lord causes a great swarm of quail to fall on the camp so that the people might have meat. But in his anger at those who are lustful, he strikes them with a plague. After they bury those who die from the plague, they continue their journey. Moses' brother, Aaron, and sister, Miriam, speak against Moses, because he married a Cushite woman. This angers the Lord, and he strikes Miriam with leprosy. Moses intervenes, and the Lord agrees that she will recover after seven days.(Nu. 9 - 12)

The Spy Team. At the Lord's direction, Moses sends a spy team into the land of Canaan to determine conditions there. There are 12 men on the team, one from each tribe. After 40 days they return, reporting that the land is very productive. Two men bring back a large cluster of grapes which they carry between them on a pole. [NOTE: Today in Israel one frequently sees a picture or a logo depicting two men carrying a large bunch of grapes. This is Israel's symbol for tourism.] As to their ability to take the land, 10 of the team issue a majority report which is negative, for these men fear defeat at the hands of the warlike people they have seen. Two members, Joshua and Caleb, file a minority report, saying that because the Lord is with the Israelites they can defeat the inhabitants. But the children of Israel refuse to enter Canaan. They would prefer to return to Egypt to die or remain in the wilderness rather than to be slain as prey by the Canaanites. The Lord tells Moses that he is appalled that they have seen all the miracles which he has performed in Egypt and the wilderness and refuse to enter the promised land. He then decrees that they shall wander in the wilderness for 40 years, until all those who were from 20 years old or older when they left Egypt have died. Of this age group, the only ones who will enter are Joshua and Caleb.(Nu. 13 - 14)

Forty Years of Wandering. The wandering of the children of Israel is carried out by moving in a very precise order according to tribes, with the Levites leading the way, carrying the Ark of the Covenant and the tabernacle parts and furnishings. When they camp, the tabernacle is erected, the ark placed in the holy of holies, the tribes encamping around the tabernacle. During this 40 years there is a constant undercurrent of rebellion. Led by a Levite named Korah, certain tribal leaders challenge Moses. If they are successful, it could thwart God's plan for carrying his word to the world through his chosen nation. This rebellion is quickly dealt with, the rebels paying with their lives.(Nu. 16)   [In the New Testament Korah is mentioned in Jude 11.] To symbolize the divine nature of Aaron's appointment as high priest, God causes a wooden rod carried by Aaron to bud.(Nu. 17) Additional laws are given regarding the support of the priests and Levites, offerings, purification of the unclean (Nu. 15, 18, 19,

28), the law of inheritance (Nu. 27, 36), the sabbath, holy feast days, and the making of vows.(Nu. 28 - 30)   Near the close of the 40 years Miriam and Aaron come to the end of their days. Aaron's son, Eleazar, is appointed high priest.(Nu. 20; 33:38-39)

Nearing the Promised Land. As they near the promised land, they complain about the journey and speak out against God and Moses. God puts a plague of snakes upon them. When they repent, God orders the erection of a bronze replica of a snake on a pole, and as long as they look upon this symbol, they are safe. [NOTE: Hundreds of years later Hezekiah destroyed this bronze replica, because people were worshiping it as an idol and burning incense before it.(2 Ki. 18:4)   In the New Testament Jesus refers to Moses' lifting up the serpent as symbolic of the manner of his own being lifted up, that is, his death and his resurrection.(John 3:14)] The Israelites are attacked by the Canaanites and the Amorites, but with the Lord's help, Israel is victorious in battle. Israel is now at a point opposite Jericho, east of the Jordan River in the land of Moabites and Midianites. Balak, king of Moab, imports a prophet named Balaam from Mesopotamia to lay a curse upon Israel. The Lord warns Balaam not to go to Moab; that if he does he will speak only the words which the Lord will give him. Three times sacrifices are made, and three times Balaam speaks. But his speeches are all on behalf of Israel. He also prophesies of a great one, "a star of Jacob and a scepter" which will arise out of Israel and have complete dominion. Balak is frustrated and disappointed and sends Balaam home. However, Balaam provides the Moabites and Midianites with a scheme. They are advised to try to corrupt the Israelites by enticing them to engage in the worship of Baal and the immoral practices which are a part of it. The scheme is put into effect, but the Lord puts a stop to it at the cost of many lives. Midian is conquered, and Balaam is eventually executed.(Nu. 21 - 25, 31; Josh. 13:22)   [The sin of Balaam is referred to in the New Testament in 2 Pet. 2:15, Jude 11, and Rev. 2:14.]

Preparations for Entering Canaan; Joshua Appointed As New Leader. The Lord Directs the taking of a census which reveals that there are 601,730 men 20 years of age or older fit for battle. Also, there are 23,000 Levites. None of these men had been included in the first census 40 years earlier. When the Israelites enter Canaan, it is to be divided among the tribes by lot.(Nu. 26) However, the tribes of Reuben and Gad and half the tribe of Manasseh request land east of the Jordan River (today in the country of Jordan). This request is approved on condition that they participate in the campaign to take over Canaan.(Nu.

32)   In the years since leaving the Sinai region, the Israelites have moved camp 31 times. Having now reached the point of entry, the Lord gives some final instructions. The inhabitants of Canaan are to be totally defeated; their idols are to be destroyed and their "high places" torn down. If they do not completely defeat them, the inhabitants will remain as "pricks in your eyes and thorns in your sides"; and the Lord will do to Israel as he thought to do to the pagans.(Nu. 33)   As the end of Moses' days approaches, the Lord selects Joshua to succeed Moses, and Moses lays hands on him and commissions him.(Nu. 27:22-23)   The Lord outlines the boundaries of Israel and appoints Joshua and Eleazar, the high priest, along with a representative from each tribe who will occupy west of the Jordan River, as the commission to oversee the division of land.(Nu. 34)

Provision for Levites: Cities of Refuge; Laws on Murder. The Israelites are directed to provide the tribe of Levi the right to live in 48 cities and have use of the land outside these cities for their possessions, cattle, and other animals. Six cities are to be "cities of refuge" to which any person who has killed another person unintentionally may flee. The slayer will be judged, and if it is found that the killing was not intentional, the slayer will be allowed to live unharmed in the city of refuge. If the slayer is found outside the city of refuge by the "revenger of blood," he may execute the slayer. When the high priest in office at the time dies, the slayer is free to return to his former home. No one is to be convicted of murder except on the testimony of two or more witnesses. Murder includes intentional killing or killing by use of a deadly weapon such as iron, stone or wood, by laying in wait, or by striking or hurling the victim out of hate or enmity, with or without a deadly weapon.(Nu. 35)

DEUTERONOMY: Moses' Farewell (c. 1410 B.C.). All of those who were from 20 years and older when they left Egypt have died except Moses, Joshua, and Caleb. Moses is now 120 years of age. He speaks to a generation of Israelites who either had been very young while in Egypt or had been born in the wilderness. He recounts their experiences up to this point and how God has told him that he will see the promised land from the top of Mount Pisgah but will not enter the land. They should heed the word of the Lord, for no other nation has all the statutes, judgments, and laws of righteousness which they have. They are to be diligent lest they forget and are to teach the law to their children and their children's children. They should worship the one true God and remember that he is a jealous God and a consuming fire. If they do not hearken to God, they will be defeated and made captives by other nations. He reviews the Ten Commandments and the other laws; he predicts that they will have judges and kings. A king should have a copy of the law with him, the same law which the priests and Levites have before them. There will be many prophets, and the Lord will raise up another prophet like Moses. There will also be false prophets. One can discern a false prophet, for the thing which a false prophet speaks does not come to pass.(Dt. 1 - 18)   After the children of Israel enter Canaan, they are to build an altar of stone and plaster on Mount Ebal and write on the stones all the words of the law very plainly.(Dt. 19 - 27)   Moses explains the blessing and the curse and exhorts the people to choose the blessing that they might live.(Dt. 28 - 30; compare: Lev. 26)   He brings Joshua before the people and announces his appointment as their new leader. Moses, having completed the book of the law, gives it to the priests and Levites with instructions to keep it with the Ark of the Covenant. Moses speaks a song of praise in which he refers to God as their Father and the Rock of Salvation, whose words and ways are true, just, and right. With his help one may chase a thousand, and two put ten thousand to flight. After blessing each tribe, Moses ascends Mount Pisgah, and the Lord shows him the extent of the promised land. Moses dies in Moab where he is buried, but the location of his grave remains unknown.(Dt. 31 - 34)

JOSHUA: Entry into the Promised Land (c. 1410-1390 B.C.); the Spies and Rahab. God speaks to Joshua and assures him that they will have divine help and protection when they claim the land of promise. The Lord reminds Joshua to be attentive to the law which Moses has recorded and to meditate upon it day and night. Then he will be confident of success and prosperity. Before leading Israel into Canaan, Joshua sends two spies to Jericho to view the land. Their presence becomes known, but they are saved by Rahab who hides them. She tells the spies that she and the others have heard how the Lord has helped Israel to escape from Egypt and defeat enemies on the way. They know that God has given Israel the land, and there is no courage among her people. Rahab recognizes that Israel's God is the God of heaven. She obtains the spies' pledge that she and her family will be spared.(Josh. 1 - 2)

Entry into Canaan. The Israelites cross the Jordan River from the east. The river is at flood stage, but the waters are miraculously divided and held back as the priests stand in the river with the Ark of the Covenant. At Gilgal, not far from Jericho, they encamp. Men who had not been circumcised in the wilderness undergo circumcision. Then the Passover is observed.

When they begin to take food from the land, the manna ceases. Near Jericho Joshua encounters a man with a drawn sword. When Joshua asks whose side he is on, the man replies that he is "the captain of the host of the Lord" and that Joshua should regard this place as holy.(Josh. 3 - 5)

Fall of Jericho and Ai. The Lord speaks to Joshua saying that he has given Jericho to the Israelites; that they should go around the city for six days, seven priests carrying the Ark of the Covenant. On the seventh day the priests are to blow trumpets. When they hear the trumpets, the people are to shout, and the walls of the city will crumble. They do as directed, the walls collapse, and they capture the city. Rahab and her family are saved. After an abortive attempt to take the city of Ai fails, the Israelites finally capture it by using two groups of men, one to entice the fighters to come out of the city, the other to enter and take it.(Josh. 6 - 8:29)

Recording the Law at Ebal. As Joshua had been commanded (Dt. 27:1-8), he builds an altar to the Lord at Mount Ebal and writes the words of the law of Moses on stones. Joshua reads the law to the assembled Israelites and the strangers among them.(Josh. 8:30-35)

Intrigue of the Gibeonites. Word of the successes of the Israelites is circulated throughout Canaan. The people of Gibeon (Samaria), desiring to escape capture and possible death, send ambassadors to Israel's encampment at Gilgal. They appear in old clothes with moldy provisions and tell the princes of the Israelites that they are from a far country and want to assure peace in the future; that they are willing to be Israel's servants. Without consulting the Lord, Joshua and the princes agree to a treaty. Then the Israelites learn that the Gibeonites actually live not far away, and they arrive in their region a few days later. No action is taken, because they have given their word in the Lord's name. But the Gibeonites are decreed to be Israel's servants from then on, to be hewers of wood and drawers of water for the congregation of Israel and for the altar of the Lord.(Josh. 9)

Canaan Conquered. Moving quickly south then north, Joshua leads the Israelites in a series of victories over the inhabitants. Of the various groups, only the Gibeonites sought to make a treaty of peace. Some groups are not entirely eradicated, and this situation poses a continuing problem for Israel. As Joshua begins to experience the effects of old age, the Lord directs that the land be divided among the tribes. Each tribe is expected to possess its land and to continue the campaign against paganism.(Josh. 10-13)

Assignment of Land. Territory is assigned the tribes by lot. The tribe of Joseph is actually two tribes, the tribes of Ephraim and Manasseh, for Joseph received a double portion through his sons when Jacob blessed them.(Gen. 48:20-22) Three groups, Reuben, Gad, and half of Manasseh, have already been granted land on the east side of the Jordan River. The other part of Manasseh settles west of the Jordan as do the rest of the tribes. Thus, from north to south on the east side of the Jordan are Manasseh, Gad, and Reuben. From north to south on the west side are Asher, Naphtali, Zebulun, Issachar, part of Manasseh, Ephraim, Dan, Benjamin, and Judah. Some Danites also settle in a small area north of the Sea of Galilee. Simeon receives cities in the southern part of Judah. The Levites are not assigned any territory but are given the right to live in 48 designated cities, the right to be supported by the people, and the right to graze cattle. They have the duty to take care of the tabernacle and to teach the law to the people. Cities of refuge are selected: Kedesh, Shechem, Hebron, Bezer, Ramoth, and Golan. (See map) Caleb receives land in the region of Hebron in Judah for his leadership in ridding the area of pagans. The tabernacle with the Ark of the Covenant, which was at Gilgal, is moved to a more central location at Shiloh. When Joshua nears death, he gives a farewell address in which he urges the leaders of the tribes to keep the law written by Moses, to worship the true God and not the idols of the pagans who are still in the land. Their freedom of choice between the blessing and curse is again explained. And all the people say that they will do as Joshua says. Joshua writes his book; then, at age 110, he dies and is buried in Ephraim. Joseph's bones, which were brought from Egypt, are buried in Shechem in a parcel of land which Jacob had bought.(Josh. 14 - 24)

JUDGES: the Period of the Judges (c. 1390-1040 B.C.). From the time of Joshua to the selection of Israel's first king, Saul, Israel continues as a federation of tribes with a central place of worship at the tabernacle in Shiloh. During this period there is no central or national government. Everyone does whatever "seems right" in his or her "own eyes."(Judg. 17:6; 21:25) The Israelites worship pagan idols, taking part in immoral practices. Much of the time they are oppressed by the pagan nations. This underscores their failure to conquer all of the pagan inhabitants as God had directed. And yet God is patient and forgiving, for when the Israelites remember their God and call upon him for help, he raises up a judge who leads them to victory over their enemies. A period of peace and spiritual renewal follows each victory, but eventually they return to their wicked ways.(Judg. 1 -2) The outstanding judges, and the nations they successfully defend against are:

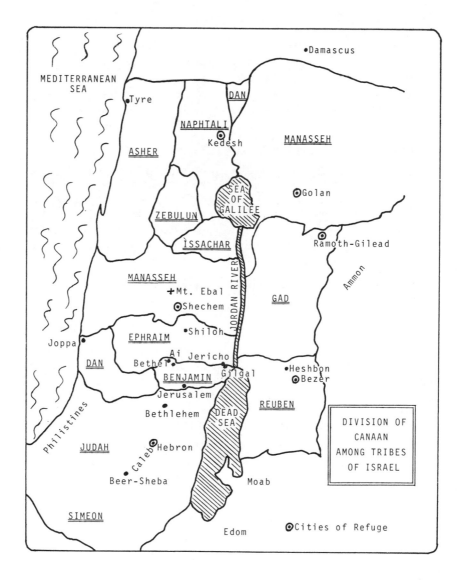

Othniel, nephew of Caleb — Mesopotamia (Judg. 3:1-11)

Ehud — Moab (Judg. 3:12-30)

Shamagar — Philistines (Judg. 3:31)

Deborah and her general, Barak — Canaan (Judg. 4 - 5)

Gideon — Midian (Gideon's faith was strengthened through God's sign of the fleece).(Judg. 6 - 8) Gideon's son, Abimilech, appoints himself king of Israel, but his "kingship" is short-lived. He is killed by a rock thrown by a woman, and Israel continues under the rule of judges.(Judg. 9)

Jephthah — Ammon (Judg. 10 - 12)

Samson — Philistines (Samson, the man of great strength, was a judge for 20 years).(Judg. 13 - 16) [The Philistines were a nation of people located in the western and southern regions of Palestine. The Israelites were continually plagued by the Philistines throughout their history until about 605 B.C. when all Palestine was conquered by the Babylonians under Nebuchadnezzar.]

Another judge is Samuel whose period of service overlaps that of Samson. Samuel is the last judge.(1 Sam. 7:15) The tabernacle and the Ark of the Covenant remain at Shiloh.(Judges 18:31; see 1 Sam. 4:4)

[NOTE RE JUDGES 17 - 21: These chapters dealing with the idol made by one Micah (not the later prophet Micah) and with the problem of the Benjamites comprise an appendix of episodes showing how bad things got in Israel. They illustrate the last verse of Judges which says, "In those days there was no king in Israel; every man did right in his own eyes."]

RUTH: a Love Story (c. 1120 B.C.). The book of Ruth is a vignette showing customs in the time of the Judges and a love story with a happy ending. Its historical importance lies in the fact that Boaz and Ruth are ancestors of David and also Joseph, foster father of Jesus. It is also an example showing that under the law a non-Israelite was eligible for the same blessings as those of the chosen nation by walking with the one true God.

A Hebrew woman, Naomi, living in Moab, is widowed, and her two sons also die. She decides to return to her homeland near Bethlehem. She advises her two daughters-in-law, natives of Moab, to remain in their own country. But one, Ruth, loves her mother-in-law and wants to stay with her. Ruth says, "Your people shall be my people, and your God my God." After they return to Bethlehem, Ruth meets Boaz, a prosperous farmer who is a relative of her deceased husband. Ruth invokes a Hebrew custom regarding "redemption" of a deceased relative's land and a deceased relative's widow if she is childless. After a "nearer kinsman" declines the privilege, Boaz buys land from Naomi and marries Ruth. Boaz and Ruth become great-grandparents of David.

1 and 2 SAMUEL; 1 CHRONICLES: from Judge Samuel to Kings Saul and David (c. 1070-970 B.C.). The first book of Samuel continues Israel's history from the time of the judges to the selection of Saul as king and David's appointment as his successor. Second Samuel and 1 Chronicles cover David's kingship and the problems of his reign, concluding with his purchase of the site for the temple. These books cover a period of about 100 years. [NOTE: We need to say a word about the books of 1 and 2 Chronicles at this point. While these two books deal mainly with events in Judah, they do cover many of the same events as 1 and 2 Samuel and 1 and 2 Kings. To get the fullest picture, one should check 1 and 2 Chronicles for parallel accounts. This situation is similar to that of the four Gospels in the New Testament which relate the life and ministry of Jesus.]

Samuel, the Last Judge (c. 1070 B.C.). Samuel's mother pledges her son to the Lord, because God has answered her prayers and has ended her childlessness. Samuel is raised by the high priest, Eli whose own sons are wicked. On Eli's death, Samuel is chosen by the Lord to be high priest, judge, and prophet. The Philistines capture the Ark of the Covenant, but when their people suffer and their idols fall from their places, they give the ark back. Under Samuel there is a spiritual reawakening in Israel, and the Israelites are successful in resisting attacks by the Philistines. Samuel moves the tabernacle from Shiloh to Nob in the territory of Benjamin.(1 Sam. 1 - 7)

Kings Saul and David (c. 1050 B.C.). In Samuel's old age he appoints his sons as judges; however, they turn out to be corrupt. The people demand a king (as Moses predicted they would). Samuel brings the people's request to the Lord. The Lord points out to Samuel and the people all that is involved in having a king: a military draft, a labor draft, a taking of property, the expense of raising an army. The people insist and the Lord acquiesces, selecting the tallest and best-looking man in Israel, Saul, son of Kish, a Benjamite, to be the first king of Israel.(1 Sam. 8 - 9)   Saul is anointed by Samuel, and Saul picks his hometown of Gibeah, just north of Jerusalem, as the nation's capital. Saul and his son Jonathan have success in defending against the Philistines and

Amalekites. But Saul proves to be unreliable, and the Lord picks David, youngest son of Jesse of Bethlehem in Judah, to succeed Saul as king. Samuel anoints David in his home, but he is not to become king right away. Saul becomes plagued by an evil spirit, and his advisers suggest that David be appointed court musician because of his ability to play the harp and because it is known that the Lord is with him. This is done, and Saul obtains relief whenever David plays.(1 Sam. 10 - 16)

Strife between Saul and David. When David kills the Philistine giant, Goliath, Saul makes him a leader in his army. David gains such a reputation as a mighty warrior that women in all the cities sing and dance in the streets, singing a popular song: "Saul has slain his thousands, and David his ten thousands."(1 Sam. 18:6-8; 21:11; 29:5)   Out of jealousy and fear, Saul tries to kill David. The more dangerous the assignments, the more David prospers. David and Saul's daughter, Michal, wish to marry. Saul gives his consent only after David completes a test in foray against the Philistines. Saul's fear continues, and he instructs his son Jonathan and others to kill David. Jonathan loves David as a brother and intercedes, but Saul continues his efforts even to the point of trying to murder David in his bed. Forewarned, his wife, Michal, helps him escape. David then visits Samuel at Ramah. Saul follows. In the presence of Samuel and the other prophets, he apparently relents and even prophesies in the spirit with them. But David realizes that there is no real hope of reconciliation between himself and the king. He seeks Jonathan's advice on the king's real intentions. Jonathan reveals that his father is determined that David should die. David flees to Nob, site of the tabernacle. The priests at the moment have no food to give David, but at his request they allow him to take some of the consecrated bread. They also return to him Goliath's sword which has been in their care. David leaves and hides in the forest. Saul, pursuing, arrives at Nob. Having learned of the priests' help of David, and in a fit of rage, Saul orders the execution of all the priests and their families. One priest, Abiathar, escapes and joins David and his band of 600 chosen men. Saul's continued pursuit of David is unsuccessful. Actually, David twice has opportunities to capture or kill Saul, but he has such respect for the king that he restrains himself. During this time Samuel dies and is buried at Ramah.(1 Sam. 25:1)   Later, in Carmel, David takes as a wife a young widow named Abigail who has provided food for him and his men.(1 Sam. 17 - 26)

Death of Saul. David and his men live among some friendly Philistines and help in their struggles against other nations. But when they propose to attack Israel, they send David away. The Philistines approach Israel ready for battle, and when Saul gets sight of their encampment, he panics. In desperation, he asks that he be taken to a medium, a "woman with a familiar spirit." This is unusual, for Saul had previously issued orders prohibiting all forms of sorcery and spiritism. Saul is taken incognito to a medium, the so-called witch of Endor, but she is reluctant to see him because of Saul's order. He insists and demands that she bring Samuel up for him. Saul has no sooner voiced his request when an apparition of Samuel is in their midst asking why he has been disturbed. Saul beseeches Samuel to tell him what to do, for seemingly the Lord has deserted him. Samuel answers that since Saul has failed to obey the Lord, David has been ordained as king of Israel; that Saul will be defeated by the Philistines; that Saul and his sons will be with Samuel the next day. Saul prostrates himself in fear. The woman, out of pity for her frightened king, prepares a meal for him and his men and tries to comfort him. After eating, they go out into the night. On the following day the Philistines attack. Saul, Jonathan, and two other sons of Saul are slain. In a psalm David laments their deaths, because they were the great of Israel. "How the mighty are fallen and the weapons of war perished." David especially mourns the death of Jonathan because of their close bond of friendship. After a period of mourning, David inquires of the Lord where he should go, and the Lord answers, "Go up to Hebron." So David and his two wives, Ahinoam and Abigail, and his men journey to Hebron and establish residence there.(1 Sam. 27 - 2 Sam. 2)

King David (c. 1010 B.C.). In Hebron David is made king over Judah, the southern region of the nation. He appoints Joab as his general. In the north Ishbosheth, a surviving son of the deceased king Saul, is made king. His military leader is Abner, Saul's cousin and general of his army. A lengthy civil war between the north and the south ensues which lasts for seven years. Toward the end of this period the northern forces prove ineffective, and strife develops between Abner and Ishbosheth. Abner defects and sends David an offer of his allegiance. He also advises the northern elders to align themselves with David. In the meantime, David has demanded of Ishbosheth and obtained the return of his first wife, Michal, whom Saul had espoused to another man in David's absence. Abner visits David in Hebron, and a pact is finalized. But on his way back to his home territory, Abner is murdered by David's general, Joab, to avenge Abner's killing of Joab's brother some time before. News of Abner's death weakens the resolve of Ishbosheth and the northern tribes. When Ishbosheth is assassinated by his own men, all the tribes join with David, and he becomes king of all Israel at the age of 30. David then conquers the city of Jerusalem (Jebus), taking it from the Jebusites who had held that stronghold for hundreds of years. Jerusalem becomes Israel's capital city (also called the "stronghold of Zion" and "city of David").(2 Sam. 2 - 5)

God's Covenant with David. As king, David and his armies fight many battles, push back the pagan nations, and expand the boundaries of Israel. David recognizes two high priests, Abiathar and Zadok. However, God speaks through the prophets, Nathan and Gad. The tabernacle is moved from Nob to Gibeon, a matter of a few miles and not far from Jerusalem. David also builds a duplicate tabernacle in Jerusalem and has the Ark of the Covenant (including the scripture written up to the time) brought there. David desires to build God's temple, but God informs him through Nathan that he is not to build the temple; that one of David's sons will do so. The Lord also makes a covenant with David that through one of his descendants God's kingdom and David's throne will be established forever (**Covenant No. 5**). David proceeds to prepare plans and to lay up money and supplies for the building of the temple. As an act of charity, he provides for Mephibosheth, son of his late friend, Jonathan.(2 Sam. 6 - 10; 1 Chron. 12 - 17)

David and Bathsheba. David's personal life becomes complicated. In Hebron he had seven wives — Michal, Ahinoam, Abigail, Maacah, Haggith, Abitel, and Eglah. Sons are born to each wife. Two sons who come to prominence later are Absalom, son of Maacah, and Adonijah, son of Haggith.(2 Sam. 3:2-5; 13 -16)   In Jerusalem he takes more wives and concubines and has additional sons and daughters. [Of these sons, Solomon and Nathan are significant. Both are included in New Testament genealogies.(Matt. 1:6; Lk. 3:31)] Michal and David become estranged when Michal criticizes David for dancing before the Lord when the Ark of the Covenant is brought into Jerusalem.(2 Sam. 6:20-23)   On an occasion when David rests from battle, leaving the army in Joab's charge, he becomes enamored of Bathsheba, wife of Uriah, one of his soldiers at the front. David has an affair with her, and she later informs him that she is with child. Uriah is brought home but does not go near his wife, vowing to forego pleasure until the battle has been won. David sends him back to the front with orders to Joab to assign him to the most dangerous fighting. As a result, Uriah is slain. David then marries the widowed Bathsheba. The Lord is displeased with David's conduct and through the prophet Nathan conveys the message to David that he will suffer for his transgressions.

David confesses his sin and is forgiven; nevertheless, strife and tragedy within his family will be his lot. Bathsheba gives birth to a boy, but he becomes ill as foretold by Nathan. Even though David fasts and prays for the boy's recovery, he dies. Upon hearing this, David ends his fast. When asked about this, David replies, "While the child was alive, I fasted and wept, for I said, 'Who can tell whether God will be gracious to me and the child may live?' But now he is dead. Why should I fast? Can I bring him back again? I shall go to him, but he shall not return to me." Another child is born to David and Bathsheba. He is named Solomon by David but Jedidiah (the Lord's friend) by the Lord.(2 Sam. 11 - 12)

Absalom's Revolt. David's son Ammon takes advantage of his half-sister Tamar. In reprisal, her brother Absalom has Ammon killed. David is shocked by what is happening in his family. Absalom goes into hiding, but David loves him and longs for his return. General Joab acting as an intermediary obtains permission for Absalom's return to Jerusalem. Absalom, desiring to be king, gathers a small army and forces David to flee Jerusalem. During a battle between the two factions, Absalom is killed by General Joab. After mourning for his son, David returns to Jerusalem. The 10 northern tribes who had supported Absalom again accept David as king. As a result, David appoints Absalom's military leader, Amasa, as one of his generals, much to the displeasure of General Joab. During a maneuver to put down another northern rebellion, Joab murders Amasa. (Joab's punishment for his various killings is meted out some time later by Solomon.) By virtue of an evil influence (satan in 1 Chronicles 21:1), David orders General Joab to take a census of Israel. The Lord is angered over this move (perhaps because a census could mean an increase in taxation and civil war. See: 1 Ki. 12:14-20), and the Lord sends a pestilence on the land. Many die from the plague which finally stops at the threshing floor of Araunah (or Ornan) the Jebusite. David buys the site and erects an altar there, designating it as the location for the future temple. David also makes sure that the priests and Levites conduct the worship services and sacrifices prescribed by the law given to Moses.(2 Sam. 13 - 24; 1 Chron. 18 - 29)

1 and 2 KINGS; 1 and 2 CHRONICLES: King Solomon; Later Kings (c. 970-586 B.C.). Just before the end of David's reign, another of his sons, Adonijah, tries to assume authority as king. At this point David's general, Joab, and the co-high priest, Abiathar, switch their allegiance to Adonijah. Zadok, the other co-high priest, remains loyal to David. Nathan (the prophet) and

Bathsheba confer with David about the situation, and David appoints Solomon as his successor. David dies, having ruled for 40 years, seven years as king of Judah plus 33 years as king of the whole nation.(1 Ki. 1 - 2; 1 Chron. 29)   [During his lifetime David wrote many songs or psalms which may be found in the book of Psalms.]

Solomon Becomes King (c. 970 B.C.). Solomon assumes his office before his father's death, and a civil war is averted when Adonijah backs down, recognizes his brother as king, and asks for forgiveness. Later, Adonijah's interest in his late father's nurse is interpreted as a power move, and he is executed. Acting on David's last instructions, Solomon also has General Joab executed for his previous crimes. Abiathar is dismissed as priest, but his life is spared. Zadok continues as sole high priest.(1 Ki. 2)

Solomon's Wisdom and Wealth. The Lord appears to Solomon in a dream and asks what he would have from God. Solomon prays only for an understanding heart and wisdom. Thereafter, Solomon's wisdom and his wealth become known far and wide. An example of his wisdom is shown in the way he brings out the truth in a dispute between two women, both claiming to be the mother of a certain child. When Solomon orders the child to be cut in two and half given to each woman, the real mother pleads for the child's life and agrees to give up her claim. The other woman says to go ahead and divide the child. Solomon then decrees that she who wants the infant's life saved should be given the child. Through alliances with other nations the boundaries of Israel are further expanded. Israel becomes a strong and wealthy nation. The Queen of Sheba visits Solomon seeking his counsel and bringing him great tribute. Solomon writes 3,000 proverbs and 1,005 songs.(1 Ki. 4:32)

The Building of the Temple. Solomon directs the building of the temple, his own palace, and a house for the Egyptian princess he married after making an alliance with the pharaoh. He also has a wall built around Jerusalem. When the temple is completed, Solomon brings in the ark containing the books of the covenant and the tabernacle. He dedicates the temple to God with prayer and supplication. The Lord appears to Solomon, tells him that he has consecrated the temple, and repeats the covenants made with Israel, including the blessing and the curse and the freedom of the people to make a choice between them. He warns Solomon that if the people do not adhere to his commandments, the temple will be destroyed, and they will be cut off from their land.(1 Ki. 3 - 10; 2 Chron. 1 - 9)

Solomon's Last Days. Solomon has wives from many nations, and when he is old, he builds places for several pagan idols worshiped by them. And he also turns to idol worship. God's anger is leveled against Solomon, but out of respect for David, he vows to take no action until Solomon's death. During his reign Solomon has adversaries in Hadad the Edomite, Rezon of Damascus and Jeroboam, an official in Solomon's government. Ahijah, a prophet, relays a covenant offer of the Lord to Jeroboam to the effect that the Lord will make him king over the 10 northern tribes and continue his line if he follows the commandments and laws. When Solomon seeks to capture him, Jeroboam flees to Egypt. Solomon dies after reigning over Israel for 40 years.(1 Ki. 11; 2 Chron. 9)

Divided Israel; Two Kingdoms (931 B.C.). Solomon's successor, his son Rehoboam, inherits a strong Israel whose boundaries have been extended beyond those of David's kingdom. However, Solomon's extensive expenditures have caused an increase in taxes. Rehoboam is advised to lessen the burden on the people, but instead he declares that he will increase taxes and rule harshly. As a result, the northern tribes, including those located east of the Jordan River, declare their independence from the house of David and form their own country under the kingship of Jeroboam who has returned from his exile in Egypt. This new nation appropriates the name Israel. The tribes remaining loyal to Solomon's son, Rehoboam, are Judah, Simeon (presumed to be merged with Judah), Benjamin, and Levi. The priests and Levites living in the northern kingdom migrate south to Judah, for the temple is in Jerusalem which is located on the border between Judah and Benjamin. Henceforth the southern kingdom is called Judah.(1 Ki. 12 - 14; 2 Chron. 10 - 11)

Israel, the Northern Kingdom (931-721 B.C.). Jeroboam realizes that if his people go to the temple in Jerusalem to worship, they may soon want to be reunited with Judah; so he builds places of worship at Bethel and Dan, erects idols, golden calves to represent their god, and appoints priests who are not of the tribe of Levi.(1 Ki. 12 - 14; 2 Chron. 10 - 11)   The two nations exist side-by-side with occasional skirmishes, but Judah is directed by the Lord through a prophet not to invade Israel. All of the kings of Israel are described as doing evil in the sight of God. Their history is characterized by intrigue, suicide, and assassination. Attacked frequently by the Assyrians and Syrians, Israel is finally taken over by Assyria in 722/721 B.C. Most of the Israelites are deported to other areas, and other people are brought in to populate the region. Through intermarriage a mixed group results called Samaritans. Israel becomes a province of Assyria ruled by governors. The deported tribes lose their identity and disappear from history (the so-called 10 lost tribes of Israel).(1 Ki. 12 - 2 Ki. 17)

Judah, the Southern Kingdom (931-586 B.C.). In contrast to the changing dynasties in Israel, all the kings of Judah are of the house of David. However, with a few notable exceptions, they also have a penchant for doing evil in the sight of God. Judah is oppressed by the Egyptians, the Assyrians, the Syrians, and the Babylonians. After Israel's defeat in 722 B.C., Judah struggles through until 605 B.C. when all Palestine is taken by the Babylonians under the leadership of Nebuchadnezzar, the conqueror of Assyria and Egypt. He permits Judean kings to remain as governors, but they plot rebellion. Nebuchadnezzar puts down Judean revolts in 597 B.C. and 587/586 B.C., the last time destroying the temple, the palace, and the walls of Jerusalem. The contents of the temple are carried away to Babylon. Each time Nebuchadnezzar attacks Judah he takes a certain number of highly skilled people and those of great potential back to Babylon. In 586 the Judean king, Zedekiah, and the rest of the Judeans are made captive, with the exception of "the poor of the land" who are kept in Judah as laborers. Judah becomes a province under a Babylonian governor.(1 Ki. 13 - 2 Ki. 25; 2 Chron. 11 - 36)

The Heroes of Faith during the Divided Kingdom Period. During the period of the kings who followed Solomon, there was a loyal remnant of God's people who kept the faith — prophets, the good kings of Judah, and those priests and Levites and scribes who maintained the scripture. According to scripture, the Lord tried to correct the ways of the northern kingdom (Israel) principally through the prophets Elijah, Micaiah, Elisha (non-writing prophets) and Amos, Jonah, and Hosea (writing prophets.)

Faith Heroes of the Northern Kingdom; Elijah. Elijah's ministry occurs during the days of King Ahab and his wife Jezebel (c. 874-853 B.C.). Jezebel came from Phoenicia (Lebanon) and introduced the worship of the pagan god Baal complete with a contingent of priests of Baal.(1 Ki. 16:31) Elijah successfully opposes these priests in a contest, and Ahab repents temporarily, but the pagan practices continue. Elijah tries to bring the northern kingdom back to worship of Jehovah through his preaching and miracles. He enlists Elisha who works with him. When Elijah is taken up to the Lord in a whirlwind, his mantle falls on Elisha who has asked for a double portion of Elijah's spirit.(1 Ki. 17 - 2 Ki. 2)   [Elijah is mentioned several times in the New Testament, particularly in connection with John the Baptist.(Matt. 11:14)]

Elisha. Elisha's ministry extends through the reigns of several kings of the northern kingdom, and he becomes known far and wide as "the man of God." He performs many miracles and healings. One of those healed is a Syrian general named Naaman. [Jesus mentions this healing in Lk. 4:27.] Elisha lives to see the destruction of the dynasty of Ahab and Jezebel and the eradication of Baal worship in Israel. This is accomplished by Jehu, an Israelite commander who leads a revolt and usurps the throne. But Jehu does not eliminate the idols built by Jeroboam and continues a mixed idol-Torah religion. Just before his death Elisha prophesies that Israel will defeat the Syrians three times. This prophecy comes about under King Joash.(2 Ki. 2 - 13) [NOTE: During the lifetimes of Elijah and Elisha there were many prophets who were their followers in both the northern and southern kingdoms. They are referred to in scripture as "sons of the prophets."(2 Ki. 2:3-5)]

Warnings to Israel. During the reign of Jeroboam II (782-753 B.C.; 2 Ki. 14:23-29), the Lord speaks to the northern kingdom through the writing prophets Hosea, Amos, and Jonah.

HOSEA: an Object Lesson. The Lord has Hosea marry a prostitute who leaves him, then returns, being redeemed by Hosea. This is an object lesson for Israel who has played the harlot and forsaken her husband, God. God will call a people who are not his people "the sons of the living God."(Hos. 1:10)   But God still loves Israel and will redeem her if only she will turn from backsliding and walk in the ways of the Lord.(Hos. 1 - 14)

AMOS: Love the Good. Amos brings the message that God is displeased with both Israel and Judah. They will suffer the consequences of their sinful practices, as will the pagan nations. The Lord is particularly upset with Israel, because the rich have been allowed to prosper at the expense of the poor of the land. Israel is exhorted to hate the evil and love the good. If she does not repent, she will be enslaved. But the Lord will sift Israel and restore the loyal ones among his people, raising up the tabernacle of David.(Amos 1 - 9)

JONAH: to Nineveh. Jonah provides another object-lesson. He is commissioned to go to Nineveh to preach God's word to the Assyrians. But Jonah, seeking to avoid a mission to the great enemy of Israel, gets on a ship bound for Tarshish. When the sailors conclude that the storm they encounter is due to Jonah's presence, he is thrown overboard and swallowed by a great fish. Jonah's prayer for rescue is answered, and three days later the fish throws him up on the shore. In Nineveh Jonah carries out his mission, and the Ninevites are converted, much to Jonah's chagrin.(Jonah 1 - 4) [HISTORICAL NOTE: According to Assyrian records, Nineveh was not yet the capital of the Assyrian empire in Jonah's day. The capital for the empire was Caleh (Nimrud). In 722/721 B.C., about a generation after Jonah's visit to Nineveh, the Assyrians invade Israel to put down a revolt by Israel's King Hoshea and take over the nation. The Assyrian kings, Shalmaneser V and Sargon II, both take credit for this conquest. NEW TESTAMENT NOTE: Jesus refers to Jonah and the conversion of the Ninevites as the only sign he will give to his opponents.(Matt. 12:38-41)]

Faith Heroes of Judah, the Southern Kingdom. Judah's history after Solomon's death (931 B.C.) and until the Judeans' captivity in Babylon (586 B.C.) shows an on-again, off-again compliance with the conditions of God's covenants. The good kings who see that worship at the temple and the reading of the scripture are carried out, and who take steps to eradicate pagan practices, are Asa (911-874 B.C.), Jehoshaphat (873-848 B.C.), Hezekiah (728-686 B.C.), and Josiah (640-609 B.C.). The efforts of these kings are nullified by those who return to pagan worship or who are well-meaning but take no steps to eliminate paganism. The last kings of Judah are evil in God's eyes, and God permits Egypt to gain control of Judah; however, Egypt is repulsed when Nebuchadnezzar and the Babylonians conquer the Assyrians and take over all of Palestine.(605-586 B.C.; 2 Ki. 18 - 25; 2 Chron. 14 - 36)

Warning and Hope. The prophets of the southern kingdom, Judah, carry God's message to the kings and the populace and set the message to writing. These prophets are Isaiah, Micah, Zephaniah, Nahum, Jeremiah, Obadiah, Habukkuk, and Joel.

ISAIAH and MICAH: Ears To Hear; Eyes To See. Isaiah serves under four kings and through the reign of Hezekiah (c. 770-700 B.C.).(Isa. 1:1; 2 Ki. 19:2-7; 20:1-11; 2 Chron. 32:20-32). Isaiah's commission as a prophet comes about when in a vision he hears the Lord's voice asking, "Whom shall I send, and who will go for us?" Isaiah replies, "Here am I; send me." Then the Lord instructs Isaiah, "Go, and tell this people, 'Hear you indeed, but understand not; and see you indeed, but perceive not.' Make the heart of this people fat, and make their ears heavy, and shut their eyes; lest they see with their eyes, and hear with their ears and understand with their heart, and convert, and be healed."

[NOTE: This commission is not without a certain amount of irony. All or part of it is quoted on three occasions in the New Testament — by Jesus when he explains why he begins using parables (Matt. 13:14-15; Mk. 4:12; Lk. 8:10), by the apostle John in relating the unbelief of the people (John 12:39-41), and by the apostle Paul in speaking to certain skeptics during his imprisonment in Rome.(Acts 28:26-27)]

Idolatry Must Go. The prophet Micah is a contemporary of Isaiah.(Micah 1:1; Jer. 26:18)   Both prophets speak out against worship of idols and images made with hands and other practices of paganism. The Lord will destroy graven images and cut off witchcraft and sorcery.(Micah 5:12-15)   Isaiah points out the folly of idol worship. An artisan makes an idol in human likeness from metal or wood to keep in a house. A carpenter will take wood and use part of it as fuel to bake bread, to roast a roast, or to warm himself. With the other part, he fashions a god and falls down and worships it. He falls down to a tree. Such a person is deceived. He gives credence to a lie and in effect feeds on ashes.(Isa. 44:9-20) Idolatry leads to degrading practices such as adultery, prostitution, and child sacrifice. It also results in weariness, lying, and loss of hope. When an idolator cries out, his companions cannot help him. "But the wicked are like the troubled sea when it cannot rest, whose waters cast up mire and dirt. There is no peace, saith my God, to the wicked."(Isa. 57:1-21)

Chastisement and Correction. Isaiah and Micah foretell the fall of both Israel and Judah because of the failure of these nations to forsake idolatry and to adhere to God's covenants. But God is a God of mercy and will reestablish his people if they repent and change their ways.(Micah 1 - 7)   Isaiah gives detailed prophecies of what will befall them and also the surrounding pagan nations and the conquering empires.(Isa. 1 - 35)   He records the episode of the repulsing of the Assyrians by Judah under the leadership of Hezekiah and by the grace of the Lord (Isa. 36 - 39) and sets forth prophecies of peace and comfort.(Isa. 40 - 66)   Israel will be defeated and captured. Judah will eventually be taken into captivity, but God will raise up a Gentile king, named Cyrus, who will let the captives go free to rebuild Jerusalem and the temple.(Isa. 44 - 45)

Prince of Peace. Peace, justice, and mercy will be established through a child to be born who will be "wonderful, counselor, the mighty God, the everlasting Father, the prince of peace."(Isa. 9:6-7)   "And there shall come forth a rod out of the stem of Jesse" (i.e., be a descendant of Jesse's son, David), "and a branch shall grow out of his roots. And the spirit of the Lord shall rest upon him, the spirit of wisdom and understanding, the spirit of counsel and might, the spirit of knowledge and fear of the Lord . . . The wolf also shall dwell with the lamb, and the leopard shall lie down with the kid, and the calf and the young lion and the fatling together, and a little child shall lead them."(Isa. 11:1-6) When the day of true peace comes, the nations will "beat their swords into plowshares and their spears into pruning hooks; nation will not lift up sword against nation; neither shall they learn war any more."(Isa. 2:3-4; Micah 4:3) A loyal remnant of Jews will be redeemed to continue as God's servants in bringing his word to the world.(Isa. 10:20-21; 52:1-2) "How beautiful upon the mountains are the feet of him that brings good tidings, that publishes peace; that publishes salvation; that says to Zion, 'Thy God reigns!' "(Isa. 52:7) "But who has believed our report, to whom is the arm of the Lord revealed?"(Isa. 53:1) God's servant, the Messiah, one despised and rejected of men, shall bear our griefs and sicknesses, carry our sorrows. He is to be wounded for our transgressions and bruised for our iniquities, and by his wounds (stripes) we are healed.(Isa. 53:2-5) The word of the Lord shall be carried forth, and all nations shall run to the holy one of God. God's thoughts are not our thoughts, nor his ways our ways, for as the heavens are higher than the earth, his ways are higher than our ways, and his thoughts than our thoughts. The word which proceeds from God will not return to him void, but it will accomplish that which he has ordained and that for which he sent it.(Isa. 55:4-12) No one has directed God's spirit or counseled or instructed him in judgment, knowledge, or under-standing.(Isa. 40:13-14) His word will prevail, for while the grass may wither and the flower fade, his word will stand forever.(Isa. 40:7-8) He will create a new heaven and a new earth of rejoicing (Isa. 65:17-25), and everyone who "thirsts" may "come to the waters" of God freely and eat of Godly "bread," and his or her soul will live delightfully in the Lord.(Isa. 55:1-3) [NOTE: Isaiah is the prophet most quoted in the New Testament — some 66 times.]

ZEPHANIAH and NAHUM: Warning against Assyria. During the reign of Josiah (c. 640-609 B.C.), prophets Zephaniah and Nahum bring God's warning to Judah, and they also prophesy against Assyria, with particular mention of Nineveh, now the capital of the empire. In the generations since Jonah, that city has become corrupt and degenerate. Assyria will be conquered and Nineveh leveled.(Zeph. 1 - 3; Nahum 1 - 3)

JEREMIAH and LAMENTATIONS: the New Covenant. Jeremiah serves as a spokesman of God during Josiah's reign. When the word of the Lord comes to Jeremiah appointing him as his representative, Jeremiah (like Moses) is reluctant. He says, "Ah, Lord God: behold, I cannot speak, for I am a child." The Lord assures him that he need have no fear. Then the Lord puts forth his hand, touches Jeremiah's mouth, and says, "I have put my words in your mouth."(Jer. 1:4-9) Josiah is a good king, but through an error of judgment he is killed during a battle against the Egyptians. Judah is then ruled by Josiah's unprincipled offspring. Judah soon comes under the control of Egypt, but both fall to the Babylonians, the conqueror of Assyria. During this latter period of his ministry, Jeremiah is persecuted for speaking the word of God. In about 586 B.C., when the Jews are deported to Babylon, Jeremiah and his secretary, Baruch, are taken to Egypt by Judeans escaping capture and deportation.(Jer. 43:5-8) In his book Jeremiah records God's warnings to all nations opposing Judah. In particular, Babylon will be conquered by an assembly of nations. The Jews will remain in Babylon for 70 years.(Jer. 25:12; 50; 2 Chron. 36:21) A remnant will return to Judah, and God will provide shepherds for the flock.(Jer. 23:3-4) A chastised Judah will have the promise of a new covenant (**Covenant No. 6**). The Lord says, "Behold, the days come . . . that I will make a new covenant with the house of Israel, and with the house of Judah; not according to the covenant that I made with their fathers in the day that I took them by the hand to bring them out of the land of Egypt; which my covenant they broke, although I was a husband to them . . . But this shall be the covenant that I will make with the house of Israel: after those days, I will put my law in their inward parts and write it in their hearts; and I will be their God, and they shall be my people. And they shall teach no more every man his neighbor and every man his brother, saying, 'Know the Lord'; for they shall all know me, from the least of them to the greatest of them . . . for I will forgive their iniquity, and I will remember their sin no more."(Jer. 31:31-34; Heb. 8:6-13) Jeremiah, saddened by the fall of Jerusalem and the destruction of the temple, expresses his grief in the book of Lamentations.

OBADIAH, HABAKKUK, and JOEL: the Ministry of the Holy Spirit. The prophets — Obadiah, Habakkuk, and Joel — also convey God's message to the Judeans about the discipline which they will undergo so that they might yet become a purified instrument for the accomplishment of God's work and the continuation of his revelations to mankind. Of special significance is God's promise of the outpouring of his Holy Spirit upon "all flesh"; that "whoever shall call upon the name of the Lord shall be delivered."(Joel 2:28-32; Acts 2:16-32)

DANIEL and EZEKIEL: Judah in Babylon. The scriptural scene now shifts from Judah east to Babylon. The Judeans (Jews) are in captivity there; yet they are given a certain amount of freedom. The most skilled are put to work and are given training. During the time of Nebuchadnezzar's initial subjugation of Judah (c. 605 B.C.), Daniel is brought to Babylon as a young man and given the Babylonian name of Belteshazzar. His three companions — Hananiah, Mishael, and Azariah — are also renamed as Shadrach, Meshach, and Abednego, respectively. They learn well and are given important posts in the government.(Dan. 1)   Ezekiel is brought to Babylon later, about 593 B.C., a few years before the final capture and destruction of Jerusalem in 586 B.C.(Ezek. 1:1-2; 17 - 20)   Ezekiel has a vision in which he sees wheels and beings with many faces — then the vision of one with the appearance of the glory of the Lord resting on a throne. He speaks to Ezekiel, and the spirit enters into him. Ezekiel is commissioned to prophesy to the Judeans in Babylon. From that time until the fall of Jerusalem, Ezekiel does so, also prophesying the fall of other nations.(Ezek. 21 - 32)   News comes that Jerusalem has fallen, and the Lord has Ezekiel prophesy about the restoration of Israel. The Lord will care for his flock, make a covenant of peace with them, and give them a new heart and a new spirit.(Ezek. 33 - 37)   Future enemies, such as Gog of the land of Magog, will arise, but the Lord will protect his people.(Ezek. 38 - 39)   In a vision the Lord gives Ezekiel instructions for a new temple and designates the descendants of Zadok as the chief priests.(Ezek. 40 - 46)   The promised land is once again to be apportioned according to the 12 tribes of Israel.(Ezek. 47 - 48)

The Supremacy of Daniel's God. While Ezekiel's ministry is among the Jewish people in Babylon, their elders coming to him at his home (Ezek. 14:1), Daniel's work is at the palace where he eventually rises to a position second only to the king of the Babylonian empire.(Dan. 6:1-2)   He and Shadrach, Meshach, and Abednego stay true to their God being steadfast in worship, prayer, and even the dietary laws.(Dan. 1:8-20)   They successfully resist the pressure to worship pagan gods and statues or the king. God's hand is upon them as Daniel interprets Nebuchadnezzar's dreams and later is saved from the ordeal of the lion's den. His friends are saved from the fiery furnace by an angel of the Lord. Nebuchadnezzar and later kings recognize and officially declare the supremacy of the God of Daniel. In 539 B.C. the Medes and Persians under Cyrus conquer Babylon and take over the empire as predicted by Daniel when he interprets the handwriting on the wall. Daniel continues to serve and is given even more responsibility.(Dan. 1 - 6)

Prophecies of Daniel. Daniel's role as a spokesman for God is seen in his interpretation of Nebuchadnezzar's dream about a large statue whose feet of clay and iron are smashed by a rock hewn without hands. Control of the empire will change hands, but God will create a kingdom which will be supreme over all others and will last forever.(Dan. 2) Also, Daniel has visions in which he sees and is told many things of the future. He sees one like the son of man who comes before the "ancient of days" seated on a throne, and he is given an everlasting dominion over a kingdom which will not be destroyed. Various animals which also appear in the vision are symbolic of various world powers, the greatest of which will oppose the "most high," but the greatness of the kingdom and all dominions will be given over to the people of the most high.(Dan. 7) In another vision a voice instructs the angel Gabriel to tell Daniel the meaning of another array of animals. This symbolism refers to the coming conquest of the Medo-Persian empire by the king of Greece. Another will arise in greater power, oppose even the "prince of princes" but be "broken without hand."(Dan. 8)

Daniel's Prayer. In a prayer Daniel beseeches the Lord to release the Judean captives so that they can return to Judah, for the 70 years of captivity prophesied by the prophet Jeremiah have been fulfilled. Daniel repeatedly confesses the transgressions of the Jews and asks that God be merciful. The angel Gabriel comes to Daniel and tells him that 70 "sevens" are to transpire before there will be full reconciliation with God and an end to sin. From the time of the commandment to rebuild the temple and the time of the anointed one (messiah) will be 69 "sevens." In that period the streets and the wall will be rebuilt. After 62 "sevens" the anointed one will be cut off. A prince will come who will destroy the city, and there will be a flood. This prince will confirm the covenant for one "seven." But in that time he will cause sacrifice and offering to cease, and he will spread abomination and desolation until the consummation.(Dan. 9) [NOTE: In most English translations the Hebrew word for "seven" in Dan. 9 is translated as "week."]

Future Deliverance. In another vision one having the appearance of a man finely dressed comes to Daniel, saying that he has come in response to Daniel's prayers. He would have come sooner but was delayed by the "prince of the kingdom of Persia." But Michael, "one of the chief princes," came to help him so that he could come to Daniel. He tells Daniel that a mighty king of Greece will some day conquer Persia, but his empire will be divided into four. Thereafter there will be constant conflict and intrigue. But there will come a day when Michael will stand forth for the people, and everyone whose name is written in the book will be delivered. Those who sleep shall awake to eternal life and some to eternal contempt. The wise will turn many to righteousness forever. The time from the stopping of the daily sacrifice to the setting up of the abomination of desolation will be 1290 days. Blessed is the person who waits and comes to the 1335 days. Daniel does not understand all these things, and the man tells him that his words are closed up and sealed till the time of the end. Many will be purified; the wicked will not understand; but the wise shall understand. To Daniel he says, "But go your way till the end, for you shall rest and stand in your lot at the end of the days."(Dan. 10 - 12; Matt. 24)

EZRA, NEHEMIAH, ESTHER, HAGGAI, ZECHARIAH, MALACHI: Return to Judah; Rebuilding of the Temple. When the Persian King Cyrus begins his rule of the empire, he issues a proclamation permitting the Judeans (Jews) to return to Judah, for, as prophesied by Isaiah, the Lord has directed Cyrus to rebuild the temple at Jerusalem (c. 538 B.C.). Cyrus also directs that the royal treasury finance the project. Zerubbabel (Sheshbazzar), a prince of the Davidic line, is appointed governor. He leads about 50,000 Jews back to Judah, and the construction of the temple at Jerusalem is begun with great joy.(Ezra 1 - 3)   But enemies in the land oppose the rebuilding of Jerusalem and the temple; they appeal to a new Persian king, Darius. They question whether there is any royal proclamation as claimed by the Jews. This confrontation causes a delay in construction while the records are searched.(Ezra 4 - 6)

Exhortation by Haggai and Zechariah. The Lord speaks to the Jews, to Zerubbabel, and the high priest, Joshua, in particular, through the prophets Haggai and Zechariah. The work on the temple is not to be delayed; the people have become complacent, and they are exhorted to get on with the work.(Ezra 5:1, 6:14; Hag. 1 - 2; Zech. 4:6-10; 6:11-15)   In their writings the prophets point to the success to be enjoyed by Zerubbabel (Hag. 2:22-23) and to the blessings to be poured forth for Judah and Jerusalem.(Zech. 8, 14)   In the future a champion will arise and come riding on a colt. Thirty pieces of silver shall be paid for his life. The shepherd of the people, he will be smitten and pierced. But the Lord shall reign, and all nations will worship him.(Zech. 9 - 14)

Completion of the Temple. The decree of Cyrus is found in a palace in Achmetha, a city of the Medes (today in Iran), and Darius issues a decree that the work continue on the temple. The

Jews' opponents are ordered not to interfere. The temple is completed during the reign of Darius (c. 515 B.C.), and the Jews dedicate it with great joy.(Ezra 6)

Esther, Queen of the Empire. The next recorded event in the book of Ezra is the arrival of Ezra, the ready scribe, in Jerusalem some 58 years after the completion of the temple.(Ezra 7)   In that interim events crucial to the Jews occur as related in the book of Esther. In Susa (Shushan), capital of the Persian empire, the king, Xerxes (Ahasuerus, Darius' son, 486 B.C.), holds a great feast for many princes and sends a message to Vashti, his queen, that she attend so that they might see the royal crown and the queen's beauty. Vashti is presiding over a banquet for the women and refuses to come. Xerxes, taking this as an act akin to treason, divorces her and holds a beauty contest to select a new queen. A Jew (actually a Benjamite) named Mordecai believes that his young cousin, Esther whom he has raised as his own daughter, might have a chance because of her outstanding beauty. The selection process is a drawn-out affair, but Esther is chosen as queen. One day Mordecai overhears a plot on the king's life which he relays to Esther who discloses it to Xerxes. The plot is uncovered and the plotters executed. The incident is set down in the official records.(Esther 1 - 2)

Order for Death of Jews. Of the princes who advise Xerxes, one Haman is the chief and by decree entitled to be reverenced by the people. But Mordecai consistently refuses to bow down to him. When Haman learns that Mordecai is a Jew, he confers with the king and convinces him that there are people throughout the empire who ignore the king's laws and follow laws of their own. If the king will issue an appropriate decree, Haman will see that these people are destroyed, and he will also pay a large sum into the king's treasury. The king agrees, but he is not aware that Haman is referring to the Jews. Haman secretly sends an edict in the king's name throughout the kingdom that on a certain day all Jews are to be killed and their belongings confiscated. Mordecai asks Esther to appeal to the king. Esther is hesitant, for if anyone intrudes on the king, not having been summoned, a law requires the death penalty unless the king grants a reprieve. Also, Esther has not told the king that she is a Jewess. Mordecai pleads with Esther on behalf of all Jewry. Esther finally decides that she must take the risk and sends a message to Mordecai. He is to have all the Jews in Susa fast for her for three days. She will go see the king. She says, "If I perish, I perish."(Esther 3 - 4)

The Jews Are Saved. Esther finds the king in a good mood, and he asks her if she has a request. She asks that the king and

Haman have dinner with her. At dinner she invites the king and Haman to a banquet the following evening. It is agreed; Haman goes home and brags about his good fortune. He also orders that a gallows be prepared for the execution of Mordecai. At the royal palace Xerxes retires but is unable to sleep. He has the official records brought to him, and while reviewing the entries, he comes across the account of how Mordecai had reported the plot on his life and recalls that Mordecai has not been honored for his faithful act. The next day he directs Haman do the honors by leading Mordecai on horseback through the city declaring that this man is a man whom the king delights to honor. Haman complies, realizing that the situation bodes no good for him.(Esther 5 - 6)   But before he can plan another move, he must attend Esther's banquet. At the banquet the king asks Esther what her request is. She reveals that she and her people are to be killed through the treachery of Haman. The king becomes angry and orders Haman to be hanged on the gallows which Haman had built for Mordecai. As for Mordecai, he is appointed to a high position in the king's government. But it is still necessary to reverse the orders which Haman had published throughout the land. The king permits Esther and Mordecai to issue orders in his name to be published abroad that the Jews may resist anyone who tries to carry out Haman's plan. Some attempts are made against the Jews, but they are quickly put down. Thus, through the bravery of Esther and Mordecai, the Jews are saved from extinction. The Jewish feast of Purim commemorates this episode in Jewish history.(Esther 7 - 10)

Ezra to Judah. Several years later (c. 458 B.C.), during the reign of Xerxes' son, Artaxerxes, Ezra is sent as the king's envoy to Judah with authority to see that the Jewish law and worship are being properly observed. Ezra's main goal is to study the law of the Lord and to teach it to the Jews. He discovers that many who have returned from Babylon have foreign wives who do not honor God, and a procedure is set up to interview those involved to correct the situation. Those who are priests readily agree to put away wives who remain as idol worshipers.(Ezra 7 - 10)

Nehemiah and the Walls of Jerusalem. Although the temple has been rebuilt, the protective wall around Jerusalem and its gates remain in shambles. An attempt was made to fortify the city, but this work was stopped by an order of Artaxerxes.(Ezra 4:20-23)   Later in Artaxerxes' reign (c. 444 B.C.) his Jewish cupbearer, Nehemiah, hears that the walls have not been rebuilt and prays that the Lord will permit the full restoration of the city. The king reverses his position about the walls of Jerusalem and appoints Nehemiah as governor of Judah so that he can oversee completion of the work. While Judah's enemies deride the Jews' attempts to build the walls and gates, Nehemiah is able to coordinate the work and get it completed but only after arming the workers to ward off the attempts at harassment.(Neh. 1 - 7)   When the time for the feast of the tabernacles is at hand, the people congregate in Jerusalem, living in booths made for the occasion from tree branches. Ezra and others stand before the people on a large platform, reading and explaining the Mosaic law to the assembly. There is great rejoicing in the city for eight days. The people recount their history and rededicate themselves to God's covenant, as they are told, "The joy of the Lord is your strength." Shortly thereafter a ceremony is held to dedicate the walls. Men, women, and children rejoice that God has been so good to them. When the celebrations are over, Nehemiah turns his attention to enforcement of the regulations concerning the Sabbath and speaks out against intermarriage with pagans.(Neh. 8 - 13)

MALACHI: the Last Old Testament Prophet. The writing prophet in this latter phase of Old Testament history (c. 444-425 B.C.) is Malachi. Through Malachi the Lord lets the priests and the people know that he does not appreciate sacrifice and offering made in a perfunctory way. He prefers sincere prayer. Priests speak for God and should give the best example in their conduct. The Jews must keep in mind that God's name is to be great among the Gentiles and the heathen. All nations can be blessed by the Jews only if they return to God and provide a good witness in obeying the covenant-law and being faithful with their tithes and offerings. Also, people cannot make a practice of treachery and expect God to be swayed by their offerings. One must take heed of his or her own spirit, for God as spirit is the creator of all. Husbands must be considerate of their wives. God does not change. He remembers his covenant and will send his "messenger of the covenant" who will pass judgment upon sorcerers, adulterers, false-swearers, and upon those who oppress widows, workers, orphans, and strangers. God will return to those who return to him, and for their sakes he will rebuke the devourer. A day of judgment is coming, but the "sun of righteousness" with his healing rays will shine upon the one who fears the Lord's name. The Jews must adhere to the laws and commandments given to Moses. God will send Elijah the prophet before the coming of the great and terrible day of the Lord.(Mal. 1 - 4)

Chart E

PROPHETS, KINGS, LEADERS OF DIVIDED ISRAEL AND JUDAH (931-425 B.C.)

*Asterisk denotes writing prophet

Prophets	Kings of Judah	Kings of Israel
Shemaiah, Ahijah, Iddo	Rehoboam (931-913)	Jeroboam I (931-910)
	Abijam (913-911)	Nadab (910-909)
Azariah, Hanani, Jehu	Asa (911-874)	Baasha (909-886)
		Elah (886-884)
		Zimri (884)
		Omri (884-874)
Elijah, Elisha	Jehoshaphat (873-848)	Ahab & Jezebel (874-853)
Elisha, Jehu, Jahaziel	Jehoram (853-841)	Ahaziah (853-852)
Elisha, Eliezer, Micaiah	Ahaziah (841)	Jehoram (852-841)
Elisha	Athaliah (Queen, 841-835)	Jehu (841-814)
Elisha, Zechariah of Jehoida	Joash (835-796)	Jehoahaz (814-798)
	Amaziah (796-767)	Jehoash (798-782)
Hosea*, Amos*, Jonah*, Isaiah*, Micah*	Uzziah (Azariah) (791-739)	Jeroboam II (793-753)
		Zachariah (753)
		Shallum (752)
Isaiah, Micah	Jotham (750-731)	Menahem (752-742)
Isaiah, Micah	Ahaz (743-715)	Pekahiah (742-740)
		Pekah (740-732)
Isaiah, Micah	Hezekiah (728-686)	Hoshea (732-722) (Israel conquered by Assyrians)
	Manasseh (697-642)	
	Amon (642-640)	
Nahum*, Zephaniah*, Hulda (prophetess) Jeremiah*, Habakkuk*	Josiah (640-609)	
Jeremiah, Obadiah*, Joel*, Uriah	Jehoahaz (609)	
	Jehoiakim (609-597)	
	Jehoiachin (597)	
	Zedekiah (597-586) (Judah taken into Babylonian captivity)	

JUDAH'S BABYLONIAN CAPTIVITY

Prophets	Kings and Judean Leaders
Jeremiah (in Judah & Egypt) Daniel*, Ezekiel*	Nebuchadnezzar, King of Babylon (605-562 B.C.)
Daniel	Belshazzar (562-539 B.C.), subruler under Nabonidus, King of Babylon
Daniel	Cyrus, King of Persia (539-529 B.C.)

RETURN TO JUDAH FROM CAPTIVITY

Haggai*, Zechariah*	Zerubbabel (Sheshbazzar), governor of Judah; Cyrus, Darius, Xerxes, Kings of Persia (539-465 B.C.)
	Ezra, priest, scholar, governor; Artaxerxes, King of Persia (465-423 B.C.)
Malachi*	Nehemiah, governor; Artaxerxes, King of Persia (465-423 B.C.)

CHART F

PERIOD OF OLD TESTAMENT WRITING
IN RELATION TO OLD TESTAMENT HISTORY

(Not to scale)

Creation Adam & Eve Cain Abel Seth	Flood Noah Ark Ham Shem Japheth	Tower of Babel Confusion of Languages	Abraham Sarah Isaac Jacob (Israel) Joseph (2100- 1800 BC)	Israel in Egypt (1880- 1450 BC)	Moses Exodus of Israel from Egypt (1450- 1410 BC)	Joshua Caleb Canaan Period of Judges (1410- 1050 BC)	Kings of Israel Saul David Solomon (1050- 931 BC)	Divided Kingdom Israel Judah Period of Kings (931- 586 BC)	Judah's Captivity in Babylon Return to Judah (586- 425 BC)	Intertesta- mental Period

2100 B.C.

425 B.C.

Period of Writing
of 39
Old Testament Books
(1450 B.C. - 425 B.C.)

Period of
the
Writing
Prophets
[Last 17
Books]
(750-425 BC)

1450 B.C.

750 B.C.

425 B.C.

CHAPTER FIVE

OLD TESTAMENT WISDOM AND POETRY BOOKS

The five Old Testament books known as wisdom and poetry books are Job, Psalms, Proverbs, Ecclesiastes, and Song of Solomon. [There is poetry in other books, such as the Song of Moses (Ex. 15:1-19); the Song of Miriam (Ex. 15:20-21); the Blessing of Moses (Dt. 33); and the Song of David.(2 Sam. 22-23) Likewise, there is a great deal of wisdom in all the books. The term "wisdom and poetry" is merely a means to categorize these particular five books.] The writing is in the Hebrew poetic form for the most part, and even the prose portions have a poetic quality about them, viz., Ecclesiastes. Some versions of the Bible, such as The New American Standard Bible and the Open Bible, show poetic passages in the poetic form.

JOB

Job was written by an unknown scribe or prophet, although Jewish tradition says that Moses wrote it. It is a very ancient account and was undoubtedly well known in both oral tradition and the written form. As indicated earlier, conservative scholars place the writing of the available Hebrew text in the 900's B.C. In the book Job is very wealthy living in Uz which is thought to have been located somewhere in Mesopotamia. The patriarchal setting indicates a time in the 2000 - 1500 B.C. era.

Job is an upright man who fears God and avoids evil. He is married and has seven sons and three daughters. These children engage in continual rounds of feasting and drinking. Job has been praying for them regularly in case they have been guilty of blasphemy against God. On a certain day when satan appears among those who come to present themselves before the Lord, satan and God discuss the merits of Job, God recognizing him as an upright man of great faith. But satan challenges God, saying that he believes he can cause Job to lose his faith and curse God if enough calamity comes upon him. God agrees that satan may try, but he is prohibited from taking Job's life. Then one day satan causes the house in which Job's children are partying to collapse from a great wind, and they are killed. Bandits and thieves make off with Job's cattle and kill his servants. Nevertheless, Job praises God, saying, "Naked came I out of my mother's womb and naked shall I return. The Lord gave, and the Lord has taken away. Blessed be the name of the Lord."(Job 1:21)   Then satan afflicts Job with a great illness which renders him hideous to look upon. Mrs. Job says to him, "Do you still retain your integrity? Curse God and die." But Job answers, "What? Shall we receive good at the hand of the Lord, and shall we not receive evil?" And Job refuses to complain.(Job 2:9-10)

Job is nonetheless grief-stricken. Three friends come by to comfort him, and they sit with him for seven days, no one saying a word. Job breaks the silence by cursing the day he was born, saying, "That which I feared has come upon me."(Job 3:25)   The three friends and Job engage in many rounds of philosophical discussion in which the friends' basic point is that Job must have been guilty of some great transgression for God to have permitted these things to happen. Job defends himself against this line of talk. A fourth friend, Elihu, has come by and hears what they are saying. The position of the first three — Eliphaz, Bildad, and Zophar — is that God is just and faithful; that he upholds believers who are innocent of wrongdoing. Job concedes that he has sinned, but he is entitled to God's forgiveness and relief from his difficulties. He wishes that a "daysman" (a mediator) be appointed to hear his case and make a just judgment. Job says that his friends are not helping him and are poor comforters. They should be pleading to God on his behalf. Why does God want to destroy one who is not wicked?

Elihu, the fourth friend, enters the discussion, saying that he speaks with the spirit of God. He rebukes Job and the others, Job for trying to justify himself rather than God, the three friends because they have no answer yet sit in judgment of Job. Surely they realize that God made all things and that he has made men wiser than animals. But God does not hear nor regard vanity. To be righteous is to trust God, for God does not act wickedly, nor does he pervert justice. God is powerful, majestic, and wonderful, doing great things which cannot be comprehended. He is both just and merciful, giving heed to the cries of the afflicted.(Job 32 -37)

Then, out of a whirlwind, God speaks. They must realize that he laid the foundations of the earth and measured and fastened it; that he knows the way of light and darkness; divides the watercourses; causes the lightning, thunder, and rain; provides the food; has set the times for birth; commands the animals; and puts wisdom in the inward parts of people and understanding in their hearts. Has any of them done these things? Do they not know that contending with God is trying to instruct him, to reprove him, and to disannul his judgment?

After hearing these words from the Lord, Job answers that he knows that he has lacked understanding, but now he says, "My eye sees you," and he repents.(Job 38 - 41) God's anger is against the three friends, because they did not speak correct things of God. The Lord directs them to offer sacrifices, and, at the Lord's direction, Job prays for his friends. After these things have been accomplished, Job is restored to good health and to prosperity. His property exceeds his previous wealth; he has 10 more children, and he lives to a ripe old age.(Job 42)

In your reading of Job, it may help you to notice that while God told satan that Job was righteous, he did not say that Job was perfect in the sense that God is perfect. Job was human, one of God's creations. Job and his four counselors were all believers. They agreed on God's sovereignty and control, as well as the need for mankind to worship him, confess sins, and lead a moral life. The first three advisors thought that Job must have sinned greatly in order to have such calamity befall him. Job essentially said, "I have been faithful, and I want to plead my case to God as I would to my neighbor." In other words, he wanted to justify himself. On the other hand, he also said that if God would speak, he would do whatever God directed. Elihu pointed out that Job's case was before God and that Job should wait for God to give direction.

Note also that there was silent misery for seven days; then Job broke the silence by cursing the day he was born. Thus, we do not find Job and the others in an attitude of prayer. We see a lot of philosophizing, complaining, and trying to figure out the problem through rationalization. Both Elihu and God said that mankind cannot solve all problems of creation through human reasoning and that all they needed to do was to let their faith go to work, worship God, pray for others, and wait upon God, because all things emanate from him. When these principles were followed, Job not only was healed and restored, but also his prosperity exceeded his previous wealth twofold. Satan's scheme did not work. Job did not curse God; he learned that full trust in God, as he is revealed through all his unchanging attributes, brings beneficial results.

PSALMS

The book of Psalms is a collection of 150 psalms or songs. The word "psalm" comes from a Greek word meaning "song." This book in the Hebrew text is called "Praises." Some psalms have titles showing the author as David or other named persons. David wrote 73 of the psalms, Moses one (Ps. 90), and Solomon two(72, 127). The rest are ascribed to others or are anonymous. The writing of the psalms covers a 500-year period from about 1000 B.C. to about 500 B.C. In the New Testament the Psalms are attributed to David. Other psalms of David are found in 2 Sam. 1:19-27; 3:33-34; 22; 23:1-7; 1 Chron. 16:7-36; 25:6-7; 2 Chron. 29:30.

Hebrew poetry was not written to rhyme or to have a particular rhythm except as imparted by stanzas of similar or contrasting thoughts. For example —

Similar: The kings of the earth set themselves,
And the rulers take counsel togcther
Against the Lord and against his anointed.
(Ps. 2:2)

Contrasting: For the Lord knows the way of the righteous,
But the way of the ungodly shall perish.
(Ps. 1:6)

Psalms is divided into five sections or books in many Bibles. Note the designations before Ps. 1, Ps. 42, Ps. 73, Ps. 90, and Ps. 107. Tradition has it that these were an allusion to the five books of the Torah, but there are no headnotes clarifying this fact. Certain Hebrew words indicate a type of psalm, such as, "maskil" or "michtam," or a pause or interlude, "selah"; however, the precise meaning of these words has been lost to antiquity. It is clear that the psalms were recited or sung to the accompaniment of musical instruments. This is indicated by the headings of Ps. 4, 5, and 6 and others; also, Ps. 148 exhorts us to sing praises to God and Ps. 150 to praise him with the sounds of musical instruments.

David was a poet, a prophet, and a king. His prophecies are in his psalms. It is here that he outlines the attributes of God, the ways for people to praise the Almighty; he underscores God's lovingkindness and patience with his creatures and his role as our protector, our healer, and our provider. Several of David's psalms are messianic, that is, they prophecy the coming of the anointed one (Messiah, Hebrew; Christ, Greek). These are Psalms 2, 8, 16, 22, 69, 110. Psalms 110 is the most quoted Old Testament passage in the New Testament. Other messianic psalms are 45, 72, 89, 118, and 132.

The Psalms are probably the most beautiful, inspiring, and comforting literature ever written. What writer could ever surpass Ps. 23 or Ps. 91 or find more joy in the Lord expressed than in Ps. 148, 149, and 150. By way of example and to close this quick run-through of this important book, we quote three psalms from the KJV.

PSALM 23
A Psalm of David

The Lord is my shepherd; I shall not want.

He maketh me to lie down in green pastures: he leadeth me beside the still waters.

He restoreth my soul: he leadeth me in the paths of righteousness for his name's sake.

Yea, though I walk through the valley of the shadow of death, I will fear no evil: for thou art with me; thy rod and thy staff they comfort me.

Thou preparest a table before me in the presence of mine enemies: thou anointest my head with oil; my cup runneth over.

Surely goodness and mercy shall follow me all the days of my life: and I will dwell in the house of the Lord forever.

PSALM 91

He that dwelleth in the secret place of the most High shall abide under the shadow of the Almighty.

I will say of the Lord, He is my refuge and my fortress: my God; in him will I trust.

Surely he shall deliver thee from the snare of the fowler, and from the noisome pestilence.

He shall cover thee with his feathers, and under his wings shalt thou trust: his truth shall be thy shield and buckler.

PSALM 91 (Cont.)

Thou shalt not be afraid for the terror by night; nor for the arrow that flieth by day;

Nor for the pestilence that walketh in darkness; nor for the destruction that wasteth at noonday.

A thousand shall fall at thy side, and ten thousand at thy right hand; but it shall not come nigh thee.

Only with thine eyes shalt thou behold and see the reward of the wicked.

Because thou hast made the Lord, which is my refuge, even the most High, thy habitation;

There shall no evil befall thee, neither shall any plague come nigh thy dwelling.

For he shall give his angels charge over thee, to keep thee in all thy ways.

They shall bear thee up in their hands, lest thou dash thy foot against a stone.

Thou shalt tread upon the lion and adder: the young lion and the dragon shalt thou trample under feet.

Because he hath set his love upon me, therefore will I deliver him: I will set him on high, because he hath known my name.

He shall call upon me, and I will answer him: I will be with him in trouble; I will deliver him, and honour him.

With long life will I satisfy him, and show him my salvation.

PSALM 150

Praise ye the Lord. Praise God in his sanctuary: praise him in the firmament of his power.

Praise him for his mighty acts: praise him according to his excellent greatness.

Praise him with the sound of the trumpet: praise him with the psaltery and harp.

Praise him with the timbrel and dance: praise him with stringed instruments and organs.

Praise him upon the loud cymbals: praise him upon the high sounding cymbals.

Let every thing that hath breath praise the Lord. Praise ye the Lord.

PROVERBS

Proverbs is a collection of long-established, short expressions of truth written in poetic form. Most of the proverbs are attributed to Solomon (about 950 B.C.), that is, Chapters 1 through 29. Chapter 30 contains the words of one Agur, and a King Lemuel speaks in Chapter 31. Prov. 25:1 indicates that Chapters 25 through 29 are the proverbs of Solomon transcribed by the men of Hezekiah. Solomon's authorship is declared in Prov. 1:1 and attested by 1 Kings 4:32.

The underlying theme of this book is the proper teaching and definition of wisdom which is often referred to in the feminine gender. Another feature of the proverbs is that they convey a practical, moral principle, contrasting good and evil. A person possessing true wisdom will live a trouble-free and peaceful life, but one without appropriate knowledge will be beset with all kinds of difficulties and ultimate defeat. Wisdom and folly are opposites, and only a fool would ignore the instructions set forth. The only way to attain wisdom is to fear the Lord (Prov. 2:5), for he protects and gives knowledge to godly people.(Prov. 2:6-22) A reader of the proverbs cannot help but notice both the practicality and the humor of them. The book is concluded with a description of the many attributes and activities of the virtuous wife.(Prov. 31:1-31) Here are some examples from the KJV.

Trust in the Lord with all thine heart; and lean not unto thine own understanding. In all thy ways acknowledge Him, and He shall direct thy paths.(Prov. 3:5-6)

Let thy fountain be blessed: and rejoice with the wife of thy youth.(Prov. 5:18)

How long wilt thou sleep, O sluggard? When wilt thou arise out of thy sleep? Yet a little sleep, a little slumber, a little folding of the hands to sleep: so shall thy poverty come as one that traveleth, and thy want as an armed man.(Prov. 6:9-11; 24:33, 34)

Receive my instruction, and not silver; and knowledge rather than choice gold. For wisdom is better than rubies and all the things that may be desired are not to be compared to it.(Prov. 8:10-11)

Righteousness exalteth a nation: but sin is a reproach to any people.(Prov. 14:34)

A soft answer turneth away wrath: but grievous words stir up anger. The tongue of the wise useth knowledge aright: but the mouth of fools poureth out foolishness. The eyes of the Lord are in every place, beholding the evil and the good. A wholesome tongue is a tree of life: but perverseness therein is a breach in the spirit.(Prov. 15:1-4)

A good name is rather to be chosen than great riches, and loving favor rather than silver and gold.(Prov. 22:1)

Withdraw thy foot from thy neighbor's house; lest he be weary of thee and so hate thee.(Prov. 25:17)

Confidence in an unfaithful man in time of trouble is like a broken tooth, and a foot out of joint.(Prov. 25:19)

A wrathful man stirreth up strife: but he that is slow to anger appeaseth strife.(Prov. 15:18; see also: 16:32)

The rich and poor meet together: the Lord is the maker of them all.(Prov. 22:2)

My son, attend to my words; incline thine ear unto my sayings. Let them not depart from thine eyes; keep them in the midst of thine heart. For they are life unto those that find them, and health to all their flesh. Keep thy heart with all diligence; for out of it are the issues of life.(Prov. 4:20-23)

Go to the ant, thou sluggard; consider her ways, and be wise: which having no guide, overseer, or ruler, provideth her meat in the summer, and gathereth her food in the harvest.(Prov. 6:6-8)

The wicked flee when no man pursueth: but the righteous are bold as a lion.(Prov. 28:1)

My son, keep my words, and lay up my commandments with thee. Keep my commandments, and live; and my law as the apple of thine eye. Bind them upon thy fingers, write them upon the table of thine heart. Say unto wisdom, thou art my sister; and call understanding thy kinswoman that they may keep thee from the strange woman, from the stranger which flattereth with her words.(Prov. 7:1-5)

If thine enemy be hungry, give him bread to eat; and if he be thirsty, give him water to drink: for thou shalt heap coals of fire upon his head, and the Lord shall reward thee.(Prov. 25:21-22)

As coals are to burning coals, and wood to fire; so is a contentious man to kindle strife.(Prov. 26:21; see also: 29:22)

It is better to dwell in the corner of the housetop, than with a brawling (contentious, NASB) woman and in a wide house.(Prov. 25:24; 21:9; see also: 21:19)

Drink waters out of thine own cistern, and running waters out of thine own well.(Prov. 5:15)

The Lord is far from the wicked: but he heareth the prayer of the righteous.(Prov. 15:29)

The spirit of man is the candle of the lord, searching all the inward parts of the belly.(Prov. 20:27)

ECCLESIASTES

The opening verse of Ecclesiastes attributes this book to Solomon (950 B.C.): "The word of the Preacher, the son of David, King in Jerusalem." The title comes from a Greek word meaning "assembly." The Hebrew name meant "preacher" or one who "gathers proverbs." Most of Ecclesiastes is in prose with several sections in the poetic form, notably, 1:2-11; 3:2-8; 7:1-14. Many people say that this is a difficult book to understand, because the author finds so much in life that is futile, "striving after wind" (NASB, Ampl.), that the book must have been written by a pessimist. Actually, the only parts which are pessimistic are those pointing out the futility of life without God in the midst of a godless society. In one sense, you can cry with the ones who have missed the peace and joy of true spiritual living and at the same time laugh with the "preacher" as he recounts all the worldly pleasures and attainments that brought him no satisfaction at all. As in the case with the book of Job, it helps to read Ecclesiastes with a sense of realism, empathy, and humor, zeroing in on those passages which show the realization that only a life with God brings true success and satisfaction.

The "preacher" realizes that in piling up wealth, he is only preparing an estate which on his death will pass to others who did not work for it.(Eccl. 2:21) He makes a discovery: "Lo, this only have I found, that God hath made man upright; but they have sought out many inventions (or devices, NASB)."(Eccl. 7:29) He advises, "Cast your bread upon the waters: for thou shalt find it after many days."(Eccl. 11:1) He extolls the wife who has stayed with a husband all the days of his struggling under the sun.(Eccl. 9:9) He has also learned that mankind (as was the case with Job) cannot know all the ways of God and that the righteous, the wise, and their works are in the hands of God.(Eccl. 8:17; 9:1)   Solomon ends his treatise recognizing that upon death the body returns to the dust of the ground; and that "the spirit shall return to God who gave it."(Eccl. 12:5-7)   He says, "Let us hear the conclusion of the whole matter: Fear God, and keep his commandments, for this is the whole duty of man. For God will bring every work into judgment with every secret thing, whether it be good, or whether it be evil."(Eccl. 12:13-14)

THE SONG OF SOLOMON

Written by Solomon (950 B.C.), the "Song" is one of the most beautiful pieces of literature in the Bible. It is a poetic drama featuring the declarations of love by Solomon for his wife, the Shulamite maiden, and her equally emotional expressions of love for him. In the drama a chorus is present which responds to some of the action. In some versions a change in speakers is indicated by headnotes or space between the verses. Jewish people have always regarded this book to be symbolic of God's love for his people, just as Jesus and the apostle Paul compare his relationship with believers to the marital status.(Mk. 2:19, 20; Eph. 5)   Some of the more familiar verses of Song of Solomon are (KJV):

Let him kiss me with the kisses of his mouth: for thy love is better than wine.(S of S 1:2)

I am the rose of Sharon, and the lily of the valleys.(S of S 2:1)

He brought me to his banqueting house, and his banner over me was love.(S of S 2:4)

The flowers appear on the earth, the time of the singing of the birds is come, and the voice of the turtle (turtledove) is heard in our land.(S of S 2:12)

Take us the foxes, the little foxes, that spoil the vines: for our vines have tender grapes.(S of S 2:15)

This is my beloved, and this is my friend, O daughters of Jerusalem.(S of S 5:16b)

I am my beloved's, and my beloved is mine: he feedeth among the lilies.(S of S 6:3)

CHAPTER SIX

THE PERIOD BETWEEN THE TESTAMENTS
(Intertestamental Period)

While Rome was still a growing nation and before Greece became a world power, the Old Testament was complete (about 425 B.C.). The nation Israel had had its heydays under David and Solomon, experienced a split into two nations, Israel and Judah, had been conquered and its people dispersed. Only the tribes of Judah (including Simeon), Benjamin, and Levi remained to return to their land and rebuild the temple at Jerusalem. The nation continued as Judah, later called Judea by the Greeks. The Judeans were also called Jews. Thus the word "Jew" refers to a descendant of the tribe of Judah.

The Persian Period. After the temple was rebuilt, being completed in 515 B.C., the Jews were allowed by the Persians to be self-governing. The High Priest (a Levite and descendant of Aaron) ruled with the help of a council. Not much is known of the history of Palestine during the period from the time of Nehemiah until the arrival of the Greeks upon the scene, but apparently it was a time of peace. The work of preserving and copying the scriptures was carried on by a group of scribes called the "Sopherim." Also, this may have been the time when a group of devout laymen established the sect known as "Hasidim." (There are Hasidim in Jerusalem today.) Many scholars believe that the Pharisees and Sadducees came from the Hasidim.

The Greek Period. The Persians were conquered by the Greeks under Alexander the Great in 334-331 B.C., and the ancient Near East came under Greek rule. There was a Jewish tradition that Daniel's prophecy about the arrival of the Greeks (Daniel 11:2-3) was told to Alexander, that he was delighted upon hearing it, and that the Jews were well treated as a result. It is known that the Greeks accorded Jews many privileges in Judea and North Africa. These privileges were recognized by subsequent rulers including the Romans for a time.

Greek Empire Divided. When Alexander died suddenly at the age of 33 (323 B.C.), his empire was divided by his generals into four kingdoms. Two became the leading powers in the Near

East: Egypt under the Ptolemies and Syria under the Seleucids. These were Greek dynasties which endeavored to force everyone in their kingdoms to become Greeks. As a result, Greek became the universal language and the language of the marketplace. It remained so even well into New Testament times and after. The Greek-Egyptians and the Greek-Syrians fought each other for supremacy, marching up and down Palestine with their armies. Judea was sometimes under Egyptian rule and sometimes under Syrian rule. It was during a period of Egyptian rule in about 250 B.C. that the Old Testament was translated into the Greek, that is, the Septuagint version.

Antiochus IV. The Syrians wrested Palestine away from the Egyptians in 198 B.C. In 174 B.C. the Syrian king, Antiochus IV, began a campaign against Judaism. He tried to destroy all copies of scripture and took over the temple. He placed a statue of Zeus in the temple and in mockery of the Jews had pigs sacrificed on the altar. He also tried to Hellenize the Jews, that is, force them to worship the Greek pagan gods and adopt Greek culture. The Jews resisted this interference with their biblical observance and mode of life. Many Jews were martyred during this period. When the resistance took the form of guerilla warfare, Antiochus rescinded his order, and the Jews regained their religious freedom.

Zadokites in Egypt. But beginning in 171 B.C., Antiochus controlled the selection of the Jewish high priest. The Jew who came up with the largest bribe got the office whether or not he was a Zadokite, that is, a descendant of Aaron through the line of Zadok, the only Aaronic line the Jews accepted for high priesthood at that time.(See 1 Chron. 6:8; Ezek. 48:11) The Zadokites, offended by this Syrian interference, all left Judea in 161 B.C. and went to Leontopolis, Egypt. Here they built their own temple and continued their observance of the Torah. This situation continued through New Testament times and until A.D. 70 when the Romans destroyed the temple at Jerusalem and ordered the observances stopped at Leontopolis. Thus, during the rest of the intertestamental period and during the time of Christ, those considered to be the rightful candidates for the position of high priest of Judea and the Jerusalem temple were in Egypt.

The Maccabees; Jewish Independence. The military resistance by the Jews began in 167 B.C. and grew into an all-out effort to gain freedom for Judea. The event which triggered the revolt transpired in the Jewish town of Modeim. Some Syrian soldiers tried to make a Jewish priest named Mattathias sacrifice a pig. He refused. Another man stepped forward and said that he would do it. Mattathias became angry, killed the man and the chief

Syrian official, and fled to the hills. Thereupon, many discontented Jews rallied to the leadership of Mattathias' son, Judas who was nicknamed "Maccabeus" (the hammer). The Jews defeated the Syrians being helped by their superior ability in mountain warfare and also by the fact that Antiochus faced a greater threat on his eastern border, diverting much of his army to the eastern front. Judas Maccabeus was killed, and his brother, Simon, became the leader and was made high priest. This was the beginning of a series of high priest-kings of the Hasmonean dynasty. (Hasmon was the family name of Mattathias and his sons, this family being descendants of Aaron but not of the Zadokite line.)

The Roman Takeover. After the Syrians were defeated, Judea became an independent state ruled by the Hasmoneans until the Romans took over in 63 B.C. The Hasmoneans were not moral rulers, and there was much intrigue and political maneuvering. This situation enabled the Roman general, Pompey, to annex Palestine, including Judea, as Roman territory. Under Roman policy the local rulers were not deposed if they recognized Roman authority, kept the peace, and paid taxes to Rome. Continuation of Hasmonean rule in Judea was aided by the ensuing power struggles in Rome which culminated in the ascendance of Julius Caesar as dictator in 45 B.C.

The Caesars. In his Egyptian campaign Julius became enamored of Cleopatra, the Egyptian queen, last of the Ptolemy line, and brought her to Rome. Caesar was assassinated in 44 B.C., and Cleopatra returned to Egypt. Caesar had given her control over a small area of Judea near Jericho which she retained. Another contest for rulership of the Roman empire arose following Caesar's death between his nephew Octavian and Marc Antony. At first they agreed that Octavian would rule over the western part of the empire and Antony over the eastern part which included Egypt and Palestine. Antony eventually visited Egypt and, like Julius Caesar, fell under the spell of Cleopatra's charms and her ambition. Antony was also ambitious to become sole dictator of the empire. He and Cleopatra had two sons as a result of their union. Antony, perhaps at Cleopatra's urging, made a gift of some eastern provinces to these two sons. Octavian became enraged at this action for two reasons. First, Antony was giving away a part of the empire, and secondly, Antony was already married to Octavian's sister Octavia whom Antony had left in Rome. As a result, Octavian set out to take control of the eastern part of the empire. His naval forces defeated those of Antony in the Battle of Actium in 31 B.C. The following year

Antony and Cleopatra committed suicide, leaving Octavian as the sole ruler. The Roman Senate designated him as emperor, and he took the name of Augustus Caesar.

Esau Returns. The events in Rome just described had their effect on the situation in Judea. While the Hasmoneans remained in charge of Judea for a time after 63 B.C., the end of their rulership was in the making. In 47 B.C. an official in the Jewish government named Antipater gained a great amount of power. Antipater was not Jewish but was an Idumean (an Edomite, descendant of Esau) whose family had been converted to Judaism, historians say, by force. He made a deal with the Romans and was appointed governor of Judea. He was assassinated in 43 B.C. When Palestine came under the rule of Marc Antony, he appointed Antipater's sons, Phasael and Herod, as joint governors. But the Parthians invaded Palestine and put a Hasmonean back on the Judean throne. Phasael was killed; Herod escaped to Rome. The Roman Senate, Antony, and Octavian together appointed Herod king of the Jews, on condition that he regain the territory from the Parthians. Parthia was a country located north of Palestine and east of Syria. Parthians were fierce fighters and had defeated every attempt of the Romans to subdue them. Herod leading a Roman army was able to defeat them and to bring Palestine back to Roman control in 37 B.C. Herod deposed the Hasmonean ruler, Antigonus, who had been appointed by the Parthians. Antigonus was eventually executed. None of these actions endeared Herod to the Jews. To appease them, he married a Hasmonean princess, but the Jews never accepted him or his family. Herod ruled strictly as a representative of Rome. When Antony and Cleopatra were defeated by Octavian, Herod quickly made friends with the new emperor who found him to be useful in controlling a potential trouble spot.

Death of Herod I. Herod I, also called Herod the Great, reconstructed the temple on a grand scale and sought to win over the Jews. He ran an efficient government but suffered from a touch of insanity when it came to the security of his position. He had two of his 10 wives and two of his sons executed, because he thought they were plotting to seize the throne. It is said that on his deathbed he ordered Jewish priests locked in a warehouse under orders that they be killed when he died so that there would be lamenting in Judea at the time of his own death. When he died in 4 B.C., this order was not carried out. The account in Matthew about Herod's killing of children in Bethlehem is consistent with the character of this man.

Tetrarchs and Procurators. After Herod died, the Romans split Palestine into four provinces and appointed a tetrarch to govern each one. ("Tetrarch" means ruler of one-fourth.) When Jesus was born, Herod I was king of Judea. When Joseph and Mary brought Jesus back to Judea from Egypt, Herod was dead, and Archelaus, a son of Herod, was tetrarch of the Judean province. Archelaus was more cruel than his father, so much so that the Romans removed him from office and sent him into exile in Europe. Thereafter, procurators such as Pontius Pilate were dispatched from Rome to govern Judea. Another of Herod's sons, named Herod Antipas, was made tetrarch of territory north and east of Judea, namely, Galilee and Perea. Descendants of Herod show up in various places in the New Testament.

Appointment of the High Priests. Herod I's position as king included the authority to appoint the Jewish high priest. These he appointed as a matter of politics. After Archelaus became tetrarch of Judea, he appointed three high priests in nine years. When Archelaus was removed from office, the Roman governors of Judea made the appointments, and the office of high priest ususally went to the Jew who came up with the largest bribe. From A.D. 6 to A.D. 70 the appointees were wealthy Sadducees. Relating this situation to the New Testament period, we find that Annas served as high priest from A.D. 6 to A.D. 15. Even after he was deposed, he retained a great deal of power. His son-in-law, Caiaphas, was high priest for 18 years, including the years of Christ's public ministry. When Christ was brought to trial, Annas and Caiaphas played major roles in the proceedings.

Jewish Religious Sects and Political Groups

Hasidim, Pharisees, Sadducees. We mentioned the Hasidim, Pharisees, and Sadducees previously, and there were other groups which formed in Judea during the intertestamental period. These groups were actually politico-religious sects or parties which were composed of lay persons. They were not the official religious leaders of the Jews as required under the law in the Torah. The official leaders were the priests and Levites. The priests were descendants of Aaron, and the Levites had charge of the upkeep and care of the temple and its contents. They were all of the tribe of Levi. The groups we discuss here were composed of laymen who wished to fill what they perceived as a religious gap resulting from the corrupt practices of temple officials who owed their positions to secular rulers. However, the Sadducees and Pharisees also got into the political arena. During the days of the Hasmonean dynasty they vied for influence, siding with different factions. Both groups were represented on the Sanhedrin, the

Jewish governing council, retaining their positions under Roman rule, as evident in the Gospels and the book of Acts. Jesus considered them as having seated themselves on Moses' seat.(Matt. 23:2) [As we have seen, the descendants of Aaron considered to be the rightful candidates for the position of High Priest, i.e., the Zadokites, were in Egypt.] The Sadducees represented the wealthy families, including some of the priestly class. They accepted only the Torah, the first five books of the Old Testament, and did not believe in a personal resurrection. The Pharisees were mainly professional and business men, and some were also rabbis or scribes. They did believe in the resurrection of the dead.(Acts 23:6-8) Their interpretations of scripture were looked to by the populace at large who held them in high regard.

Essenes, Zealots, Herodians, Scribes. The Essenes thought the other groups were too worldly and developed their own communities in the first century B.C. One of these was Qumran near the Dead Sea whence came the Dead Sea Scrolls now in the Shrine of the Book in Jerusalem. The Zealots were fiercly loyal Jews who attacked Roman soldiers whenever they could. Herodians were supporters of the claim of the Herod family to the rulership of Palestine. The scribes were men who copied and interpreted scripture.

Rabbis and Synagogues. Another group were the rabbis who taught in the synagogues. The synagogues were places where the Jews went for meeting and instruction after the first temple was destroyed in 586 B.C. After the temple was rebuilt, the synagogue system continued because of the needs of the people. The word "synagogue" originally meant "assembly of people" but came to mean the place where they met. "Rabbi" means "master" or "teacher." A rabbi might also be a member of one of the other groups mentioned. Education of Jewish children concerning the Law and Prophets was the duty of parents.(Prov. 1:8, 6:20; 2 Tim. 3:15) In the intertestamental period additional instruction was available at the local synagogue. Eventually, schools or academies arose, such as those of Hillel and Shamai. In the New Testament we learn that Paul was educated in the school of Gamaliel, a leading Pharisee.(Acts 22:3) The teachings emanating from rabbinical schools became the basis for such later Jewish books as the Mishna. In the Gospels Jesus criticized many ideas of these groups as inconsequential legalisms which obscured the deeper meanings of scripture.

Other Religions and Philosophies

Paganism and Mythology. In contrast to the scripture of the Jews and their belief in one sovereign God, most of the western and near-eastern world was pagan, that is, most of the people worshiped a group of gods each of whom had a special area of interest or duty. People had their favorites (viz. Diana (Artemis) of Ephesus in Acts 19:24-41) whom they worshiped. Each group of mythological gods and goddesses had a chief god as leader who was hard pressed to keep them in line, because they possessed all the foibles of the human race. (Augustine once wrote to a Roman soldier that one would hardly seek instruction on mortality at a party thrown by the Roman gods.) Some systems included worship of the sun, the stars, and even certain animals. Also common was resort to astrologers, soothsayers, magicians, and all forms of fortune telling.

Philosophy and the Soul. Thoughtful people during this period realized the inadequacies of a pagan religious system and began searching for principles which would provide answers to questions about the human soul and spiritual life. In Persia Zoroaster (about 600 B.C.) taught that there is one supreme creator-God (Ahura Mazda, meaning "God is light") who activates pious people through his holy spirit. Greek philosophers, including Heraclitus (500 B.C.), Plato (380 B.C.), Aristotle (330 B.C.), and Zeno (300 B.C.), wrote about "metaphysics" and concluded that there must be a supreme intelligence and creator of the universe. Such terms were used as "supreme reality," "uncaused cause," "prime mover," "universal soul," "eternal reason." The Greek word "logos" came to represent these concepts. It means literally "reason" or "word," but in the world of philosophy it took on the meaning of the everlasting totality of creation, intelligence, wisdom, and reason. The Jewish philosopher, Philo (20 B.C. - A.D. 50), saw in the logos the personification of God's wisdom operating as the intermediary and advocate between God and the world. "Logos" is found in the New Testament with reference to the "word of the kingdom" (Matt. 13:19), "word of God" (Lk. 8:11), and the "word" as existing from the beginning with God and becoming flesh to dwell among us.(John 1:1-14)

The Apocrypha

During the latter half of the intertestamental period, that is, from about 200 B.C. to the time of Christ, devout Jewish authors produced considerable religious literature. Much of it has been preserved, some being included in the Dead Sea Scrolls discovered in 1947. This literature includes history, fiction, and visionary (apocalyptic) writings dealing with the future. Those writings deemed to be of the most importance were called the Apocrypha (hidden things). While they were highly thought of, the Jewish people never considered them as scripture. When the Old Testament was translated into Greek, some of the Apocrypha were also translated and appended to the Septuagint version. The Christians used the Septuagint, and when the early Christians compiled the canonical books of the Christian Bible, they also included the Apocrypha. The Catholic Church considers the Apocrypha to be scripture, but Protestant denominations and theologians do not. Early English translations, including the King James version, had the Apocrypha in a separate appendix, and later most publishers eliminated it. The historical and literary importance of the Apocrypha has always been recognized, for they give a picture of Jewish life, morals, and beliefs just before the commencement of the Christian era. Of historical interest are the books 1 and 2 Maccabees which depict the Jewish struggles with the Syrians and the successful revolt led by the Maccabees, that is, Judas Maccabeus and the Hasmonean family.

Bibles with the Apocrypha and text material on the subject are available at Christian bookstores. The Good News Bible now has a version which includes the Apocrypha. The cost is about $4.00 if ordered from the American Bible Society. Also, the Apocrypha are included in Catholic versions of the Bible. A readable book on the subject is **An Introduction to the Apocrypha** by Bruce M. Metzger, published by Oxford University Press, New York.

The Apocrypha include:

1 and 2 Esdras: Ezra recounts the history of the Jews from the time of Josiah to the rebuilding of the temple; seven visions and prophecies of Ezra.

Tobit: A morality story of Tobit and his son Tobias, showing God's mercy and goodness.

Judith: A beautiful Jewish widow saves Judah from destruction.

Additions to the Book of Esther: Adds details and prayers to the book of Esther.

Wisdom of Solomon: A book of Jewish wisdom including ideas borrowed from Greek philosophy.

Ecclesiasticus (Sirach): Wisdom material and a defense of Judaism.

Baruch: A short book attributed to Baruch, secretary of the prophet Jeremiah; setting is Babylon.

Letter of Jeremiah: A letter attributed to Jeremiah condemning idolatry.

Prayer of Azariah and Three Young Men: Prayers attributed to the men as they walked about in the fiery furnace in Daniel 3.

Susanna: Daniel saves Susanna from false accusation of adultery.

Bel and the Dragon: Two stories; in one, Daniel's detective work unmasks crooked pagan priests; Daniel kills a dragon worshiped by Babylonians.

Prayer of Manasseh: Prayer of repentance attributed to Manasseh, a wicked king of Judah.

1 and 2 Maccabees: History of Maccabean period.

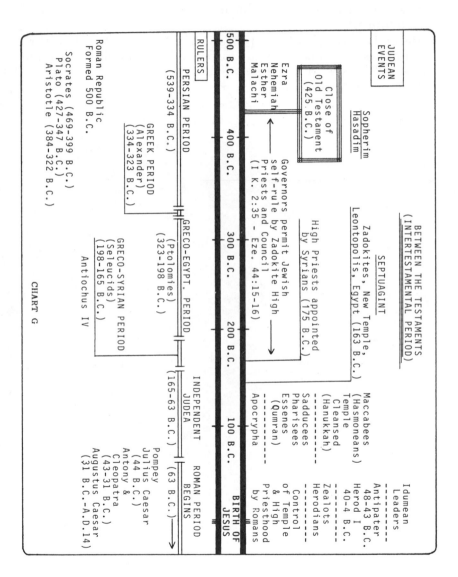

CHART G

BETWEEN THE TESTAMENTS
(INTERTESTAMENTAL PERIOD)

JUDEAN EVENTS						
Close of Old Testament (425. B.C.)	Sopherim Hasadim			SEPTUAGINT		Idumean Leaders ------------ Antipater 48-43 B.C. Herod I 40-4 B.C.
Ezra Nehemiah Esther Malachi		Governors permit Jewish self-rule by Zadokite High Priests and Council (I K. 2:35 - Eze. 44:15-16)	Zadokites, New Temple, Leontopolis, Egypt (163 B.C.) High Priests appointed by Syrians (175 B.C.)	Maccabees (Hasmoneans) Temple Cleansed (Hanukkah) Zealots Herodians ------------ Sadducees Pharisees Essenes (Qumran) Apocrypha	Control of Temple & High Priesthood by Romans	Pompey (63 B.C.) Julius Caesar (44 B.C.) Antony & Cleopatra (43-31 B.C.) Augustus Caesar (31 B.C.-A.D.14)

RULERS

PERSIAN PERIOD (539-334 B.C.)	GREEK PERIOD (Alexander) (334-323 B.C.)	GRECO-EGYPT. PERIOD (Ptolomies) (323-198 B.C.)	GRECO-SYRIAN PERIOD (Seleucids) (198-165 B.C.) Antiochus IV	INDEPENDENT JUDEA (165-63 B.C.)	ROMAN PERIOD BEGINS (63 B.C.)

500 B.C.	400 B.C.	300 B.C.	200 B.C.	100 B.C.	BIRTH OF JESUS

Roman Republic
Formed 500 B.C.

Socrates (469-399 B.C.)
Plato (427-347 B.C.)
Aristotle (384-322 B.C.)

CHAPTER SEVEN

INTRODUCTION TO THE NEW TESTAMENT

The New Covenant. In the ancient Greek manuscripts of the New Testament, the word for "covenant" is **diathekē** which also appears in the Septuagint version of the Old Testament as the translation of the Hebrew word **b'rith. Diathekē** can mean either a contract or a testament (as "last will and testament"), depending upon the context in which it is used. In the New Testament there are instances of both meanings. Jesus Christ of Nazareth, the central figure in the New Testament, is presented as the fulfillment of the new covenant prophesied by Jeremiah.(Jer. 31:31-34) Jesus is the mediator or administrator of the covenant as a contract between God and the world. Jesus is also the testator, executor, and heir under his own testament.(Heb. 1:2; 9:15-18; 10:14-22) Anyone can become a joint heir with him by believing and following him.(Rom 8:17) Jesus told the disciples that his was the blood of the new covenant serving as the sign and seal of it in the same way that Moses sealed the old covenant with the blood of a bull.(Lk. 22:20; Ex. 24:8; Heb. 9:20)

The New Testament Books. Thus we see that the group of books called the New Testament got its name from the new covenant (or testament) promised in the Old Testament book of Jeremiah. The four Gospels — Matthew, Mark, Luke, and John —relate Jesus' birth, ministry, and death on the cross and also his resurrection, post-resurrection appearances, and ascension. ("Ascension" refers to his ascending to the Father.) The book of Acts begins with the ascension and carries through with the coming of the Holy Spirit, the beginnings of the first-century church, with emphasis on the adventures and ministries of Peter and Paul. The 21 epistles are letters to specific congregations, or to Christians generally, explaining Christ and his teachings, relating these principles to the everyday problems of the people. The book of Revelation depicts a vision experienced by the apostle John in which he is given a message by God to be relayed to the churches. In his vision he sees heaven, the throne of God, and Jesus as the triumphant leader of angelic forces against satan and the forces of evil. With the exception of John's writings, the books of the New Testament were written during part of the historical period covered by the book of Acts (Chapters 15 - 28), that is, from about A.D. 47 to 64. John's writings are assigned to the A.D. 85-95 period.

The Gospels and the Messiah. In the four Gospels Jesus is revealed as the long-awaited Messiah whose coming was foretold by the prophets.(Matt. 16:16-17; Dan. 9:25) He left no doubt of his claim. He was the "son of man" of Dan. 7:13-14 (Mk. 2:28); the "son of God" of Ps. 2; 110 (Matt. 27:43; John 5:23-30); the prophet predicted by Moses in Dt. 18:15.(John 5:45-47) But further than this, he claimed to be equal to God, to be God visiting earth in the form of a man. He said that if they have seen him, they have seen the Father (John 14:9), for "I and my Father are one."(John 10:30) John makes the point clearly in his Gospel: "the word (logos) was with God, and the word was God ... And the word was made flesh and dwelt among us ..."(John 1:1, 14) "the Gospels attest to Jesus' birth of the virgin Mary who conceived by virtue of the Holy Spirit.(Matt. 1:18; Isa. 7:14) Her child would be ruler of the house of Jacob (Israel) forever and of an everlasting kingdom.(Lk. 1:32-33) When Jesus began his ministry, a voice from heaven said, "You are my son in whom I am well pleased."(Mk. 1:11) According to the apostle Paul, Jesus "being in the form of God thought it not robbery to be equal with God"; that he was "made in the likeness of men."(Phil. 2:6-7; see also 1 Tim. 3:16) Both John and Paul credit Jesus with having been integral in the creation of all things visible and invisible in heaven and on earth.(John 1:3; Col. 1:16) Jesus told his accusers that his kingdom is not of this world (John 18:36) and, "Hereafter shall the son of man sit on the right hand of the power of God."(Lk. 22:69) The risen Christ affirmed that "all power is given to me in heaven and earth."(Matt. 28:18) The disciples referred to Jesus as "Master and Lord" (John 13:13; see also Lk. 24:3; John 20:13; 21:7), and they worshiped him.(Lk. 24:52) When he saw Jesus' wound, Thomas exclaimed, "My Lord and my God."(John 20:28; see also Heb. 1:8) After Jesus' ascension his followers referred to him as "Lord and Christ" (Acts 2:36), "Lord Jesus Christ" (Acts 28:31), "Jesus Christ our Lord" (Rom. 1:3), "the Lord Jesus Christ."(Jas. 1:1) In Revelation an angel refers to him as "Lord of lords and King of kings" (Rev. 17:14), and this name is on Jesus' vesture as he leads angelic forces in his successful battle against the evil forces.(Rev. 19:16)

Jesus, a Different Kind of Prophet. Up to the time of his crucifixion Jesus' ministry was one of teaching, healing, miracles, and prophesying. The principles he taught and the way he taught, especially about himself, were not as the scribes

taught, for he taught as one having authority.(Matt. 7:28-29)
Jesus spoke to individuals, to small groups, and large crowds. He
used many teaching methods: lecture, conversation, question and
answer, demonstration and example, as well as parable and other
forms of symbolism. He showed his authority through miracles of
healing, control over the elements, and even raising the dead. He
illustrated his message of God's kingdom with over 60 parables. A
parable has been called an earthly story with a heavenly
meaning. Perhaps the best known of these is the parable of the
Good Samaritan.(Lk. 10:25-37)   Jesus' ministry, based upon the
principle of a kingdom not of this world, was not what was
expected of the Messiah. The Jewish people were expecting
another David with the wisdom of Solomon who would lead
Judea as a nation to independence from the Roman yoke, just as
the Maccabees had freed Judea from Syrian control during the
intertestamental period. They longed for a return to the glorious
days of Solomon when Israel was at its zenith as a nation among
nations. Even the disciples thought this was one of Jesus'
objectives right up to the time of his ascension. ["Lord, will you at
this time restore again the kingdom to Israel?"(Acts 1:6)] The
Judeans were aware of the predictions of their prophets: that
some such as Elijah and Elisha had the ability to heal sickness;
that the prophets exhorted Israel to repent, that is, to turn away
from evil and follow God's commandments. They were familiar
with God's direction to love him and one's neighbor and to help
the strangers and the unfortunate among them.(Dt. 6:5; Lev.
19:18) They even had a form of baptism for Gentiles who
embraced the Jewish faith. They probably would have accepted
Jesus as an Old Testament prophet had he also embraced the
institutional religion of Judea. They were surprised and amazed
at his teaching of personal freedom and each person's right to
seek the kingdom of God independently. As Peter later said,
believers are a "holy nation" and a "royal priesthood."(1 Pet. 2:9)
Jesus taught that he came to save sinners and that the way to
salvation is through him and his teachings.(John 10:9; 14:6)   He
said that he is "the way, the truth, and the life" (John 14:6) and
that whenever two or three are gathered together in his name,
there he is in their midst.(Matt. 18:20)   This points up the prime
mystery of the New Testament — Jesus' death on the cross, his
resurrection, and his ascension. The four Gospels show Jesus'
awareness that he must die physically at the hands of men as a
sacrifice or propitiation for the sins of the world.(Mk. 10:45; Lk.
18:31-33; 1 John 2:2; Heb. 10:12)   Yet a risen Christ continues his
ministry in a spiritual plane seated at God's right hand ready to
judge both the living and the dead.(Acts 10:42; 1 Pet. 4:5)   The

Holy Spirit is ever present to assist seekers and believers, and his human representatives individually and collectively carry his message to the world.(John 16:7-14; Acts 1:7-8; 2:32-33)

Apostles, Evangelists. Jesus had many disciples, that is, learners or students. He chose 12 disciples as an inner core of assistants to help him in his ministry and to receive special instruction. He also appointed them as apostles to carry the gospel message to the world.(Lk. 6:13) ["Apostle" means "one who is sent," implying one sent with some authority.] The Gospels relate how he sent the 12 on an evangelistic journey, giving them the authority to preach in his name, heal the sick, and cast out demons.(Matt. 10:6-42) Jesus also showed that evangelism was not confined to the 12 when he also sent out 70 disciples on the same kind of mission with the same authority and capability.(Lk. 10:1-20) Jesus' plan for continuation of his work after his departure included the commissioning of 11 of the 12 to be the leaders of the Christian movement, originally called "the way."(Acts 9:2; 19:9) Followers of Christ did not become known as "Christians" until several years later, being so called for the first time in Antioch, Syria.(Acts 11:26) On the night before he died, at the Last Supper, Jesus told the 11 (Judas Iscariot having defected) that he had chosen them and ordained them. When he was with them after his resurrection, he said, "Peace be to you. As my Father has sent me, even so send I you. Whose sins you remit, they are remitted to them; whose sins you retain, they are retained."(John 15:15-16; 20:21-23) He also said, "Go you therefore and teach all nations, baptizing them in the name of the Father, and of the Son, and of the Holy Spirit, teaching them to observe all things which I have commanded you; and, lo, I am with you always, until the completion of the age."(Matt. 28:19-20) ". . . And these signs shall follow them that believe: in my name they shall cast out demons; they shall speak with new tongues; they shall take up serpents; and if they drink any deadly thing, it shall not harm them; they shall lay hands on the sick, and they shall recover."(Mk. 16:17-18) When the 120 gathered in the upper room after Jesus' ascension, the first order of business was the selection of an apostle to fill the office left vacant by Judas Iscariot. Matthias was appointed as the twelfth apostle.(Acts 1:15-26) Some time later Saul of Tarsus (Paul) was converted and commissioned by the risen Christ to be "a chosen vessel" to bear Christ's name "before the Gentiles, the kings, and the children of Israel."(Acts 9:15) Paul became known as the thirteenth apostle. As stated in Mk. 16:20, "And they went forth and preached everywhere, the Lord working with them and confirming the word with signs following."

The Individual in the New Testament. The teachings of Jesus stress human values, the spiritual worth and freedom of each individual. He said, "God so loved the world that he gave his only begotten son that whoever believes in him shall not perish but have eternal life" (John 3:16); that salvation depends upon one's being "born again" of the Holy Spirit.(John 3:8) Jesus' ministry was to the lost (Matt. 18:11; Lk. 15:24), to the sinner (Mk. 2:17) to Jew and Gentile alike.(Matt. 10:6; 12:17-21) He said that he did not come to condemn the world but to save it, and each person who does the truth "comes to the light" and his or her deeds become manifest as being done through God.(John 3:17-21) Some very specific spiritual and material blessings or rewards were declared by Jesus for true followers: forgiveness of sins (Lk. 7:47-48); answered prayer (Matt. 7:7-8); Mk. 11:24); provision of necessities (Matt. 6:31-33); prosperity now, spiritually and materially, and eternal life (Mk. 10:28-30); receiving measure for measure as one gives (Lk. 6:38); living with peace (John 14:27) and joy (John 15:11); having freedom from anxiety (Matt. 6:25-34) and fear (Lk. 12:32; see Rom. 8:15); receiving the spiritual power to do works as Jesus has done (John 14:12); being seated with Christ in heaven.(Rev. 3:21; John 14:3) Jesus also taught the concept of a spiritual oneness, a unity of the Father and the Son with each believer and of believers with each other.(John 17:11-26; 1 John 4:12) A believer also receives the baptism of the Holy Spirit whose indwelling endows him or her with spiritual gifts.(Mk. 1:8; Matt. 3:11; Acts 1:5; 2:4; 1 Cor. 12-14) It is stressed that the risen Christ has a special affinity for each individual, having empathy for human weaknesses, since in his earthly walk he had been "in all points tempted as we are, yet without sin."(Heb. 4:15) "Wherefore, he is able also to save them to the uttermost who come to God by him, seeing he ever lives to make intercession for them."(Heb. 7:25) A believer need have no fear of physical death, for he or she will enjoy a resurrection to a higher life, being raised with a spiritual body in power and glory. (See: Matt. 22:30; Lk. 20:36; 1 Cor. 15:42-44.)

Faith; Counting the Cost. Jesus said that if a person has faith as a grain of mustard seed, he or she could move mountains.(Matt. 17:20) The faith Jesus talked about is the belief that Jesus is who he said he is; that his words are God's words; that Jesus lives to intercede for the seeker and believer; that God answers prayer and does what he has promised.(Rom. 4:21; 8:32; 15:8; Jude 24) Faith is the confidence that a person may "come boldly to the throne of grace" and obtain mercy and find grace to help in time of need.(Heb. 4:16) Faith is defined as "the substance of things hoped for, the evidence (assurance) of things not seen."(Heb. 11:1)   The faith of Abraham and Sarah is a prime example of steadfastness, along with that of other Old Testament figures.(Heb. 11:2-40)   It is by God's grace through the believer's faith that he or she is saved and not by works previously performed without faith. And a believer is "created in Christ Jesus" for Christian good works, as God has ordained.(Eph. 2:8-10)   James says, "Show me your faith without works and I will show you my faith by my works."(Jas. 2:18)   In this vein Jesus said that one must "count the cost," for faith involves forsaking the things of the world (Lk. 14:28-33) without forsaking a world in need.(John 17:15-18; Rom. 12:2)   Jesus said, "Seek first the kingdom of God and his righteousness, and all these things shall be added to you."(Matt. 6:33)   He also said that his message is a sword and that a believer may encounter persecution because of his or her beliefs.(Matt. 10:34-39; Mk. 10:29-30)   The epistles exhort believers to remain steadfast in the faith in the face of trials and tribulations.(1 Pet. 1:7; Heb. 12:3-4) Repentance (a turnaround or turning away from sinful conduct and thought) is also a requirement, and steadfastness includes staying clear of sin and resisting temptation.(Heb. 6:1-8)   In this respect, God provides the means to escape, to bear temptations and testings.(1 Cor. 10:13; Jas. 1:2-4)   A precondition for God's forgiveness is the forgiving of others (Matt. 6:14-15; Eph. 4:32), and if "we confess our sins," God is "faithful and just to forgive us our sins and to cleanse us from all unrighteousness."(1 John 1:9) A believer must also guard against doubt and unbelief which can be a hindrance to a truly spiritual life and receipt of blessings.(Mk. 9:24; Matt. 17:19-20; Jas. 1:6-8)   There is that constant struggle with self, that "old man" who tries to assert himself as before, as well as the continual battle against satanic influence.(Eph. 4:22-24; Rom. 7:15-25; 1 Pet. 5:8)   But a spirit-filled believer has victory over all these obstacles through vigilance and steadfast resistance.(Rom. 8:28-39; Jas. 4:7)   The "bottom line" for the seeker and believer is to be "perfect even as your Father who is in heaven is perfect." Jesus said that this goal is reachable through a spiritual love for all, even enemies, persecutors, or those who despitefully use others. God loves saint and sinner alike.(Matt. 5:38-48; Lk. 6:27-35)   One should not judge others, lest he or she be judged by the same standard.(Matt. 7:1)   A person should act toward others as he or she wants to be treated.(Lk. 6:31)   Helping another in need is the same as doing it for Jesus.(Matt. 25:40)   Spiritual gifts are to be exercised and used for the benefit and edification of others.(Rom. 12:1,5-21; Eph. 4:12-16)   These principles apply in every situation including relationships in the family (1 Cor. 7; Col. 3:18-21) and in the workplace.(Col. 3:22; 4:1)   Jesus taught that the key is having a humble heart (Matt. 23:11-12) and yet a boldness for the faith, realizing that servanthood in the kingdom of God is friendship with Christ.(John 15:14-15)

The New Commandment. Jesus said that he did not come to destroy the Old Testament (the law and the prophets) but came to fulfill it.(Matt. 5:17)   The most important commandments are to love God and your neighbor as yourself. He not only stressed the continuing validity of these principles but also added a new dimension to them. In the parable of the Good Samaritan he stressed the point that "neighbor" means all people, regardless of race, creed, or nationality.(Lk. 10:25-37)   His new commandment is "Love one another as I have loved you so that all may know that you are my disciples."(John 13:34-35)   He also stressed that love is action, saying, "Let your light shine before men that they may see your good works and glorify your Father who is in heaven."(Matt. 5:16)   The Gospels show Jesus' conception of love in action. He is the good shepherd who knows and cares for his sheep, even laying down his life for them.(John 10:1-17)   He healed all who came to him; he had compassion for the lost and the burdened.(Matt. 11:28-30)   He came to befriend and save sinners (Lk. 5:32; 7:34); to bring salvation to the world (John 12:47); to offer himself as the last sacrifice for the sins of all.(Matt. 20:28; Rom. 5:6; Heb. 9:27-28; 10:12-14)   This kind of love is necessary for he who does not love in this deeper sense does not know God, for God is love.(1 John 4:8)   Love is the greatest gift. It endures all things; it never fails.(1 Cor. 13:1-8)

Spirituality and the Kingdom of God. Jesus' teachings expanded the concept of the spiritual nature of mankind as a part of the spiritual existence of the Creator-God. Realization of this through faith brings one within the realm of a spiritual kingdom referred to as the "kingdom of God" (Mk. 4:11) and the "kingdom of heaven."(Matt. 13:31)   This kingdom is not of the world but is found in the truths spoken by Jesus.(John 18:36-37)   He taught that the kingdom is "at hand."(Matt. 4:17)   It is come (Lk. 11:20); it is near (Lk. 10:9); it is present.(Lk. 17:21)   Jesus said, "The kingdom of God comes not with observation...the kingdom of God is within you."(Lk. 17:20-21)   Paul explains that the "kingdom of God is not meat and drink, but righteousness and peace and joy in the Holy Spirit."(Rom. 14:17)   The kingdom of God is also future. The Old Testament taught that upon death, a person's body returns to the dust whence it came, and his or her soul (spirit) "returns to God who gave it."(Eccl. 12:7)   Jesus' teachings expand this thought through the principle that spiritual life is eternal (John 17:2-3), and in heaven ("in the resurrection") human souls "are as the angels of God."(Matt. 22:30)   An example of this angelic state is seen in Rev. 22:8-9, when an angel in heaven reveals himself to John as one of the brethren.

  The Holy Spirit, Spiritual Gifts. As we observed in Chapter THREE, the Holy Spirit is described in the Old Testament as falling upon various individuals, and Moses expressed his wish that the Spirit would fall on all the Lord's people.(Nu. 11:29)   In the New Testament we see the Holy Spirit in action throughout: in the virgin birth of Jesus (Matt. 1:18; Lk. 1:35); in Jesus' baptism (Lk. 3:22); in Jesus' resistance of satan (Lk. 4:1); in the exorcism of demons (Matt. 12:28); in the evangelism and establishment of churches as described in the book of Acts and the epistles.(Acts 2; Rom. 5:5)   Blasphemy of the Holy Spirit was named as the only unforgivable sin.(Matt. 12:31-32)   The increased ministry of the Holy Spirit in the world depended upon Jesus' departure; and then the Holy Spirit would come as a paraclete, that is, an advocate and comforter for the people.(John 14:26; 16:7-15)   As previously mentioned, Jesus told his disciples that they would be endued with power from on high; that they were to evangelize, baptizing in the name of the Father, the Son, and the Holy Spirit, having the ability to cast out demons, heal the sick, speak with new tongues, and be protected from poisonous substances.(Matt. 28:19; Mk. 16:17-18; Lk. 24:47; Acts 1:8)   These "signs following" (Mk. 16:17) are seen in the book of Acts in the manifestation of the Holy Spirit in a dramatic way and in the exercise of spiritual gifts by various people.(Acts 2:4; 3:11; 10:44-47; 16:18; 28:3-9)   The principle is expressed that one may open himself or herself to receive the Holy Spirit but may also put a damper on the operation of the Holy Spirit in his or her life. Paul says, "Be not drunk with wine, . . . but be filled with the Spirit"; and again, "Quench not the Spirit."(Eph. 5:18; 1 Thess. 5:19)   The "spiritual gifts" are designated in the epistles and are declared to be a potential of every believer. "Now, there are diversities of gifts but the same Spirit."(1 Cor. 12:4)   The categories of gifts are set out in Romans 12:6-13; 1 Cor. 12-14; Eph. 4:11:

Apostles	Exhortation	Faith
Prophets and	Giving	Healing
prophecy	Ruling and	Miracles
Ministry	governing	Discerning of
Teaching	Showing mercy	spirits
Evangelists	Word of wisdom	Tongues
Pastors	Word of knowledge	Interpretation
Helping	Hospitality	of tongues

The purpose of spiritual gifts is to serve God, help and edify others, and strengthen believers collectively comprising the "body of Christ."(Rom. 12:11-13; 1 Cor. 12:25-26; Eph. 4:12-13; 1 Pet. 1:12; 4:8-10) These gifts are a means for the exercising of the greatest gift — the love which never fails.(1 Cor. 13:1-13)

Prayer. Jesus affirmed the importance of prayer, stressing the prayer life of the individual. He recognized charitable giving, material offerings, and voluntary fasting as forms of prayer, teaching that the most vital aspects of prayer are one's private communication with God and a clean heart.(Matt. 6:1-18; Lk. 11:1-13) He preached against hypocrisy and paying only lip service to God. He said, "Not that which goes into the mouth defiles a man; but that which comes out of the mouth, this defiles a man."(Matt. 15:7-11; Mk. 7:6-23) Having a clean heart involves confession of sins and repentance.(Mk. 6:12; Lk. 5:32; 18:10-14) God forgives the repenting sinner, but his forgiveness is dependent on one's forgiveness of others, and getting misunderstandings with others straightened out is more important than making an offering.(Matt. 5:24; 6:14-15; Lk. 11:4) Effective prayer is not a matter of repeating words without meaning; it is sincere, confident, and private conversation with God, for he knows one's needs before he or she asks.(Matt. 6:6-8; 21:22) Prayer need not be in any particular form. Jesus frequently used the word "ask" in referring to prayer. He said, "Ask, and it shall be given to you; knock and it shall be opened to you. For everyone who asks receives, and he who seeks finds, and to him who knocks it shall be opened."(Matt. 7:7-8) Whatever is asked in Jesus' name shall be granted by the Father (John 15:16; 16:23-24) and by the Son.(John 14:13-14) Jesus provided a model prayer, called the "Our Father" or "Lord's Prayer," which indicates that prayer is to God as the eternal Father. Intercession by the Son may be invoked by asking in Jesus' name.(Matt. 6:9-13; Lk. 11:2-4; John 14:13-14) God hears prayer and wants to give good things to those who ask him (Matt. 7:11), even before they ask.(Matt. 6:8) God receives prayer as ascending to him with incense.(Rev. 5:8; 8:3-4) Jesus gave the example, for he was constantly in prayer himself.(Lk. 3:21-22; 9:28; 21:37; 22:39-41) At the Last Supper he prayed for the spiritual unity of believers with each other and the Father and the Son (called Jesus' "high priestly" prayer; John 17). In the garden of Gethsemane just before his being seized by authorities, he prayed, "O my Father, if it be possible, let this cup pass from me; nevertheless, not as I will but as you will." Then to his disciples he said, "Watch and pray, that you enter not into temptation. The spirit indeed is willing, but the flesh is weak."(Matt. 26:39-41; Mk. 14:36-38) Being persistent in prayer is illustrated by two of Jesus' parables, The Persistent Widow (Lk. 18:1-7) and The Friend at Midnight.(Lk. 11:5-10) Prayer in the Spirit is shown in the book of Acts.(Acts 2:4, 33)   The account of Cornelius' conversion illustrates God's consideration of the prayers of one seeking his truth. An angel told Cornelius, "Your prayers and your alms are come up for a memorial before God."(Acts 10:4)   The Lord then arranged for Peter to visit Cornelius and explain the gospel of Christ.(Acts 10:4-48)   Another example of effective prayer is seen in the prayers of Paul and Silas in the Philippian jail. They "prayed and sang praises to God," when suddenly an earthquake opened the prison doors and the prisoners' bonds were loosed.(Acts 16:25-26) In Romans Paul explains the help which the Holy Spirit gives in prayer, "Likewise the Spirit helps our infirmities, for we know not what we should pray for as we ought; but the Spirit himself makes intercession for us with groanings which cannot be uttered. And he who searches the hearts knows what is the mind of the spirit, because he makes intercession for the saints according to God."(Rom. 8:26-27; see also Eph. 6:18)   Paul also exhorts us to "pray without ceasing."(1 Thess. 5:17)   Peter points out that failure to consider others properly, especially one's spouse, may be a hindrance to effective prayer.(1 Pet. 3:7)   In this vein James says that "you have not because you ask not. You ask and receive not because you ask amiss, that you may consume it on your lusts."(James 4)   James underscores the effectiveness of prayer and singing psalms, particularly in the healing of the sick and forgiveness of sins.(Jas. 5:13-18)   "The effectual fervent prayer of a righteous man avails much."(Jas. 5:16)   John gives this assurance: "And this is the confidence that we have in him, that if we ask anything according to his will, he hears us. And if we know that he hears us, whatever we ask, we know that we have the petitions we desired of him."(1 John 5:14-15; see also 1 John 3:22)

   Satan. In the Old Testament the tempter and originator of evil is called the "serpent."(Gen. 3:1-15)   (Rev. 12:9 identifies "that old serpent" as satan.) In Job he is the accuser.(Job. 1:6)   The word "satan" means "accuser" or "adversary" in Hebrew. Whenever mentioned in the Old Testament, satan is always in opposition to the best interests of humans.(1 Chron. 21:1; Zech. 3:1; Ps. 109:6)   In the New Testament satan is mentioned often as the personification of evil. (There are more than 60 references to satan or the devil and other references to demons and evil spirits.) His actions are calculated to bring people within his sphere of influence. He is opposed to God and God's redemptive plan for the world.(Matt. 13:37-43)   Jesus successfully resisted satan's temptations, and satan departed from him for a season.(Lk. 4:13)   The Gospels show satan's continuing work against people through demonic influence and the possession of people by demons (also called devils, evil spirits, unclean spirits). Jesus said that they are agents of satan.(Matt. 12:25-28)   During his public ministry Jesus showed his dominion over satan through the casting out or exorcism of demons from certain people, and he accomplished this by virtue of the Spirit of God.(Matt. 12:28)   Other names for satan in the New Testament are "Beelzebub" ("lord of filth"; Matt. 12:24), the "tempter" (Matt. 4:3), the great "dragon" (Rev. 12:9), "the father of lies" (John 8:44), "the evil one" (Matt. 13:38 NASB), "prince (ruler) of this world" (John 14:30), "prince of the power of the air" (Eph. 2:2), and "murderer."(John 8:44) Jesus declared a complete victory over satan, saying that satan has already been judged.(John 12:31; 16:11; 1 John 3:8; Heb. 2:14)   The book of Revelation discloses the execution of this judgment through consignment of satan to the lake of fire along with death and hades.(Rev. 20:10,14)   Until then, satan's operations are limited.(John 14:30)   While he "as a roaring lion walks about seeking whom he may devour," (1 Pet. 5:8; 1 John 3:8; 5:18) vigilance in the faith provides protection (1 Pet. 5:9-10), and if satan is resisted in his efforts, he will flee.(Jas. 4:7)   In the words of Paul, our struggle in this world is not with flesh and blood but with the devil and his minions (principalities and powers) who perpetrate wickedness in high places. The defense against these denizens of evil is in the putting on the whole spiritual armor of God.(Eph. 6:11-13)

Resurrection. Jesus' death on the cross and his resurrection on the third day thereafter are considered central to the gospel message. Paul said that he preached "Jesus Christ and him crucified."(1 Cor. 1:23; 2:2)   During his public ministry, Jesus foretold his own death and resurrection on many occasions, but no one understood the significance of what he was saying.(Mk. 8:31; 9:30-32)   When he was asked for a sign of his authority, he said that the only sign he would give them was the sign of Jonah. Just as "Jonah was three days and three nights in the whale's belly, so shall the son of man be three days and three nights in the heart of the earth."(Matt. 12:39-40)   He said that he came not to be ministered to but to minister to others and give his life as a ransom for many.(Matt. 20:28; Mk. 10:45)   He was giving his life that others might live in a true spiritual sense, for God is spirit.(John 4:24)   He approached his death in the attitude of the good shepherd who lays down his life for his sheep (John 10:11) and as one who is willing to sacrifice his own life for a friend (John 15:13), and in his death both the Father and the Son

111

are glorified.(John 12:23-28) Jesus assured his disciples that while he was returning to the Father who sent him (John 7:33), he was laying down his life that he might take it again (John 10:17); he will yet live that others might live (John 14:19) and will come again (John 14:28); that on being lifted up he will draw everyone to himself.(John 12:32) It was necessary that he depart so that the Holy Spirit might begin his ministry.(John 16:7) Thus it was that the Christian movement became based upon the teaching that Jesus lives, sits at the right hand of the heavenly Father, making intercession for the human race.(Mk. 16:19; Heb. 7:25) This is apparent in the book of Acts, the Epistles, and the book of Revelation. For example, Peter told Cornelius, "That word you know which was published throughout all Judea and began from Galilee after the baptism which John preached; how God anointed Jesus of Nazareth with the Holy Spirit and with power, who went about doing good and healing all who were oppressed of the devil, for God was with him. And we are witnesses of all things which he did both in the land of the Jews and in Jerusalem, whom they slew and hanged on a tree (cross). God raised him up the third day and showed him openly —not to all the people but to witnesses chosen before by God, to us who ate and drank with him after he rose from the dead. And he commanded us to proclaim to the people and to testify fully that it is he who was ordained of God to be the judge of the living and the dead. To him all the prophets bear witness that through his name everyone who believes in him shall receive remission of sins."(Acts 10:37-43) The New Testament teaches that every individual will also experience a resurrection. Jesus said, "Marvel not at this, for the hour is coming in which all who are in the graves shall hear his voice and shall come forth; they who have done good to the resurrection of life; and they who have done evil to the resurrection of judgment."(John 5:28-29) After Jesus' resurrection he demonstrated several aspects of his "glorified" resurrection-body. He showed the marks of his crucifixion; he ate with the disciples and continued to teach them for 40 days. The miraculous nature of his being was shown by his appearing and vanishing instantly and in his ascension.(Mk. 16:19; Lk. 24:36-45; John 20:19-21; 21:1-25; Acts 1:9) Jesus said that in the resurrection believers will be as the angels of God in heaven.(Matt. 22:30; Lk. 20:36) Paul says, "The body which was sown a natural body" will be raised "a spiritual body" in power and glory (1 Cor. 15:42-44), a body like Jesus' own glorious body.(Phil 3:21; see also: 1 John 3:2)

Jesus' Return. The New Testament presents two aspects of the return of the risen Christ. First, there is the principle of the unity of the believer with the indwelling Christ and, secondly, the concept of a second coming of Christ to rule and to reign with power. The unity of the individual with the Father, Son, and Holy Spirit is described most clearly in the Upper Room Discourse.(John 14-17) In Matt. 18:19-20 Jesus said: "Again I say to you that if two of you shall agree on earth as touching anything that they shall ask, it shall be done for them by my Father who is in heaven. For where two or three are gathered together in my name, there I am in the midst of them." The epistle writers also make this point. For example, Paul in chapter 8 of Romans (called the "Victory Chapter") says, "And if Christ be in you, the body is dead because of sin, but the Spirit is life because of righteousness. But if the Spirit of him who raised up Jesus from the dead dwells in you, he that raised up Christ from the dead shall also enliven your mortal bodies by his Spirit who dwells in you."(Rom. 8:10-11; see also: Eph. 3:16-19) The apostle John says, "And we know that the son of God has come and has given us an understanding that we may know him who is true, and we are in him, in his son Jesus Christ. This is the true God and eternal life."(1 John 5:20) Jesus also spoke of his second coming in terms of visual symbolism. He said that after great tribulation "they shall see the son of man coming in the clouds of heaven with power and great glory. And he shall send his angels with a great sound of a trumpet, and they shall gather his elect from the four winds, from one end of heaven to the other."(Matt. 16:28; 24:30-31; Mk. 13:2-27; Lk. 21:27-28) At the time of Jesus' ascension, two men in white apparel told the disciples: "You men of Galilee, why do you stand gazing up into heaven? This same Jesus who is taken up from you into heaven shall so come in like manner as you have seen him go into heaven."(Acts 1:10-11) Perhaps one of the most quoted passages is 1 Thess. 4:16 - 5:2: "For the Lord himself shall descend from heaven with a shout, with the voice of the archangel and with the trumpet of God, and the dead in Christ shall rise first. Then we who are alive and remain shall be caught up together with them in the clouds to meet the Lord in the air; and so shall we ever be with the Lord. Wherefore, comfort one another with these words. But of the times and seasons, brethren, you have no need that I write to you, for you know perfectly that the day of the Lord so comes as a thief in the night."

Eternal Life, Reward, Judgment. The word "eternal" means without beginning and without end, denoting a continual existence including past, present, and future. As applied to human existence, the Bible indicates that the spirit or soul is indestructible and eventually returns to God who gave it.(Eccl. 12:7) This thought is expressed by Paul who attests to God's overall plan whereby God is "all in all."(1 Cor. 15:24-28) Thus, one might well say that eternal life includes the present, or "Today is the first day of the rest of your eternal life." Just as there are rewards for followers of Christ, there are judgments of the works of both believers and nonbelievers. Jesus said that all authority to judge the living and the dead is his.(John 5:22; 17:2; Acts 10:42; 1 Pet. 4:5) In a sense, failure to receive blessings because of failure to ask or asking wrongly (Jas. 4:2-3) or continued anxiety and fear by not heeding the teachings in the Sermon on the Mount (Matt. 5 - 7) are indicative of a present judgment. As the proverbs say, "The wicked flee when no one is pursuing" (Prov. 28:1) and "The way of the wicked is as darkness; they know not at what they stumble."(Prov. 4:19) As we have seen, Jesus assured his listeners that a follower of his and a doer of his words is assured of having his or her needs met and eternal life which includes the glories of the resurrection-life.(Mk. 10:28-30) The New Testament sets out a concept of a gradation of reward for believers based upon their Christian good works (Matt. 16:27), their works being tested as by fire.(1 Cor. 3:13-15; see also: 2 Cor. 5:10-12) In this respect, the epistles frequently warn believers against backsliding and the loss of reward.(Note the six warnings in the book of Hebrews: 3:7-13; 4:1-11; 5:11-14; 6:1-9; 10:26-39; 12; also, 2 Pet. 2:20-22) A righteous person will receive a righteous person's reward (Matt. 10:41), and one who shows compassion in Jesus' name will not lose his or her reward.(Matt. 10:42; Mk. 9:41) Those who reject the Father and the Son will be judged, and punishment will be meted out for the wrongs which they have committed.(Col. 3:25) They are as "cast into outer darkness where there shall be weeping and gnashing of teeth."(Matt. 22:13; 24:51; 25:30) Those who seek after the plaudits of men have their reward.(Matt. 6:2) One should enter in by the "narrow gate" to life, for "broad is the way which leads to destruction."(Matt. 7:13-14) Therefore, one should not lay up for himself or herself material treasures on earth but should lay up treasures in heaven, for "where your treasure is, there will your heart be also."(Matt. 6:19-21) God is merciful, and Jesus stands at the door and knocks. If anyone hears his voice and opens the door, he will enter and they shall dine together.(Rev. 3:20) But there is a reckoning, and the son of man will separate the "sheep" from the "goats." Those who have helped the less fortunate are deemed to have done it for Jesus and shall inherit the kingdom. Those who have not helped others have failed Jesus and receive punishment.(Matt. 25:31-46) The meting out of judgment is portrayed in Revelation depicting God as sitting on a great white throne judging the dead according to their works. The books are opened including the book of life. Anyone whose name is not found in the book of life is subject to punishment. It is decreed that the enemies of God and mankind be cast into "the lake of fire." These include satan, the false prophet, and the beast who have opposed God, death, hades, and "whoever was not found written in the book of life."(Rev. 20:10-15)   There is also described a new heaven, a new earth, and a new Jerusalem in which there reside only those who are overcomers and those who are "athirst of the fountain." These are given the water of life freely.(Rev. 21:1-27)   "And behold, I come quickly, and my reward is with me to give every man according as his work shall be. I am the Alpha and Omega, the beginning and the end, the first and the last."(Rev. 22:12-13)

Hell, Sheol, Gehenna, Hades, Tartarus. The word "hell," found in the King James and other English versions of the Bible, has its origin in Anglo-Saxon and Nordic words meaning to cover or conceal. It is akin to the Nordic word "Hel" which denoted a place for souls of the dead in Norse mythology. Hel was said to include Valhalla, an eternal home for warriors, and Niflhel, the place for the souls of the wicked. In the KJV "hell" translates the Hebrew word "sheol" 31 times in the Old Testament, and "hell" is used 22 times in the New Testament to translate the Greek words "Gehenna," "Hades," and "Tartarus." In the Old Testament "sheol" usually denotes merely the grave, and one does not find a precise concept of the afterlife of the soul. The Ecclesiastes passage (12:7) affirms that upon physical death of a person, his or her soul returns to God who gave it. "Sheol" is used many times to indicate a dreary present and future existence remote from God.(Ps. 6:5; 88:3-18; Isa. 38:16-19)   The Greek word "Gehenna" refers to the Valley of Hinnom just south of Jerusalem which had been used in Old Testament times as a site for human sacrifice to the pagan god Molech. It later became a burning dump for Jerusalem and, during the intertestamental period, many Jewish people regarded it as a symbol of punishment. "Hades" in Greek mythology was the place where all souls of the dead went, and it was also the name of the god who rules the underworld. The mythical Hades included a place called "Tartarus" where the souls of the wicked dead were punished. The word "Tartarus" appears only once, in 2 Pet. 2:4. Because there are differences in the meanings of these words, many modern English translations do not encompass them all in the one term "hell," or they use the word sparingly (for example, the RSV, NASB, and NAB (Cath.)). Also, many study Bibles have marginal notes or footnotes setting out or explaining the original words. As we have seen, when Jesus wanted to underscore the sorry spiritual state of a person who is in enmity with God, he used very descriptive language, such as, "thrown into the fire" (Matt. 7:19; 13:49-50; Mk. 9:41-48); "outer darkness" (Matt. 22:13); "weeping and gnashing of teeth" (Matt. 8:12); "eternal punishment" (Matt. 25:46); "condemnation."(Mk. 12:40) Many of these expressions are parts of parables; thus, they are symbolisms in human terms to express a spiritual thought. During the intertestamental period the Jewish term **Gehenna** and the Greek mythological terms just mentioned were popularly used in Palestine to refer to a place of judgment and punishment. Many theologians have therefore concluded that Jesus was referring to a place in which lost souls will reside and suffer punishment forever. Other scholars are of the opinion that Jesus was indicating more a condition of lostness or a status as estranged from God rather than designating a particular place. Both views recognize the principles of judgment, rewards and/or punishment, as previously discussed.

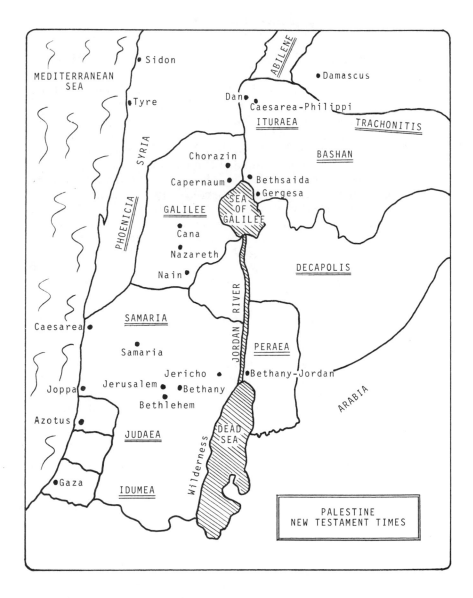

PALESTINE
NEW TESTAMENT TIMES

CHAPTER EIGHT

THE GOSPELS AND THE MINISTRY OF JESUS CHRIST

The four Gospels written by **MATTHEW, MARK, LUKE, AND JOHN** present the birth, ministry, death, resurrection, and ascension of Jesus Christ of Nazareth. To obtain the complete account, one must read all four Gospels, for each book has content not found in the others. Matthew, Mark, and Luke are referred to as the Synoptic Gospels because of their many similar (parallel) passages. The fourth Gospel supplements the first three, 92 percent of its information being reported only by John. Our effort in this chapter is to provide a synopsis-digest of the four Gospels as one chronological account with references to the book or books having the particulars. The English word "gospel" comes from an old Anglo-Saxon word "gōdspell" meaning "good news" or "good tidings." It translates a form of the Greek word **euangelizō** meaning "to bring good news." From this word the English words "evangel," "evangelist," and "evangelize" are derived.

Birth of Jesus; John the Baptist. Jesus' birth of the virgin Mary is preceded by the birth of a kinsman, John, who is to prepare the people for Jesus' ministry. God sends the angel Gabriel to a priest named Zachariah whose wife Elizabeth is a kinswoman of Mary. Gabriel informs Zachariah that he and Elizabeth will have a son to be named John who will minister in the spirit and power of Elijah and prepare the people for the coming of the Lord. Zachariah and Elizabeth are along in years, and he finds this hard to believe. Because of his disbelief, Zachariah is told that he will be unable to speak until John is born. Elizabeth does conceive, and when she is in her sixth month, Gabriel appears to Mary in Nazareth. Gabriel assures her that she need not fear; that she is highly favored and is blessed among women. She will conceive a son and call his name Jesus. ("Jesus" is Greek for "Joshua" meaning "savior.") He will be great and called "Son of the Highest," and he will have the throne of David. He will reign over the house of Jacob (Israel), and of his Kingdom there will be no end. Mary objects that she is not married, but Gabriel says that she will be overshadowed by the Holy Spirit and that she will give birth to a holy one called the Son of God. Gabriel also tells her of Elizabeth's pregnancy, saying, "With God nothing is impossible." Mary replies, "Behold the

handmaid of the Lord; be it unto me according to your word."
Later, Mary visits Elizabeth who says, "Blessed are you among
women, and blessed is the fruit of your womb." She tells Mary
how the baby in her own womb leaped for joy when Mary greeted
her, and Mary expresses her own joy. When John is born,
Zachariah gets his speech back and, filled with the Holy Spirit,
prophesies that John will be a prophet of God and prepare the
way for the Lord who will teach salvation and remission of sin
through his great mercy.(Lk. 1)

Jesus' Birth (6 B.C.). Mary, at the time of her conception, is
betrothed (i.e., legally engaged) to Joseph, a descendant of David.
He learns of her condition and thinks about putting her away
privately. But an angel of the Lord appears to him in a dream,
explaining how she has conceived through the Holy Spirit. She
will give birth to a son whom he is to name Jesus, for he will save
his people from their sins. This is in fulfillment of the prophecy
that a virgin will give birth to a son, and his name will be
Immanuel which means "God with us." Joseph does as directed
by the angel and takes Mary as his wife.(Matt. 1:18-24; Isa.
7:14)   When Mary's time to give birth is at hand, the Roman
Emperor, Augustus Caesar, orders a census to be taken, and every
family is required to register in the city identified with their
ancestors; in Joseph and Mary's case, Bethlehem, because they
are of the house of David. There Jesus is born and laid in a
manger, because there is no room for them at the inn. That
evening angels appear to some shepherds watching their flock
and tell them of the birth of a savior, Christ (Messiah) the Lord,
and that they will find him lying in a manger. The heavenly host
say, "Glory to God in the highest, and on earth peace, good will to
men." The shepherds find the child in Bethlehem, and after
seeing him, they spread the news, praising God. Joseph names
the baby Jesus, and after eight days, he is circumcised. Joseph
and Mary then go to the temple in Jerusalem to present Jesus
before God and to offer a sacrifice. At the temple, two devout
people, Simeon and Anna, having the Holy Spirit upon them,
bless the infant Jesus and prophesy that they have seen the
savior of Israel and a light for the Gentiles.(Lk. 2:1-38)

Magi Worship Jesus. Some time later Magi (wise men) from
the east come to Jerusalem and inquire where they can find the
child who has been born "King of the Jews." They have followed
his star and have come to worship him. King Herod hears about
this and learns that prophecy places the birthplace of the
Messiah in Bethlehem.(Mic. 5:2)   Herod gives this information
to the Magi, requesting that they return and tell him where the
child is after they have found him. The star guides the men to

Bethlehem and to the house in which Joseph, Mary, and Jesus are staying at that time. When they see Mary and Jesus, they fall down and worship him and present their gifts of gold, frankincense, and myrrh. Being warned by God in a dream not to go back to Herod, they return to their own country another way.(Matt. 2:1-12)

Flight to Egypt; Return to Nazareth. An angel also warns Joseph about Herod in a dream, and he takes Mary and Jesus to Egypt. Herod, seeing that he has been tricked, orders all male children in Bethlehem two years of age or younger slain. After the death of Herod in 4 B.C. Joseph brings his family back to Judea, but hearing that Herod's son, Archelaus, is tetrarch of Judea and a cruel man, Joseph takes the family straight to Nazareth (about 65 miles north of Jerusalem). This city is in the Galilean region which is under the rule of a tetrarch who is another of Herod's sons named Herod Antipas.(Matt. 2:13-23; Lk. 2:39)   Joseph and Mary have other children, half-brothers to Jesus, named James, Jude, Joses (Joseph), and Simon.(Matt. 13:55; Mark 6:3)   Jesus also has half-sisters, but their names are not recorded in the Gospels.(Mark 6:3)   Jesus grows and becomes strong, filled with wisdom, and the grace of God is upon him.(Luke 2:40)

Youthful Jesus in the Temple (A.D. 7). When Jesus is 12 years old, the family travels to Jerusalem on an annual pilgrimage to worship at the temple. When they begin their return trip, he is not with them. He is finally located at the temple. All who hear his discussion with the teachers are amazed at his knowledge. On their return to Nazareth he submits himself to his parents.(Luke 2:41-52)   The Gospels are silent about the period of Jesus' adolescence and early manhood in Nazareth, except for a general statement by Luke that Jesus increased in wisdom and favor with God and men as he matured in the human realm.(Luke 2:52)

JESUS' MINISTRY

Jesus' Baptism by John the Baptist (A.D. 27). When Jesus is about 30 years of age, he comes to a place by the Jordan River where his cousin, John the Baptist, is baptizing people with water. [The symbolism of washing was well-known to the Jews, for the Old Testament law in the Torah set forth many washing rituals, and a Gentile proselyte (a convert to Judaism, also called "God-fearer" or "fearer of God") underwent a form of baptism.] John's baptism is a baptism of repentance symbolizing a cleansing from sin and a new dedication to a moral life. John's message includes an announcement of the coming of the Messiah in the words of Isaiah 40:3, "The voice of one crying in the wilderness. Prepare the way of the Lord. Make his paths straight."(Matt. 3:3) John also says, "Behold the Lamb of God who takes away the sin of the world.(John 1:29) . . . I indeed baptize you with water for repentance, but he who comes after me is mightier than I whose shoe straps I am not worthy to stoop down and unloose. He will baptize you with the Holy Spirit and with fire."(Matt. 3:11; Mk. 1:7-8; Lk. 3:16; John 1:27) Many, including Pharisees and Sadducees, are submitting to John's baptism. Jesus insists that John baptize him. During this rite the Holy Spirit descends upon Jesus like a dove, and God's voice is heard, saying, "This is my son in whom I am well pleased."(Matt. 3:1-17; Mk. 1:1-11; Lk. 3:1-22) The Holy Spirit then leads Jesus into the wilderness where he fasts for 40 days, then is tested by satan who uses scriptural passages in an attempt to trap him. Jesus responds with scriptural principles, defeating satan at his own game. Satan departs for a time, and angels minister to Jesus.(Matt. 4:1-11; Mk. 1:12-13; Lk. 4:1-13)

First Year of Ministry (A.D. 27-28). During the first year of his three and one-half-year ministry, Jesus spends a great deal of time in Jerusalem and the surrounding area. He selects 12 men to be the "inner-core" of his many disciples. (A "disciple" is a "learner.") The 12 are Andrew and his brother Peter, James and his brother John (not John the Baptist), Philip, Nathanael (Bartholomew), Matthew, Thomas, James, son of Alpheus, Thaddeus (Judas, the son of James), Simon Zealotes (the Zealot), Judas Iscariot. All were from Galilee except Judas whose name Iscariot indicates that he was from a region in Judea. Several of the 12 were present at Jesus' baptism (John 1:35-51), and their final call to follow Jesus comes at the beginning of his Galilean ministry.(Matt. 4:18-22; Mark 1:16-20; 3:13-19; Luke 6:12-16) He also appoints them as apostles (one who is sent).(Matt. 10:2-5; Lk. 6:13) Jesus has many followers. The Gospels speak of multitudes of people, crowds, and Jesus' miraculous feeding of 5,000 men plus women and children and on another occasion 4,000.(Matt. 14:15-21, 15:32-38) He sends the 12 to preach, heal, and cast out demons in his stead and later commissions 70 disciples to do the same.(Mk. 6:12, 13; Lk. 10:1-24) Women especially play a large role in his ministry. There are his human mother Mary, Mary Magdalene, Mary and Martha, sisters of Lazarus, Mary, mother of Joses, Mary, mother of James, the less, Salome, mother of James and John, Joanna, wife of Chuza, Herod's steward, Susanna and many others who contribute to the support of Jesus and the disciples from their private resources.(Lk. 8:1-3; see also: Matt. 27:56, 28:1; Mk. 15:40, 16:1; Lk. 24:10; John 12:2-3)

Changing Water to Wine. On a visit to the Galilean region Jesus, his mother, and his disciples attend a wedding feast. During the feast Mary observes to Jesus that the host's supply of wine is depleted. Jesus asks that jars be filled with water which he then miraculously changes into vintage wine. This is the first of Jesus' signs, and it serves to convince the disciples of his power and authority.(John 2:1-11)

Chasing Merchants from Temple. Jesus returns to Jerusalem for the Passover observance at the temple. Seeing the extensive business being conducted on the temple grounds, he fashions a scourge of cords and uses it to chase the merchants and money-changers from the area, saying that they have made his Father's house a place of commerce. They ask for a sign of his authority, and he replies, "Destroy this temple, and in three days I will raise it up." They ask how he can do that, seeing that the temple has been 46 years in the building (the new temple built by Herod). But Jesus was referring to the temple of his own body. His disciples will remember these words after he has risen from the dead. While Jesus is in Jerusalem, many people become believers when they see the miracles which he performs.(John 2:13-25)

"You Must Be Born Again." One night Nicodemus, a Pharisee of importance, visits Jesus and tells him that he realizes God is with Jesus. Jesus tells Nicodemus that unless one is "born again," born of water and of the spirit, he cannot see the kingdom of God; that the light has come into the world, but people who do evil are in darkness having condemned themselves through disbelief in the one sent by the Father; that one who knows the truth will act according to the truth so that he will provide a godly witness.(John 3:1-21)   Amplifying this principle in relation to his own ministry, Jesus says:

> For God so loved the world, that he gave his only begotten Son, that whoever believes in him shall not perish, but have eternal life. For God sent not his son into the world to condemn the world; but that the world through him might be saved.(John 3:16-17)

Imprisonment of John the Baptist. John the Baptist and his disciples continue their ministry and water baptism. Jesus also includes water baptism as a part of his evangelism, the disciples doing the baptizing rather than Jesus himself.(John 4:1-2)   When asked about Jesus' ministry, John replies, "He must increase, but I must decrease."(John 3:30)   John had been openly criticizing Herod Antipas for living with his brother's wife, Herodias. To silence John, Herod imprisons him.(Matt. 4:12; Mk.

1:14; Lk. 3:19-20; John 3:24)   Sometime later when Jesus is well into his work in Galilee, John the Baptist, still in prison, sends two of his disciples to ask Jesus about his ministry. Jesus tells them, "Go and show John again those things which you hear and see: the blind receive their sight, and the lame walk, the lepers are cleansed, and deaf hear, the poor have the gospel preached to them. And blessed is whoever shall not be offended in me." Jesus takes this opportunity to underscore the importance of John and his mission. John is more than a prophet, for (as prophesied by Malachi) he is the messenger of God appointed to prepare the way for the Messiah. He is Elijah returned, if they can accept that thought.(Mal. 3:1; 4:5-6)   However, he who is least in the kingdom of God is greater than John.(Matt. 11:2-15; Lk. 7:18-30)

Martyrdom of John the Baptist. Herod fears John the Baptist, because John is a righteous and holy man. He enjoys listening to him and keeps him safe. But Herodias waits for an opportunity to have John killed. At a party given for Herod, the daughter of Herodias (Salome, according to the historian Josephus) pleases Herod by dancing before him and his guests. He grants her a request, and at the prompting of her mother, she asks for the head of John the Baptist on a platter. The deed is carried out, and Salome gives John's head to her mother. John's disciples take his body and lay it in a tomb.(Matt. 14:3-12; Mk. 6:17-29)

JESUS' GALILEAN MINISTRY (A.D. 28-29)

The Samaritan Woman. Jesus terminates the first major phase of his ministry. He has followers in Jerusalem but will not commit himself to them, because he is aware of what is in man.(John 2:23-25)   He decides to center his activities in the region of Galilee. There he can preach and teach in the areas around the Sea of Galilee (also called Sea of Tiberias; John 21:1) and easily reach other areas in north Palestine, such as Tyre and Sidon (Lebanon) and Caesarea Philippi (Syria). On his way to Galilee he passes through Samaria, and in the city of Sychar he meets a Samaritan woman by Jacob's well. When he asks for a drink of water, she is surprised, for customarily a Jew would have no dealings with a Samaritan woman. Jesus tells her that he will give her "living water" springing up to eternal life. Jesus also indicates his full knowledge of her present life style. She replies that she knows of the coming of the Messiah, and Jesus reveals to her that he is that one. The woman then spreads the news, and Jesus remains there for two days, making many converts.(John 4:27-42)

Arrival in Galilee. When he arrives in the area of Galilee, he finds many believers who had witnessed what he had done in Jerusalem.(John 4:43-45) News of his arrival spreads quickly throughout the region, and he begins teaching in the synagogues a message of repentance and belief in his gospel that the kingdom of God is at hand.(Matt. 4:17; Mk. 1:14-15; Lk. 4:14-15) After healing a royal official's son (John 4:46-54), he goes to his hometown of Nazareth where he is invited to read scripture and to speak. He reads Isa. 61:1-2, a prophecy about the coming Messiah, and declares that those assembled have seen this scripture fulfilled. He also points out situations in the Old Testament where God made special provision for certain nonIsraelite people. Sensing a negative reaction, Jesus says that no prophet is welcome in his own hometown. These statements enrage his hearers to the point of trying to throw him over a cliff, but he passes "through their midst." After this rejection by his former neighbors, he establishes his headquarters in the city of Capernaum located several miles from Nazareth on the north shore of the Sea of Galilee, not far from the point where the Jordan River enters the sea.(Lk. 4:16-31; Matt. 4:13) He had visited this city before, along with his mother, his brothers, and his disciples.(John 2:12)

Teaching, Miracles, Healing, Popularity. Jesus teaches in many cities, in the synagogues, and in the open areas of the countryside. He preaches the gospel of repentance and the kingdom of heaven as being at hand.(Matt. 4:17) He stesses that he has come not to call the righteous but rather sinners to repentance.(Mk. 2:17) His word is a sword. Whoever receives Jesus receives the one who sent him, and whoever receives one of his disciples shall not lose his or her reward.(Matt. 10:32-42) All things have been delivered to Jesus by the Father. No one knows the Son but the Father, and no one knows the Father except those to whom the Son reveals him.(Matt. 11:27) Wherever Jesus goes he attracts a crowd, and great multitudes from all parts of Palestine gather to hear him and to be healed.(Matt. 4:23-25; Mk. 3:7-8) Whenever Jesus is healing the afflicted, he can sense healing power leaving him.(Lk 6:19; 8:46) Jesus not only heals the sick and exorcises evil spirits from the demon-possessed (Matt. 4:24; Mk. 3:7-12), he also shows his ability to raise the dead.(Lk. 7:11-17; John 11:38-44) Matthew tells us that Jesus' healing ministry is in fulfillment of Isa. 53:4, "Himself took our infirmities and bore our sicknesses."(Matt. 8:17) If necessary to make a point, Jesus brings about miracles involving natural phenomena, such as assuring a catch of fish or quieting a storm.(Lk. 5-11; Matt. 8:23-27; Mk. 4:35-41; Lk. 8:22-25) As Jesus' fame spreads, he finds it difficult to have a quiet time and slips away as frequently as he can to be alone and pray.(Lk. 5:16)

Growing Opposition. It does not take long for opposition to surface. Jesus is hoping that the self-appointed religious leaders among the Jewish people will recognize him as the Messiah and support the principles which he is teaching. Many do, but some members of the religious establishment oppose him. Here in Galilee his detractors are beginning to be vocal. They ask for "signs" of his authority. They question many things which he and his disciples do, not always with relation to the Torah but usually from the standpoint of their own interpretations or customs by which they try to influence the Jewish populace and which they wish to be recognized as "law." For instance, when Jesus is criticized for eating with sinners and tax gatherers, he replies that it is the sick who need a physician, not those who are well, and that he came to call sinners to repentance, not the righteous.(Mk. 2:17)   Again his disciples are criticized for not fasting. Jesus points out by parable that there will be a proper time for fasting when he (the bridegroom) is taken away.(Mk. 2:18-20)   The disciples are also criticized for picking a small amount of grain on the Sabbath because of tradition that this is servile work. Jesus replies that the Sabbath was made for man, and the son of man is Lord of the Sabbath. He shows that David ate the consecrated bread in the tabernacle to escape starvation, even though only the priests were allowed to eat it under the Mosaic law.(Mk. 2:23-28)

Healing on the Sabbath. The question of what is servile work prohibited by the law on the Sabbath becomes the subject of running controversy between the Pharisees and Jesus. He is criticized for healing a paralyzed man and for telling him to pick up his pallet (portable bed; John 5:1-13); for healing a man's withered hand (Matt. 12:9-14); for healing a woman bent double (Lk. 13:10-21), all on the ground that these were done on the Sabbath. Jesus shows the hypocrisy involved in such interpretations by asking which of his accusers would not feed his animals or save the life of a person or animal in peril on the Sabbath.(Lk. 13:15)   What honors God more than releasing someone from satan's grip and healing him or her on the Sabbath?(Lk. 13:16-17; Mk. 3:1-6)   Upon being humiliated by Jesus' logical and merciful answers, many Pharisees begin plotting with the Herodians on how they might destroy him.(Mk. 3:6)   But Jesus' popularity with the people continues to grow.(Matt. 4:25)

Jesus' Authority from the Father. Jesus observes the Passover each year by going to Jerusalem to worship at the temple. On one such occasion he heals a paralytic by the Pool of Bethesda. Jesus is criticized for healing on the Sabbath and for calling God his father, making himself equal with God, and a faction in Jerusalem seeks to kill him.(John 5:1-18)   In reply to their criticism, Jesus outlines his relationship with the Father and the authority which the Father has given him. If they believed Moses, they would believe him, for Moses spoke of him.(Dt. 18:18-22)   If they do not believe Moses, how will they believe his (Jesus') words? They have not believed Moses, because they themselves do not possess Godly love.(John 5:19-47)

Sermon on the Mount. On his return to Galilee Jesus delivers a major public address in which he outlines ethical, moral, and spiritual principles which should guide and help every person in his or her life. The setting of the sermon is an area on the shore of the Sea of Galilee which slopes down to the sea (today called the Mount of Beatitudes). Multitudes have gathered here (Matt. 5:1), a great throng of disciples and others from Judea and Jerusalem to the south and from the northern region of Tyre and Sidon.(Lk. 6:17)   Before he speaks, he heals all who have come for healing of diseases and release from troubling unclean spirits.(Lk. 6:18-19) Positioning himself on a level spot, he begins his teaching.(Matt. 5:1-2; Lk. 6:17)   He describes eight attributes of believers (the "Beatitudes"). He stresses humility, gentleness, seeking right-eousness, purity, peacemaking and the strength to withstand persecution, insults, and false accusations. People who do these things are blessed and can rejoice, for great is their reward in heaven as sons of God.(Matt. 5:3-12; Lk. 6:20-26)   The blessed are the "salt of the earth" and the "light of the world" whose light should shine before men, and they will glorify the Father.(Matt. 5:13-16)

Meaning of the Commandments. Jesus looks with favor upon the law and prophecy of the Old Testament, saying that he came to fulfill it, not to destroy it. Recognizing the validity of the Ten Commandments, he teaches that one's negative thoughts are equal to negative action; that anger against another is the same as murder; that a person must work to obtain self-control and in case of disagreement with others, take the initiative in seeking reconciliation. He speaks out against divorce and adultery.(Matt. 5:17-32)

Jesus on Truth, Love, and Prayer. He says that one should speak the truth instead of making vows of truthfulness. One should help meet the needs of others; love one's enemies and face persecution with love, mercy, and prayer. Such is the way to perfection.(Matt. 5:29-48; Lk. 6:27-36)   Regarding worship and prayer, Jesus stresses that one should not pray, make donations, or fast with a big show but should do so secretly and directly, for the Father knows our needs before we ask.(Matt. 6:1-8; 16-18)   He prescribes a simple prayer (called the "Lord's Prayer" or "model prayer"; also "the Our Father"):

Our Father who art in heaven,
Hallowed be thy name.
Thy kingdom come.
Thy will be done, in earth as it is in heaven.
Give us this day our daily bread.
And forgive us our debts, as we forgive our debtors.
And lead us not into temptation, but deliver us from evil.
For thine is the kingdom and the power and the glory, forever.
Amen.(Matt. 6:9-13; Lk. 11:2-4)

Be Not Anxious. Jesus lectures on the issue of the material versus the spiritual. People should not pursue material wealth as an end in itself but should concentrate on seeking God's kingdom and his righteousness. Anxiety and worry, especially about the future cannot accomplish anything. Each day has its own problems. The Father knows what we need and will supply it if we seek him.(Matt. 6:19-34)   Sharing with others results in abundant blessings, for by one's standard of measure it will be measured in return.(Lk. 6:38)

Personal Relationships. Peaceable personal relationships are important not only to humans but also to the Father. Forgiveness by God is dependent on our forgiving one another.(Matt. 6:14-15)   We are not to judge others, lest we ourselves be judged. And the standard we use if we judge others will be used to judge us. We cannot judge another fairly if we have a similar or greater defect of character or habit (that is, a "beam" or "log" in our own eye). We should treat others as we want to be treated. However, care should be taken in sharing valuables with those who do not appreciate their value.(Matt. 7:1-6, 12; Lk. 6:31, 37-42)

The Narrow Gate. Again, on the Father's concern for each individual, Jesus declares that one who places reliance upon God will be recognized, and prayers will be answered in the same way that a human father looks out for the welfare of his children. "Ask, and it shall be given to you; seek and you shall find; knock, and it shall be opened to you." To qualify for such a blessed life is to "enter in by the narrow gate" avoiding the "wide gate" which leads to destruction. On the way, one has to avoid false prophets (wolves in sheep's clothing). These can be detected, for "by their fruits you shall know them."(Matt. 7:7-23; Lk. 6:43-46)

The Word, a Rock Foundation. Jesus concludes by comparing the person who hears his words and acts upon them to the wise man who built his house on a good rock foundation. Such a house will withstand rain, flood, and wind. But anyone who hears his words and does not act upon them is like the foolish man whose house has a foundation of sand and so is subject to destruction in the face of storm.(Matt. 7:24-27; Lk. 6:47-49)   The people who have heard Jesus deliver this sermon are amazed at his teaching, for he teaches as one having authority.(Matt. 7:28-29)

A Leper Healed; a Centurion's Faith. Coming down from the mountain, Jesus is followed by many people. A leper asks if Jesus will heal him. Jesus says, "I will; be you clean." He was immediately cured. Jesus advises him to tell no one except the priests in accordance with Mosaic law (Lev. 14:3) and as a testimony for the priests.(Matt. 8:1-4; Mk. 1:40-45; Lk. 5:12-16)

As Jesus enters Capernaum, he is met by a Roman centurion who asks that Jesus heal his sick servant. Jesus agrees, but the centurion says, "Lord, I am not worthy that you should come under my roof. Say but the word, and my servant will be healed. For I too am a man under authority, having soldiers under me. I say to this man, 'Go,' and he goes, and to another, 'Come,' and he comes, and to my servant, 'Do this,' and he does it." Jesus marvels at these words, declaring, "I have not found such great faith in all Israel." He issues a warning that Jewish people may miss the blessings of the kingdom, while other people "from the east and west" receive them. To the centurion he says, "Go your way. Since you have believed, so be it done for you." And the servant was healed that very hour.(Matt. 8:5-13; Lk. 7:1-10)

Healing of Peter's Mother-in-Law; Healing of a Paralyzed Man. Shortly thereafter Jesus is in the home of Peter and Andrew, along with James and John. Peter's mother-in-law is ill from a fever. Jesus enters, takes her by the hand, and lifts her up. Immediately the fever leaves her, and she begins to serve them.(Matt. 8:14-17; Mk. 1:29-34; Lk. 4:38-41)   At another time when Jesus is in the house in Capernaum, many people come to see him. He speaks to them from the doorway. Four men carrying a paralyzed man on a portable bed approach. Seeing their way blocked by the crowd, they take the sick man up onto the roof, remove some tiles, and lower him to a point near Jesus. When Jesus sees their faith, he looks at the afflicted man and says,

"Son, your sins are forgiven you." Certain Pharisees and scribes who are present reason to themselves that Jesus blasphemes, because only God can forgive sins. Jesus, knowing their thoughts, says, "Why do you reason these things in your hearts? Which is easier to say to the sick of the palsy, 'Your sins are forgiven you,' or to say, 'Arise, take up your bed and walk?' But that you may know that the son of man has power on earth to forgive sins" (he says to the sick man), "I say to you, 'Arise, and take up your bed and go your way to your own house.' "(Matt. 9:1-8; Mk. 2-1-12; Lk. 5:17-26)

The Widow's Son Raised. In the city of Nain, not far from Nazareth, Jesus has compassion on a widow whose son has died. Jesus speaks, "Young man, I say to you, 'Arise.' " When the townspeople see the man brought back to life, they begin glorifying God and saying, "A great prophet has arisen among us. God has visited his people." News of this miracle travels throughout the area and also Judea.(Lk. 7:11-17)

Cities Warned; Jesus' Load Is Light. Jesus reproaches the cities in which he has performed miracles without any change of heart by the people. In the day of judgment it will be more tolerable for Tyre and Sidon (Gentile cities) and for Sodom than for them. He gives praise to the Father for hiding the word from the wise and making it known to babes. Jesus' authority stems from the Father and is revealed through the Son to others. The invitation is put forth: "Come to me, all you who labor and are heavy laden, and I will give you rest. Take my yoke upon you and learn of me, for I am meek and lowly in heart, and you shall find rest for your souls. For my yoke is easy, and my burden is light."(Matt. 11:20-30)

A Lesson in Forgiveness. One day Jesus accepts a Pharisee's invitation to dinner. While they are reclining at the table, a woman, a sinner, enters and stands weeping, her tears falling on Jesus' feet. She wipes his feet with her hair, kisses them, and anoints them with perfume. The Pharisee thinks to himself that if Jesus were a prophet he would know what sort of woman she is. Jesus knows what the Pharisee is thinking and asks him who would love a creditor more, one who was forgiven a debt of 50 denarii or one who was forgiven 500 denarii. The Pharisee supposes the one who was forgiven the greater debt. Jesus says that he has judged correctly. Jesus points out that the Pharisee has not accorded Jesus the common courtesies of water for feet-washing, a greeting kiss, or the anointing of his head. But this sinner did all these things with regard to his feet. Therefore, her sins which are many are forgiven her, for she loved much; but the one to whom little is forgiven loves little. Jesus says to her, "Thy sins are forgiven. Your faith has saved you. Go in peace." Others at the table wonder at Jesus' forgiving of sin.(Lk. 7:36-50)

A Divided Kingdom Cannot Stand; the Sign of Jonah. Jesus continues his ministry accompanied by the 12, proclaiming and preaching the kingdom of God.(Lk. 8:1)   His opponents try to think of some propaganda which would defeat his work and turn the people against him. One day Jesus heals a demon-possessed man who is also deaf and unable to talk. This miraculous healing amazes the onlookers, but certain Pharisees lay down a serious accusation. They say that Jesus is in league with satan; otherwise he could not cast out demons. Jesus easily refutes this charge with logic. A kingdom divided against itself cannot stand. Satan would not weaken his campaign to control the world by interfering with his own agents and the work he had directed them to do. Jesus casts out demons by the Spirit of God, and anyone who claims that such exorcism is the work of satan is guilty of the unforgiveable sin of blasphemy against the Holy Spirit.(Matt. 9:27-34; 12:22-37; Mk. 3:20-30)   Then Jesus is asked for a "sign" of his authority. Now, by this time, Jesus has performed numerous signs, wonders, and miracles, and they still want another sign. Jesus refuses, except to refer to the sign of Jonah, that is, just as Jonah was in the whale three days, so shall the son of man be three days in the heart of the earth. This is a reference to his coming death and resurrection. Jesus castigates them for not recognizing that his words are greater than those of both Jonah and Solomon. His detractors need to be careful that they do not become like the man who is released from the clutches of an evil spirit, then allows himself to come under the influence of that spirit again, along with seven other evil spirits.(Matt. 12:22-37; Lk. 11:27-36)

Who Are My Mother and Brothers? While Jesus is speaking to the group, his mother and brothers approach, and someone informs Jesus that they wish to speak to him. Jesus asks, "Who is my mother and who are my brothers?" Pointing to his disciples, he says, "Behold my mother and my brothers. Whoever shall do the will of my Father who is in heaven, these are my brother and sister and mother."(Matt. 12:46-50; Mk. 3:31-35; Lk. 8:19-21)

A Turning Point and Parables. Jesus now sees that most of the religious establishment will continue to oppose him; that nothing he can say can win them over. So he begins explaining the truths of God's kingdom through parables. When his disciples ask him about the parables, Jesus explains that they (the disciples) have been granted knowledge of the mysteries of the kingdom. But others who have had the information available will lose what they have, for Isaiah prophesied that they will continue to hear but will not understand nor seek forgiveness.(Matt. 13:10-14; Mk. 4:10-12; Lk. 8:9-10; Isa. 6:9-10)

The Sower Sows the Seed. In this parable Jesus pictures four types of people who hear the word of God. First, there are those who permit satan to take away the word (the seed) from their hearts; second, those who receive the word with joy but give it up when affliction or persecution arises because of the word; third, those who worry and whose pursuit of worldly things chokes the word so that it is not fruitful; fourth, those who hear the word, accept and understand it, and hold it fast so that it bears a great deal of fruit.(Matt. 13:3-23; Mk. 4:3-25; Lk. 8:5-18)   In other parables spoken on the same occasion, Jesus expands on this theme. [These and others are called kingdom parables, because Jesus begins them with "The kingdom of heaven is like" or "The kingdom of God is like."]

The Lamp. Just as one does not hide a lamp under a cover, there is nothing secret which will not be revealed and come to light.(Mk. 4:21-22; Lk. 11:33-36)

Seed Growing Secretly. The kingdom of God is like a man who plants seed and does not know how it grows. He tends the plant and harvests it when it is ready.(Mk. 4:26-29)

The Mustard Seed. The kingdom of heaven is like this smallest of seeds. It grows into a tree in which birds build their nests.(Matt. 13:31-32; Mk. 4:30-32)

Leavened Flour. The kingdom of heaven is like leaven (yeast) which a woman puts into flour, and it all becomes leavened.(Matt. 13:33-35)

Hidden Treasure. The kingdom of heaven is like treasure hidden in a field. When a man discovers it, he sells all that he has to buy the field.(Matt. 13:44)

Pearl of Great Price. The kingdom of heaven is like a merchant looking for valuable pearls. When he finds one, he sells what he has to buy it.(Matt. 13:45-46)

The Net. The kingdom of heaven is like a net full of every kind of fish. The good fish are kept, and the bad fish are cast away. So it will be at the end of the age. Angels will come and separate the wicked from the just, casting the wicked into the furnace where there will be wailing and gnashing of teeth.(Matt. 13:47-50)

The Householder. Every scribe who becomes a disciple of the kingdom of heaven is like a householder who brings from his treasure both the old and the new.(Matt. 13:51-52)

The Wheat and the Tares. Jesus explains the parable of the wheat and tares to the disciples. Jesus is the farmer who sows good seed; the field is the world. The seeds are the sons of the kingdom; the tares (weeds) are sons of the devil sown by the devil. The harvest is the end of the age; the reapers are angels. Just as the tares are gathered and burned, so will it be at the completion of the age. Jesus will send forth his angels and gather out the stumbling blocks and lawless persons and cast them into the furnace. There will be weeping and gnashing of teeth. Then the righteous will shine forth as the sun in the kingdom of the Father.(Matt. 13:24-30; 36-43)

Calming the Storm; Demons and the Swine. Jesus and the disciples take a boat across the Sea of Galilee to the southeastern part of the lake. On the way a storm comes up causing the disciples to become frightened. Calling upon them to exercise their faith in such situations, Jesus rebukes the wind and the sea and calms the storm. The disciples witness this control over the elements in utter amazement.(Matt. 8:23-27; Mk. 4:35-41; Lk. 8:22-25) Arriving in the region of the Gadarenes (Gadara; also referred to as the country of the Gerasenes), Jesus cures two demon-possessed men, one of whom has been too strong to handle. Jesus speaks to the demons asking their name. They answer "Legion," for they are many. They ask not to be sent out of the country but to be allowed to enter a nearby herd of swine. Jesus orders them out. They enter the herd which immediately runs into the water, and all drown. The people of the area are impressed but also fearful. They ask Jesus to please go somewhere else. One of the healed men wishes to accompany Jesus, but he instructs the man to return to his home and report the great things the Lord has done. As a result, the news is spread throughout the Decapolis (an area east of the Sea of Galilee).(Matt. 8:28-34; Mk. 5:1-20; Lk. 8:26-39)

Healing Jairus' Daughter; Woman of Faith. Jesus and the disciples return across the lake to Capernaum. Here Jesus is met by a large crowd. A synagogue official named Jairus approaches and entreats Jesus to lay hands on his dying daughter and heal her. As Jesus starts toward Jairus' house, a woman acting on her faith touches Jesus' cloak and is instantly healed of a long-standing illness. Jesus, feeling a drain on his power, asks who touched him. The woman identifies herself, and Jesus says, "Your faith has cured you. Go in peace free of your affliction."

[For other occasions of people receiving healing by touching the fringe of Jesus' cloak, see: Matt. 14:36; Mk. 6:56.] On reaching Jairus' house, Jesus sees that a funeral dirge is in progress. Jesus orders everyone out saying that the girl is not dead, merely asleep. They laugh at him, because they are convinced she is dead. Jesus calls to the girl, "Child, arise." At this, she arises immediately. Jesus gives the parents directions to feed her and to tell no one what happened.(Matt. 9:18-26; Mk. 5:21-43; Lk. 8:40-56)

Disbelief, No Mighty Works. Jesus visits his hometown of Nazareth once again, but his former neighbors still take offense at him. He can do no mighty works there because of their disbelief, although he does lay hands on the few sick who have come to be healed, and they receive their healing.(Matt. 13:54-58; Mk. 6:1-6) Jesus continues his ministry in the area of Galilee, and the crowds follow him. On one occasion he turns to his disciples and says, "The harvest is plenty, but the workers are few. Pray the Lord of the harvest to send workers into his harvest."(Matt. 9:35-38)

Jesus Commissions the Twelve. Jesus then commissions the 12 to preach the gospel message to the Jewish people. They are to take no money with them, for they will subsist on what is given them. If they are not welcomed in any community, they are to shake the dust off their feet and move on. He warns them to expect rejection and persecution. Everyone who accepts Jesus through their preaching of the gospel will be confessed before the Father in heaven; whoever denies Jesus will be denied before the Father. Jesus has not come to bring peace, but a sword (i.e., the gospel). He who does not take up his cross and follow Jesus is not worthy of him. He who has found his life (in the flesh) shall lose it, but he who loses his life (of flesh) for Jesus' sake shall find it (in the spirit). He who receives the disciples receives Jesus. One who is moved by the gospel to help those in need will not lose his or her reward. After receiving these instructions, the disciples venture forth, teaching and preaching, anointing with oil, and healing the sick and demon-oppressed.(Matt. 10:5-42; Mk. 6:7-11; Lk. 9:1-6) On their return, they report to Jesus all that they have done.(Mk. 6:30; Lk. 9:10)

Feeding of the 5,000 Plus. So many people are coming to Jesus and the disciples that they do not even have time to eat. So Jesus arranges for them to go by boat to an out-of-the-way place for rest. But when they reach the other side, they are met by another large crowd. Jesus feels compassion for them, because they are like sheep without a shepherd. So he teaches them and cures those needing healing.(Matt. 14:13-14; Mk. 6:31-34; Lk. 9:10-

11; John 6:1-3)   There are 5,000 men, plus women and children.(Matt. 14:21)   When it becomes late, Jesus realizes that the people need nourishment. They do not have enough money to buy food for so many, and they only have five barley loaves and two fish which a boy has brought. Jesus asks everyone to be seated, dividing the crowd into smaller groups of 50 and 100. He then takes the loaves and fish and, after blessing the food, miraculously multiplies it so that all are fed, with enough fragments left over to fill 12 baskets.(Matt. 14:15-21; Mk. 6:35-44; Lk. 9:12-17; John 6:4-13)   The people want to make Jesus their king (John 6:14-15), but Jesus sends the people on their way and withdraws to a mountain to be alone to pray.(Matt. 14:22-23; Mk. 6:45-46; John 6:14-15)

Jesus Walks on Water. The disciples get in the boat to return to the other side of the lake but are delayed because of wind and waves. Looking up, they see Jesus walking on the water to them and are frightened. Jesus calms their fears. Peter wants to walk on the water to Jesus, and Jesus says, "Come." Peter walks on the water toward Jesus, but becoming fearful, he begins to sink, crying out, "Lord, save me." Jesus takes hold of him and asks why he doubted. The others in the boat declare that Jesus is truly the son of God. Their astonishment at this miracle stems in part from their failure to fully comprehend the significance of the miracle of the loaves and fishes.(Matt. 14:24-33; Mk. 6:47-52; John 6:16-21)

The Bread of Life. When they arrive at Capernaum, many people come to see Jesus, some by boat from Tiberias, a city on the western bank of the Sea of Galilee. Jesus speaks to them, saying that they have come because of the miracle of the loaves and fishes, and he entreats them to seek the food which he can give them which endures to eternal life, the bread of heaven. He says that he is the living bread of life; that the bread is his flesh which he will give to the world; that he who eats his flesh and drinks his blood will have eternal life, and Jesus will raise him up on the last day; that Jesus will abide in him and he in Jesus. Many, including the disciples, find these statements hard to understand. So Jesus explains that he is speaking of spiritual things. Nevertheless, many disciples (other than the 12) withdraw and stop following him. Jesus is aware of who believes and who does not, as well as who will betray him (that is, Judas Iscariot).(John 6:22-71) Jesus challenges the loyalty of the 12, but Peter speaking for all replies that there is no person to whom they can go, because Jesus is the one with words of eternal life and is the holy one of God.(John 6:67-69)

Truth versus Doctrines of Men. On one occasion some
Pharisees and scribes from Jerusalem come to Galilee and
confront Jesus and the disciples for not washing their hands in
the ceremonial way of tradition. Jesus takes this opportunity to
speak against hypocrisy, pointing out the difference between
being caught up in traditional trivia devised by men as opposed to
true worship of God, helping one's family, and refraining from
evil thoughts and speech. He quotes Isaiah's warning against
teaching as doctrine the precepts of men. Every plant not planted
by the Father will be uprooted. Those who reject Jesus' teachings
are like a blind guide of the blind. Both fall into a pit. It is not that
which goes into the mouth which defiles a man, for it is digested
and eliminated. It is what comes out of the mouth which defiles,
for it can reveal evil thoughts of murder, adultery, fornication,
theft, false witness, slander, covetousness, sensuality, deceit,
envy, pride, and foolishness. But eating without the ceremonial
washing of hands does not defile a man.(Matt. 15:1-20; Mk. 7:1-23;
Isa. 29:13)

Faith of a Gentile Woman. Jesus takes his ministry to Tyre
and Sidon (Lebanon). A Gentile woman asks him to heal her
daughter who is demon-possessed. Jesus tests her by saying that
his immediate concern is with the lost sheep of Israel; that it is not
good to take the children's bread and throw it to the dogs. She
answers that even the dogs feed on the crumbs under the table.
Seeing the woman's great faith, he heals the daughter.(Matt.
15:21-28; Mk. 7:24-30)

Feeding of 4,000 Plus. On his return to Galilee, Jesus
continues on to Decapolis. [The name of the region refers to a
league of 10 independent cities of Gentile people. Today this area
is in Syria and Jordan.] Jesus heals the sick and repeats the
miracle of feeding a large crowd, on this occasion 4,000 men plus
women and children.(Matt. 15:29-38; Mk. 8:1-9) The disciples
have difficulty understanding the full significance of these
miracles, and when Jesus tells them to beware of the leaven
(yeast) of the Pharisees, they think he is talking about bread.
Jesus reminds them of the feeding of the 5,000 and 4,000, and they
understand that he is warning them about the teachings of the
Pharisees and Sadducees.(Matt. 16:5-12; Mk. 8:13-21)

Healing a Blind Man. Near Bethsaida a blind man seeking to
be touched by Jesus is brought to him. Jesus leads the man out of
town, then spits on his eyes and lays hands upon him. At first the
man sees only dimly. Jesus again lays hands on him and directs
him to look up; whereupon, he sees clearly. Jesus sends him home,
asking him not to tell anyone about it.(Mk. 8:22-26)

135

"Who Am I?" Moving to the north, near Caesarea Philippi, Jesus asks his disciples who the people say he is. They answer that some refer to him variously as John the Baptist, Elijah, Jeremiah, or one of the other Old Testament prophets. Jesus then asks them who they say he is. Peter answers that Jesus is the Christ (Messiah), the Son of the living God. Jesus blesses Peter and tells him that he is Peter (Greek, **petros,** little rock, or piece of rock); that on this rock (Greek, **petra,** large rock or ledge) he will build his church (Greek, **ekklesia,** assembly, congregation; Matt. 16:18); that the disciples will be given the keys of the kingdom of heaven; that whatever they shall bind on earth shall be bound in heaven, and what they loose on earth shall be loosed in heaven. When Jesus begins telling them about his coming death and resurrection, Peter exclaims that such a thing should not happen. But Jesus says, "Get thee behind me satan; you are not setting your mind on things of God but of man." Jesus reiterates his teaching that whoever wishes to save his life should deny himself, take up his cross, and follow him. Whoever wishes to save his life shall lose it, but whoever loses his life for Jesus' sake shall find it. What profit is there to one who gains the whole world and forfeits his or her soul? Whoever denies Jesus and his words will be denied before the Father, but there are some who will not taste death until they see the kingdom of God.(Matt. 16:21-28; Mk. 8:27 - 9:1; Lk. 9:22-27)

The Transfiguration. About a week later Jesus takes Peter, James, and John to a high mountain where he is transfigured before them. His face becomes radiant like the sun and his clothes white and gleaming as light. Two men, Moses and Elijah, appear and begin talking to Jesus about his departure which is to be accomplished in Jerusalem. The three disciples become terrified at this sight, and Peter, not knowing what to do, offers to build shelters for them. At that moment a bright cloud overshadows them. A voice comes from the cloud: "This is my beloved son in whom I am well pleased. Listen to him." Suddenly, Moses, Elijah, and the cloud disappear, and the men see only Jesus who tells them not to fear and not to reveal this miracle until after he is resurrected. (Today Mt. Tabor, about 10 miles southwest of the Sea of Galilee, is traditionally known as the Mount of Transfiguration. This is a tradition from the earliest days of the church.) When Jesus and the three disciples come down to rejoin the others, a question comes up as to whether Elijah will return to restore the nation of Israel. Jesus replies that Elijah did return through John the Baptist, but the people allowed him to be killed; further, that in the same way the son of man will suffer at their hands.(Matt. 17:1-13; Mk. 9:2-13; Lk. 9:28-36)

Healing of Demon-possessed Boy. A multitude has been waiting for their return, and they see that at the center of the crowd are the other disciples with a man and a boy. They had been asked to exorcize a demon from the boy but could not. The father asks Jesus to help if he can. To this Jesus replies that all things are possible to one who believes. The father declares, "I believe; help me in my unbelief." Jesus rebukes the unclean spirit, and it comes out. The disciples ask why their attempt was unsuccessful. Jesus answers that the problem is their lack of faith. If they had the faith as a grain of mustard seed, they could move mountains. And a difficult task such as exorcizing a firmly entrenched demon requires not only faith but also prayer and fasting. Later Jesus tells the disciples, "The son of man shall be betrayed into the hands of men. And they shall kill him, and on the third day he shall be raised again." The disciples do not fully understand his words and are afraid to ask what he means.(Matt. 17:14-23; Mk. 9:14-32; Lk. 9:37-45)

The Fish and the Coin. On their return to Capernaum, they are confronted by collectors of the two-drachma tax. (This was also called the temple tax, collected to finance the provision of animals for sacrifice at the temple.) Jesus likens this tax to the paying of customs by aliens. One who is a true son of God is free from such a tax, but lest one should give offense, he should do as expected and pay it. Jesus directs Peter to catch a fish, and in its mouth he will find a coin which will cover the tax.(Matt. 17:24-27)

Servant of All. During the final days of his Galilean ministry, in response to events and questions, Jesus emphasizes certain of his teachings. One problem which continues right up to the time of the crucifixion is the concern of the 12 about what they are to do if and when Jesus does depart from them. In addition to this uncertainty, a degree of humanistic pride develops as to which of them will be in positions of leadership. Jesus now gives them one of several lectures on humility. He who would be first in God's kingdom must be willing to be last in this world and to be a servant of all. To illustrate, he takes a child in his arms and says that unless they are converted and become like children in their faith and humility, they shall not enter God's kingdom. And whoever receives such a one receives both Jesus and God the Father.(Matt. 18:1-5; Mk. 9:33-37; Lk. 9:46-48)

That No One Should Perish. Whoever causes a believer to stumble must answer for it. A believer must be on guard that his or her own flesh does not cause backsliding. Where others not of the immediate group preach and heal in the name of Jesus, they are not to be hindered, for one who is not against Jesus and his followers is for them. One who does an act of kindness or teaching in Jesus' name shall not lose his or her reward. Jesus came to save the lost, just as a shepherd goes to save a lost sheep. It is not the will of the Father for anyone to perish.(Matt. 18:6-14; Mk. 9:38-50; Lk. 9:49-50)

Settling Disputes. Jesus gives an important instruction for the settlement of disputes between believers. He says that if a believer has wronged another, the matter should be settled privately. But if this is of no avail, the wronged party should try again in the presence of one or two witnesses in accordance with Mosaic law.(Deut. 19:15)   If the other person will not listen, the matter may be taken to the church (Greek, **ekklesia,** assembly, congregation). If the wrongdoer continues in the sinful conduct, that person may be regarded as a Gentile (pagan) or a tax-gatherer (one who collects Roman taxes for profit).(Matt. 18:15-17)

Authority of Believers; Forgiveness. Jesus also explains that the disciples will have the authority to bind and to loose with spiritual effect. That if two or three of them agree on a petition to God in Jesus' name, it shall be granted. For where two or three are gathered together in Jesus' name, he will be there in their midst. Peter, knowing that forgiveness of others is a precondition to receiving God's forgiveness, asks Jesus how often one must forgive another who sins against him or her — perhaps, seven times? Jesus responds that it should be 70 times seven (i.e., at least 490 times). He illustrates this principle with the parable of the slave who was forgiven a huge debt but would not forgive the small debts of his debtors and as a result was punished by his master.(Matt. 18:15-35)

THE LAST SEVEN MONTHS (A.D. 29-30)

For about three years Jesus has been teaching the principles of God's kingdom, performing miracles, including the healing of all who come to him for this purpose. He has completed his work in Galilee and will be on the move in various parts of Palestine with an emphasis on Judea. [Note: In the Gospels thus far we have gone through Matthew 18, Mark 9, Luke 9:50, and John 6. The remaining chapters of the four Gospels deal with the events leading up to Jesus' crucifixion, burial and resurrection, post-resurrection appearances, and ascension, a period of about seven months. Interestingly, 45 percent of the Gospels' verses cover the first three years of the ministry, and 55 percent are devoted to the last seven months.]

Jerusalem Visit; Importance of Commitment. Jesus resolves to go to Jerusalem (Lk. 9:51), but his initial arrival there will be secret. His brothers needle him about going to the temple for the Feast of Booths (or tabernacles; see Neh. 8). They dare him to show himself publicly there, for they do not believe in him. (They are eventually converted and become pillars of the early church. See Acts 1:14, 15:13; Gal. 1:19, Jude 1.) Jesus waits until his brothers leave; then he also departs, traveling a route which takes him through Samaria.(John 7:2-10; Lk. 9:52)   One Samaritan village does not receive him, because they realize that he is going to worship at the temple in Jerusalem and not their temple in Samaria. James and John want to call down fire upon the village, but Jesus reprimands them, saying that they should realize the kind of spirit which they have, because he, Jesus, has not come to destroy men's lives but to save them.(Lk. 9:52-56)   Later on the road, men come up to him and say that they want to follow him but must first attend to duties at home, one wanting to bury his deceased father. Jesus takes this opportunity to emphasize the importance of not only making a commitment to God but also in giving preference to carrying out that commitment.(Matt. 8:19-22; Lk. 9:57-62)

Teaching in the Temple. Upon arriving at Jerusalem, Jesus goes to the temple without any fanfare and begins to teach. The people wonder at the knowledge displayed by one having little formal education. Jesus replies that his teaching is not his own but that of the one who sent him. While it seems common knowledge that some are out to kill him, no one lays a hand on him, for his hour has not yet come. Many become believers because of Jesus' words, signs, and miracles. When the Pharisees hear what is happening, they express their frustration.(John 7:11-53)   They then bring a woman to the temple who has been caught in adultery, and they ask Jesus if they shouldn't stone her as required by the law of Moses. Jesus replies that he who has not sinned should throw the first stone. One by one they leave, and Jesus asks, "Woman, where are your accusers; has no one condemned you?" She answers, "No, Lord." Then Jesus admonishes, "Neither do I condemn you. Go, and sin no more."(John 8:1-11)

The Light of the World. Still at the temple, Jesus refers to himself as the light of the world, and those who follow him will have the light of life; that if they knew him they would know his father who bears witness of him. He stresses that he is not of this world. He speaks and teaches the things the Father has taught him. Many come to believe in him.(John 8:12-30)   He says that all who abide in his word are disciples of his. They shall know the truth, and the truth shall make them free. Some continue to challenge Jesus saying that he could not be greater than their father Abraham. To this, Jesus replies that before Abraham was born "I am." They then pick up stones to throw at him, but he hides himself and leaves the temple.(John 8:31-59)

Healing a Man Born Blind; the Good Shepherd. While walking in Jerusalem, Jesus and the disciples see a man who was born blind. Jesus makes some mud, puts it on the man's eyes, and tells him to go to the pool of Siloam to wash it off. He does and gets his sight. His neighbors ask him who healed him, and he replies that he does not know, but that whereas once he was blind, now he can see. The Pharisees question him about who healed him. He says that the man must be a prophet and asks whether they want to become his disciples. In anger, the Pharisees have the man excluded from the synagogue. Jesus hears about this and seeks him out. Finding him, Jesus reveals who he is, and the man becomes a believer. Jesus declares that he came into this world that those who see may become blind and that those who do not see may see.(John 9:1-41)   Some Pharisees hear this statement and ask Jesus if he considers them blind. Jesus answers, "If you were blind, you would have no sin. But you say, 'We see'; therefore, your sin remains." Jesus continues with the symbolism of the sheep, the shepherd, and the sheepfold. Jesus is the door to the sheepfold that a man may enter and be saved. He is the good shepherd who gives his life for the sheep. He knows his sheep and his own know him. There are sheep not of this fold who will hear his voice, and there will be one fold and one shepherd. No person can take Jesus' life from him, but he lays it down himself according to the power and authority granted by the Father. Someone claims that Jesus must be demon-possessed, but another says, "A demon cannot open the eyes of the blind, can he?"(John 10:1-21)

Mission of the Seventy. After some time Jesus sends out 70 disciples to evangelize. They are commissioned to bring Jesus' message to the people and to heal the sick. On their return they report joyously that even the demons are subject to them in Jesus' name. Jesus admonishes them to consider it more important that their names are recorded in heaven, then rejoices with them and gives thanks.(Lk. 10:17-24)

The Good Samaritan. A certain expert in Mosaic law tests Jesus by asking what he must do to have eternal life. Jesus asks him to answer from the law. He answers according to Lev. 19:18 and Deut. 6:5, to love God and to love one's neighbor as oneself. Jesus agrees, but the man asks, "Who is my neighbor?" Jesus then tells the parable of the Good Samaritan who rescued an injured robbery victim when a priest and a Levite would not. In answer to Jesus' question, the doctor of law admits that of the three men the neighbor to the victim was he who showed mercy toward him. Jesus says, "Go, and do likewise."(Lk. 10:25-37)

Persistency in Prayer. When the disciples ask for more instruction on prayer, Jesus repeats his model prayer and illustrates persistency in prayer with the parable of the man who needed bread for an unexpected guest and who would not give up until he had roused his neighbor and received the needed bread. He says to the people, "Ask, and it shall be given you; seek and you shall find; knock and it shall be opened to you." He points out that even an evil person will not give his or her children harmful things. How much more does the heavenly Father wish to give the Holy Spirit to those who ask him.(Luke 11:1-13)

Ceremony versus Charity. A Pharisee who heard Jesus' words invites him to lunch with some other Pharisees and doctors of the law. When they remark about his not washing his hands in the accepted ceremonial way, he points to their hypocrisy of making a show of ceremony and trivia while failing to do really charitable things. They represent the attitude of their ancestors who killed the very prophets they say they revere. The Scribes and Pharisees then began plotting to catch him in something he might say.(Lk. 11:37-54)

Holy Spirit Provides. In speaking to his disciples later, Jesus tells them to fear God but at the same time to realize that God will protect them; that everyone who confesses Jesus before men, the son of man will confess before the angels of God; but he who denies him before men will be denied before them. Believers may be persecuted, but when they are challenged, the Holy Spirit will provide them with the words to speak.(Lk. 12:1-12)   He lectures against greed and tells the parable of the man who kept building more barns to hold his many crops but whose soul was required of him before he could use or enjoy any of his riches. He stresses that those who seek the kingdom of God are charitable and will have their needs met by the Father. The treasures of heaven endure forever, and "Where your treasure is, there will your heart be also."(Lk. 12:13-34)

Repentance and God's Patience. With the parable of the cruel and drunken servant who was caught in his misdeeds when his master returned home unexpectedly, Jesus illustrates the importance of being alert and ready to do God's will at all times. Much is required of those to whom much is entrusted, while those who do not know the master's will are to be judged by a lesser standard. Jesus' teachings will bring division among households as between those who follow these teachings and those who do not. Jesus has a baptism to undergo, and he is anxious for its accomplishment. He tells the crowd assembled before him that they are aware of the signs of nature, and in the same way they should know how to do what is right. He says that if they rely on man's justice, they better settle with their opponent on the way to court lest the judgment of the judge be against them.(Lk. 12:35-59) Someone asks him about the Galileans whom Pilate had killed. Jesus answers that the Galileans were no more or less sinful than the Judeans in the crowd. What is important is repentance with knowledge of the truth available in the gospel message. Like the grower who gave the overdue fig tree another year to produce, God is patient and merciful to those who make an effort to grow in his will.(Lk. 13:1-9)

Healing of Woman Bent Double. While teaching in a synagogue on the Sabbath, Jesus lays hands on a woman bent double by a sickness caused by an evil spirit, and she immediately recovers. Jesus is castigated by a synagogue official for healing on the Sabbath since it is a form of work. Jesus answers the man by pointing out that they all untie their animals and lead them to water on the Sabbath. At this, the people rejoice over the glorious things Jesus is able to do. He finishes his teaching with the comparison of the kingdom of God with the mustard seed which grows into a large tree and with leaven (yeast) which leavens the flour throughout.(Lk. 13:10-21)

Jesus and the Father Are One. It is now winter, and the Feast of Dedication is being observed in Jerusalem. It is about two months since Jesus left Galilee. [This "Feast" is a religious observance which is also called the Feast of Lights or Hanukkah. It commemorates the victory of the Jews under the leadership of the Maccabees and the rededication of the temple during the intertestamental period.] While Jesus is walking in the temple, people gather around him and ask him to tell them plainly whether he is the Christ (Messiah). Jesus answers, "I told you, but you do not believe. The works that I do in my Father's name, they bear witness of me. But you do not believe, because you are not of my sheep. As I said to you, my sheep hear my voice, and I know them and they follow me, and I give to them eternal life. They shall never perish, nor shall any man pluck them out of my hand. My Father who gave them to me is greater than all, and no man is able to pluck them out of the Father's hand. I and the Father are one."(John 10:22-30) At this, many pick up stones to throw at him, and Jesus says to them, "I have shown you many good works from the Father. For which of these works do you stone me?" They answered that they do not stone for good works but for the blasphemy of claiming to be God. Jesus replies by quoting Ps. 82:6 ("I said you are gods.") and asking why it is blasphemy to say he is the son of God in view of the works he is able to do. He says that if his works are the works of his Father, they should believe what he says. Instead of listening to Jesus, many try to seize him, but he eludes them.(John 10:31-39)

Lament for Jerusalem. Jesus takes his ministry to Perea and other areas near the Jordan River, teaching in the towns and villages, in preparation for his return to Jerusalem. Many become believers.(John 10:40-42; Lk. 13:22)   One question put to him is whether many are being saved. He replies, "Endeavor to enter by the narrow gate, for many will seek to enter but will not be able." There will be many who claim to be followers, but their true motives are known, and they will not attain the kingdom. "The last shall be first and first shall be last." Just then some Pharisees warn Jesus that Herod Antipas wants to kill him. Jesus replies, "Go tell that fox, 'Behold, I cast out devils and I do cures today and tomorrow, and the third day I am perfected.' It cannot be that a prophet perish outside of Jerusalem. O Jerusalem, Jerusalem, which kills the prophets and stones those who are sent to her. How often would I have gathered your children in the way a hen gathers her brood under her wings, and you would not. Behold, your house is left to you desolate; and verily, I say to you, you shall not see me until the time comes when you shall say, 'Blessed is he who comes in the name of the Lord.' "(Lk. 13:22-35)

Humility and Charity. On another Sabbath occasion Jesus is invited to eat with a leader of the Pharisees, along with other Pharisees and experts on the Mosaic law. They are watching Jesus closely when he asks them if it is lawful to heal on the Sabbath. They do not answer; whereupon he heals a man of the dropsy. Jesus then asks which of them having a son or an ox fall into a well on the Sabbath would not pull him out. The others remain silent. Jesus, noting that some present have been seeking seats of honor, gives a lecture on humility. One should take the last place and wait for the host to seat him or her higher for any honor due. In giving a luncheon or dinner, invite the poor, the lame, the crippled, and blind since they cannot repay, for such a charitable host will be repaid at the resurrection of the righteous. On hearing this, one of the men said, "Blessed are those who will eat bread in the kingdom of God."(Luke 14:1-15)   Jesus uses this setting to illustrate God's kingdom-plan by telling the parable of the man who gave a big dinner and whose invited guests gave all sorts of excuses as to why they could not come. The host directed his servant to go out and invite the poor, the crippled, and blind and lame. The servant did so, but there was still more room. The host said to go out even further and invite more so that the house might be filled, that no one who was first invited shall taste the dinner.(Lk. 14:1-24)

Counting the Cost. Some time later, as Jesus is walking, he turns and says to the crowd following him that there is a cost involved in being a follower of his. A person building a house or a king going to war calculates the requirements and costs of a project. Thus, a follower of Christ must anticipate the possibility of differences within the family and be willing to give up worldly things, even his or her own life, to be Christ's disciple. One not prepared to count the cost is as worthless as salt which has lost its savor.(Lk. 14:25-35)

The Lost Sheep; Lost Coin. On an occasion when many tax gatherers and sinners are gathered around to hear Jesus, some Pharisees and scribes criticize him for eating with sinners. Jesus replies by parable. What shepherd having found one lost sheep or woman having found one lost coin does not rejoice when the lost has been found? "Joy shall be in heaven over one sinner who repents, more than over 99 just persons who need no repentance."(Lk. 15:1-10)

The Loving Father. Jesus continues with the parable of the lost son (or loving father) in which one of two sons demands and gets his future share of his father's estate. After leaving home, he squanders his money on fast living and is reduced to abject poverty. He returns home after reasoning that the worst conditions his father might impose would be better than his present state. When he does return, his father greets him with open arms and gives a banquet in his honor. The other son objects. He has never been honored this way even though he has been diligent in his father's interests. The father says to him, "Son, you are ever with me, and all that I have is yours. It is right that we should be merry and glad, for your brother was dead and is alive again, and was lost and is found."(Lk. 15:11-32)

The Squandering Steward; Lazarus and the Rich Man. Some time later Jesus relates two parables to his disciples knowing that some Pharisees are listening. The first parable is about a rich man whose chief steward was reported for gross mismanagement. When the employer fired him and demanded an accounting, the steward called in some of his employer's debtors and changed the paper work to lessen their debts. He did this so that he would have some friends to turn to after leaving since he did not want to become either a laborer or a beggar. When the employer learned of this, he actually praised the steward for his foresight. Jesus indicates the point he is making: worldly people are more shrewd in their affairs than the "sons of light" (the

Jewish people whom Jesus is trying to reach) are in their own affairs. Comparing spiritual unrighteousness to double dealing in money matters, he says, "Make to yourselves friends of the mammon (money or property) of unrighteousness, that when you fail, they may receive you into eternal dwellings." He goes on to affirm that one who is faithful with a little is faithful also with much; that one who is unfaithful with money or property cannot be trusted with true riches. One may not serve two masters, for he or she will hate one and serve the other; one cannot serve God and mammon.(Lk. 16:1-13)   The Pharisees scoff at Jesus' remarks, but knowing that they are lovers of money, Jesus tells them that God knows their hearts. To emphasize the need to put things of God first, Jesus tells the story of a certain rich man and a poor man named Lazarus. When Lazarus died, he was carried by angels to Abraham's bosom. The rich man, who had failed to help Lazarus during his earthly life, died and was buried. Being in torment in hades, the formerly rich man called to Abraham to have Lazarus bring him water to relieve the agony of fire. But Abraham told him that there was a great gulf between them, and there could be no crossing. The man then asked that Lazarus be sent to warn his brothers so they could avoid his predicament. To this Abraham said that if they do not pay any attention to Moses and the prophets, they will not be persuaded even if someone were raised from the dead.(Lk. 16:14-31)

Faith As a Mustard Seed. Jesus continues his teachings by pointing out that believers will encounter "stumbling blocks"; that those who cause one to stumble will themselves experience woe. If a brother sins, even repeatedly, he is to be taught the right conduct and if he repents, to be forgiven. At this, the disciples ask Jesus' help in increasing their faith. Jesus says, "If you had faith as a mustard seed, you might say to this sycamine tree, 'Be you plucked up by the root, and be you planted in the sea;' it would obey you." He also reminds the disciples not to expect praise for their own ministries; that they will be content knowing that they have only done that which they are commissioned to do.(Lk. 17:1-10)

Healing of 10 Lepers. Before his final entry into Jerusalem, Jesus returns to the area between Galilee and Samaria. In one village he encounters 10 lepers who cry for mercy. He tells them to show themselves to the priests (a requirement of the Mosaic law for a healed leper). They become healed as they go. Only one, a Samaritan, comes back to glorify God and thank Jesus who asks, "Were not 10 cleansed; where are the nine? Did no one return to give glory to God, except this stranger?" (i.e., a nonJewish person). He assures the Samaritan that his faith has made him well.(Lk. 17:11-19)

The Kingdom Is among You. Some Pharisees ask Jesus when the kingdom of God is coming. Jesus answers that the kingdom of God is not coming with observation. The kingdom of God is present among them. Before the full extent of the kingdom is revealed, the son of man must suffer many things and be rejected by this generation. One should remember Noah and Lot's wife, for the events connected with this revelation will come without signs but will occur in a dramatic way.(Lk. 17:20-37)

The Persistent Widow. Jesus again teaches on being persistent in prayer and not being discouraged. He tells the parable about a widow who kept at a worldly judge about her case so resolutely that he gave her justice just to avoid her verbal barrages. If it is this way in the world, imagine how much more will God bring justice for believers who are constant in their prayer life. Jesus asks how much faith the son of man will find when he comes. Referring to humility in prayer, he contrasts the man who makes a big show of his piety and contributions with the man who humbly asks God to be merciful to him, a sinner. One who exalts himself or herself will be humbled, but one who is humble will be exalted.(Lk. 18:1-14)

Lazarus Raised from the Dead. When Jesus is about two days' journey from Jerusalem, he receives word that a friend named Lazarus is sick (not the same Lazarus as in the parable). Lazarus, his sisters, Mary and Martha, and his father, Simon, live in Bethany which is only two miles from Jerusalem. Jesus visits them often when he is in the Jerusalem area. Previously he had told Martha that Mary's learning of the gospel message from him was more important than helping her to prepare dinner.(Lk. 10:38-42) Now their brother is ill, and the sisters are asking Jesus to come and heal him. Jesus decides to go, ignoring his disciples' warning not to get too near Jerusalem. However, he purposely waits two days before starting out. As he approaches Bethany, Martha meets him and admonishes him, saying that if he had come earlier her brother would not have died. He assures her that Lazarus will rise. Martha says she understands that he will rise in the resurrection. Jesus replies that he (Jesus) is the resurrection and that whoever believes in him shall live even if he or she suffers physical death. Martha affirms her understanding of this and her belief that Jesus is the son of God who has come into the world. Mary and some friends who have come to mourn Lazarus' passing join them. Mary also expresses her feeling that Jesus could have saved her brother's life. Upon seeing Mary and the mourners in tears, Jesus is so moved in the spirit that he also begins to weep. When they reach the tomb, a cave, Jesus orders the stone door removed. Martha observes that there might be a stench since Lazarus' body has been in the tomb for four days. Jesus gives her assurance that she will see the glory of God. After giving thanks to the Father, Jesus cries out, "Lazarus, come forth!" Then Lazarus appears still covered with his gravecloths which Jesus orders removed. Many of the onlookers are convinced by what they have seen, but others return to Jerusalem and report the miraculous event to the Pharisees.(John 11:1-46)

One Should Die for Many. Quickly the high priest, Caiaphas, other priests, and some Pharisees hold a meeting. They agree that if Jesus is allowed to continue performing miracles, everyone will believe in him and that they will lose their privileged positions, and perhaps their nation, at the hands of the Romans. The high priest prophesies that it would be expedient that Jesus die for the nation; that by his death the children of God who are scattered abroad might be gathered together. Knowing what they plan to do, Jesus avoids Jerusalem. He and the disciples reside for a time in Ephraim, a city near the wilderness area.(John 11:47-57)

Jesus' Lecture on Divorce. Returning to the area of Perea, Jesus is met by large crowds. Any who come for healing are healed. A Pharisee asks him whether a man may divorce his wife for any cause. Making reference to the book of Genesis (1:27, 2:24, 5:2), Jesus answers that a man and wife are one flesh. "What therefore God has joined together let not man put asunder (separate)." But they ask why the Mosaic law provides for a bill of divorce. He answers that the rule in the law was ordained because of the hardness of their hearts. [NOTE: Before this law in Deut. 24:1-4, there was no requirement for a written bill of divorcement. Also, by custom or premarital contract, when a wife was divorced, the husband had to return any dowry she brought to the marriage.] Jesus says that whoever divorces his wife except for fornication and marries another woman commits adultery. When the disciples hear this, they say that perhaps it is better not to marry. Jesus replies that not everyone can accept what he is saying. Some remain unmarried by preference, some to serve the kingdom of heaven. But those who can accept what he says should accept it.(Matt. 19:1-12; Mk. 10:1-12)

As a Little Child. When some children are brought to Jesus for prayer and the laying on of hands, the disciples think this would bother him. But Jesus tells them not to hinder the children, for the kingdom of God belongs to them. One must receive the kingdom of God as a little child. Taking the children into his arms, he blesses them.(Matt. 19:13-15; Mk. 10:13-16; Lk. 18:15-17)

147

The Rich Young Ruler. As Jesus prepares to go to another location, a certain young ruler kneels before him and asks, "Good Teacher, what shall I do that I may inherit eternal life?" Jesus says, "There is no one good but one, God"; and feeling love for the young man, he instructs him to abide by the commandments which he already knows. The ruler claims to have done this from his youth but still feels incomplete. Jesus replies that if he wants to work toward perfection in earnest, he should sell his possessions, give the money to the poor, and follow him. This statement grieves the man, because he is very wealthy, and he leaves. To his disciples Jesus says, "How difficult it is for those who trust in riches to enter the kingdom of God. It is easier for a camel to go through the eye of a needle than for a rich man to enter the kingdom of God." The disciples are greatly astonished at these words, and they ask, "Then who can be saved?" Jesus answers, "The things impossible with men are possible with God." Peter asks, "We have forsaken all and followed you. What shall we have therefore?" Jesus tells them that they who have followed him will follow him in the regeneration when the son of man will sit on his throne. They will sit on 12 thrones judging the 12 tribes of Israel. He adds: "In truth I say to you, there is no one who has left house, or brothers, or sisters, or father, or mother, or wife, or children, or lands for the sake of me and of the good news (gospel) who shall not receive a hundredfold, now in this time, houses, and brothers, and sisters, and mothers, and children, and lands, with persecutions, and in the age that is coming life eternal. But many who are first shall be last, and the last first."(Matt 19:16-30; Mk. 10:17-31; Lk. 18:18-30)

Parable of the Laborers. Continuing his teaching, Jesus likens the kingdom of heaven to the landowner who paid all his laborers, whom he had hired at various times of the day, the same amount, a full day's wages. When those who had worked the longer hours complained, the employer explained that he had paid each man the amount agreed upon. "Is it not lawful for me to do what I will with my own? Is your eye bad (envious) because I am good (generous)?"(Matt. 20:1-16)

Honor and Servanthood. Jesus and the disciples now begin their last journey to Jerusalem. He informs them that they are going there, because the time is at hand when the son of man will be seized, tried, and crucified. But on the third day he will rise again. The disciples do not understand and are fearful.(Matt. 20:17-19; Mk. 10:32-34; Lk. 18:31-34) The disciples James and John and their mother approach Jesus with a request. Their mother asks if her sons could sit at his right and left when he comes into his kingdom. Jesus explains to the 12 that they will suffer for the gospel as he is to suffer but that he does not give positions of honor; they must be earned. "Whoever will be chief among you, let him be your servant; even as the son of man came not to be ministered to but to minister and to give his life a ransom for many."(Matt. 20:20-28; Mk.10:35-45)

Blind Bartimaeus. Jesus and the 12 now come to Jericho and encounter two blind men, one of whom is named Bartimaeus. They cry out to Jesus for mercy. When he asks them what they want him to do, they ask that their sight be restored. Jesus heals them, saying that their faith has made them well. On regaining their sight, they praise God and follow Jesus.(Matt. 20:29-34; Mk. 10:46-52; Lk. 18:35-43)

Salvation of Zaccheus. As they pass through Jericho, a chief tax collector named Zaccheus climbs into a tree because of his short stature to get a better look at Jesus. As Jesus comes near the tree, he looks up and says, "Zaccheus, make haste and come down, for today I must abide in your house." Zaccheus does as bidden with great joy. Onlookers grumble, saying that Jesus will be the guest of a sinner. But to Jesus, Zaccheus says, "Behold, Lord, the half of my goods I give to the poor; and if I have taken anything from any man by false accusation, I restore him fourfold." Jesus says, "This day has salvation come to this house, inasmuch as he is also a son of Abraham. For the son of man has come to seek and save those who are lost."(Lk. 19:1-10)

THE FINAL WEEK (A.D. 30)
Saturday, Nisan 9

Investing Wisely. Because Jesus is now nearing Jerusalem, some people suppose that the kingdom of God is going to appear immediately. Because of this, Jesus relates the parable of a certain nobleman who had many enemies and who went off to a distant country. He left 10 servants in charge of investing money. Only two earned money by investing it. They were greatly rewarded. Another who earned nothing had his money taken from him and was told he would be judged for his failure. The nobleman also had his enemies executed.(Lk. 19:11-28)

Jesus Anointed in Bethany. Jesus and the disciples arrive in Bethany on Saturday, Nisan 9 on the Jewish Calendar (March/April), and stay with Simon, Mary, Martha, and Lazarus. The Passover observance is about a week away on Friday (Nisan 15, A.D. 30). While they are assembled in the house, Mary begins to anoint Jesus' head and feet with expensive perfume. The disciples object to her extravagance, saying that the perfume could be sold and the money given to the poor. But Jesus asks them not to interfere, because she is anointing him for burial. The poor they will have with them always, but they do not always have him. A large crowd is outside, people having come to see both Jesus and Lazarus whom he raised from the dead. At the same time in Jerusalem the chief priests are planning to kill Lazarus, for because of him people are following Jesus.(Matt. 26:6-13; Mk. 14:3-9; John 12:1-11)

Sunday, Nisan 10

Jesus' Triumphal Entry into Jerusalem. The next day, Sunday, Jesus makes his triumphal entry into Jerusalem. The city is full of pilgrims who have come from many parts of the empire to observe the Passover.(John 11:55 - 12:1; see also Acts 2:9-11)   When Jesus and the crowd from Bethany reach the Mount of Olives near Jerusalem, he directs two disciples to obtain a certain donkey colt. They do as directed and place garments on it for Jesus to sit upon. This is done in fulfillment of prophecy that salvation will come (Isa. 62:11) riding the foal of a donkey.(Zech. 9:9)   As Jesus and the crowd cross over to the city, many spread garments on the road, and others cut palm leaves and branches and spread them on the road before him. The people acclaim him, crying out joyfully, "Hosanna to the son of David. Blessed is he who comes in the name of the Lord. Hosanna in the highest."(Ps. 118:26)   Looking at the city, Jesus is saddened, for he foresees its ultimate destruction. Once inside the gates he goes directly to the temple teaching and healing the blind and lame. The temple officials are indignant about this and the praise accorded him. But Jesus quotes to them Ps. 8:2 which refers to preparing for praise out of the mouths of infants. He then returns to Bethany.(Matt. 21:1-17; Mk. 11:1-11; Lk. 19:29-44; John 12:12-19)

Monday, Nisan 11

The Glory of God's Name. On Monday Jesus returns to the temple and again casts out the merchants and money changers. The temple officials are not happy about this, but the crowds are attending to his words.(Matt. 21:12-13; Mk. 11:15-18; Lk. 19:45-58)   Some worshipers from Greece want to see Jesus, but Jesus is in prayer with a troubled heart. First he asks if he should pray to be spared but quickly says, "But for this cause came I to this hour. Father, glorify your name." Then a voice from heaven comes, "I have both glorified it and will glorify it again." Some people hearing it think it was thunder. Others say that an angel spoke to him. Jesus turns to the crowd, telling them that the voice came for their sakes; that judgment is on the world, and its ruler will be cast out; that he, Jesus, is to be lifted up to draw all to himself. He senses opposition, saying, "Yet a little while the light is with you. Walk while you have the light, lest darkness come upon you; for he that walks in darkness knows not where he goes. While you have the light, believe in the light that you may be the children of light."(John 12:20-36)

Jesus' Lament over Disbelief. Leaving the temple area, Jesus goes into seclusion. While meditating, he recalls the words of Isaiah, "Lord, who has believed our report? And to whom has the arm of the Lord been revealed?"(Isa. 53:1) Jesus laments over the amount of disbelief he has encountered; yet there are many of the Jewish religious leaders who do believe in him. But they are not publicly acknowledging their belief for fear of the Pharisees and fear of being put out of their synagogues. Jesus recounts that he has come to be a light to the world; that his message is the truth which the Father has directed him to reveal. If only the people could understand that believing what Jesus says results in a greater belief in God the Father who sent him.(John 12:20-50)

The Withered Fig Tree. As Jesus and the disciples are returning to Bethany that evening, they see the fig tree which Jesus that morning had ordained would no longer bear fruit, for the reason that it had no fruit, even though it was not the season for figs. The tree is now withered. The disciples ask how this could happen. Jesus had set up this situation as a visual parable, for he replies that if they have faith they can not only possess a similar authority but also move a mountain. Such faith depends upon prayer, forgiveness of others, and confidence that they will receive that for which they pray and ask.(Matt. 21:19-26; Mk. 11:12-24)

Tuesday, Nisan 12

Who Was John the Baptist? On Tuesday Jesus returns to teach at the temple. The chief priests and elders approach him and ask by what authority he does these things. Jesus says that if they will answer a question, he will tell them. His question is whether the source of the baptism of John the Baptist was from heaven or men. The questioners reason that if they say, "From heaven," Jesus will ask why they did not believe him. They cannot say, "From men," because they fear being stoned by the many people who believe that John was a prophet. Their answer is, "We cannot tell." Jesus says, "Neither do I tell you by what authority I do these things."(Matt. 21:23-27; Mk. 11:27-33; Lk. 20:1-8) Jesus then challenges them with parables.

Belief and Action. By the parable of the son who did his father's bidding after at first refusing as contrasted with the son who agreed but did not do it, Jesus teaches that one is known by what he does. Jesus illustrates the consequences of disbelief in him with the parable of the renters of a vineyard who try to gain ownership of it by killing the owner's son. Those who hear this parable agree such evil men should have their just desserts. With the parable of the wedding feast he moves the thought a step further. Those who were specially invited not only did not come, they killed or mistreated those who came with the invitation. They were punished for their actions. Then the people off the street were invited, and the wedding was furnished with guests. But one did not have on the traditional garment for attending weddings and was cast out. Jesus makes reference to Ps. 118:22-23, a messianic prophecy about the stone which the builders rejected becoming the chief cornerstone by action of God. Jesus makes sure they understand that in the parable he was talking about them in saying that the one who falls on the cornerstone will be broken to pieces, and him upon whom it falls will be scattered like dust. The officials would have seized Jesus if it were not for their fear of his followers.(Matt. 21:28 - 22:14; Mk. 12:1-12; Lk. 20:9-19)

Jesus Answers Questions; Civil Law. Jesus is now met by a series of attempts to trip him up, to catch him in a statement which his opponents can use in a trial before the Jewish council on the ground of blasphemy. Note how each sect or group has a "$64 question" which they feel will be the "cruncher" for Jesus. A question is put by some Pharisees and Herodians as to whether a Jew may pay the Roman poll tax under Jewish law. Jesus asks whose picture is on the coin. "Caesar's" is the reply. Jesus says, "Render to Caesar the things that are Caesar's and to God the things that are God's."(Matt. 22:15-21; Mk. 12:13-17; Lk. 20:20-26)

Saints As Angels. The next group are the Sadducees who do not believe in any resurrection. They refer to the Mosaic law that if a man dies without children, it is the obligation of any surviving brother to take the widow as a wife in order that the deceased's line may continue.(Dt. 25:5) If a woman goes through this procedure with six brothers of her deceased husband because they also die leaving her childless, when she dies, whose wife is she in the resurrection? Jesus replies that the Sadducees do not understand scripture or the power of God. In the resurrection there is no institution of marriage. The resurrected are equal to the angels in heaven. But regarding the basic fact of resurrection, he points out that in the Torah God says that he is the God of Abraham, Isaac, and Jacob (Ex. 3:6), implying that they still live. Therefore, says Jesus, God is the God of the living and not of the dead. Some of the scribes concede that Jesus speaks correctly.(Matt. 22:23-33; Mk. 12:18-27; Lk. 20:27-40)

The Greatest Commandment. When the Pharisees see that the Sadducees are unsuccessful, they team up with a scribe and pose a question about the greatest commandment. Jesus answers that the first is to love God with heart, soul, and mind. The second is to love one's neighbor as one's self. On these two commandments are all the law and the words of the prophets based. Some of the scribes admit that Jesus has spoken well.(Matt. 22:34-40; Mk. 12:28-34)

"The Lord Said to My Lord." After the attempts to trip him fail, no one will venture to ask Jesus any more questions. They do not have the courage to question him about anything.(Mk. 12:34; Lk. 20:40) Jesus now takes the initiative and lectures to the people about erroneous teachings they have received and about the hypocrisy of their teachers. He asks the Pharisees present a question about one of the best known messianic prophecies in Ps. 110:1: "The Lord said to my Lord, 'Sit thou on my right hand, till I make thine enemies thy footstool.' " The question is: "David then calls him Lord; why is he called his son?" The crowd enjoyed this turnaround of questioning, especially since no one was able to answer this question.(Matt. 22:41-46; Mk. 12:35-37; Lk. 20:41-44)

In Moses' Seat. Jesus warns the people that the Pharisees and the scribes have placed themselves in the chair of Moses. The people should heed their words but not their deeds, because they do not what they teach. They are mainly concerned with making a big show and getting personal recognition. Many of their teachings are merely burdens which they place upon people without any effort to help. The people should look to God and the Messiah (Christ) and remember what Jesus has said about being a humble servant, for those who humble themselves shall be exalted.(Matt. 23:1-12)

Hypocrisy Unmasked. Continuing to address the scribes and Pharisees, Jesus tells them that they are bound to suffer distress because of their hypocrisy. He outlines some of their specific transgressions: they do not enter the kingdom of heaven, and they hinder those who are entering. They do not treat widows according to the law but make pretentious prayers. They work hard to make proselytes (Gentile converts to Judaism) and make them sons of Gehenna (the city's garbage dump) like themselves. They make up conflicting and illogical rules about swearing and oaths. They carry out certain rules of the Torah to the point of stressing trivial things like tithing (donating 10 percent) even the flavoring herbs from the garden but omit the weightier things of the law, such as judgment, mercy, and faith. He likens this to cleansing the outside of the cup and leaving the inside unclean. They are more interested in outward appearance than cleanliness within. They claim they would not kill prophets as their ancestors did. But because they are full of hypocrisy within, they prove that they are sons of those who did. And their actions and attitudes demonstrate that they would do the same thing given the chance. Having said these things, Jesus again laments over Jerusalem.(Matt. 23:1-39; Mk. 12:38-40; Lk. 20:45-47)

The Widow's Offering. Jesus moves to a spot near the temple treasury and watches the people deposit their offerings. Rich people put in some large sums, but a poor widow put in two small copper coins. Jesus tells the disciples that she put in more than the others, because they gave out of their surplus; whereas, she gave all she had.(Mk. 12:41-44; Lk. 21:1-4)

Olivet Discourse. As they are leaving the temple area, the disciples comment on the beauty of the buildings. Jesus observes that they will some day be torn down, and not one stone will be left upon another. When they reach the Mount of Olives, the disciples ask Jesus to tell them the time and signs of these occurrences, as well as his coming and the end of the age. Jesus responds at some length in what is called "The Olivet Discourse." First he warns against following false messiahs. The people will hear of wars and rumors of wars, but the time is not yet. Nation will rise against nation, and there will be famines and earthquakes. People will bring tribulation upon believers, and they will be hated because of Jesus' name. But they will be aided by the Holy Spirit who will instruct them. False prophets will arise and mislead many. The love of some will grow cold, but those who endure to the end will be saved. When they shall see Jerusalem encompassed by armies, then they will know that her desolation is near. The gospel will be preached to the world, and then the end will come. When the "abomination of desolation" spoken by the prophet Daniel stands in the holy place, where it should not be, those in Judea should flee, going back for nothing, for there will be great tribulation. The days will be cut short for the elect, but otherwise no one will be spared. False messiahs and prophets will mislead many, except, perhaps, the elect. Immediately after the tribulation the sign of the coming of the son of man will appear in heaven, and he will come with power and glory and gather his elect. Just as a fig tree foretells summer by putting forth leaves, they will recognize that he is near, right at the door. This generation will not pass away until all things take place. No one knows the day or hour, only the Father. Just as the people in Noah's day did not understand until the flood came, so shall the coming of the son of man be. One of two men in a field will be taken, the other left. One of two women at a grinding mill will be taken, the other left. They must be on the alert, lest they be asleep when he comes.(Matt. 24:1-41; Mk. 13:1-22; Lk. 21:5-33)

Be Alert. By "alert" Jesus means the alertness of the servant who makes sure everything is in order at all times, since he knows not when his master returns; not like the evil servant who parties on his master's time and is punished when his master comes home early. Also not like the girls who did not have the foresight to buy oil for their lamps for the wedding festivities. When they could not light their lamps, the bridegroom refused to allow them to attend the reception. Jesus also illustrates "alert" with the parable of the man who entrusted his servants to invest money for him while he was away. Those who were diligent and showed a profit were rewarded by the master with great joy. But the one who failed to invest and hid the money was punished for his failure. Every diligent person who has shall gain an abundance, but he who has little will have even that taken away from him if he is not alert.(Matt. 24:42 - 25:30; Mk. 13:33-37; Lk. 21:34-36)

The Sheep and the Goats. When the son of man comes in his glory and with angels, he will sit on the throne of his glory. The people of all nations will be gathered, and he will separate them as a shepherd separates the sheep from the goats, sheep on his right and goats on the left. He will say to those on his right, "Come, blessed of my Father, inherit the kingdom prepared for you from the foundation of the world. For I was hungry, and you gave me food; I was thirsty, and you gave me drink; I was a stranger, and you took me in; I was naked, and you clothed me; I was sick, and you visited me; I was in prison and you came to me." The righteous will ask when did they do this, and the king will answer, "Verily, I say to you, inasmuch as you have done it to one of the least of these my brethren, you have done it to me." Those on his left are the ones who failed to do these things. They will receive punishment, but the righteous will enter into eternal life.(Matt. 25:31-46)

Wednesday, Nisan 13

The Plot To Seize Jesus. During the day Jesus teaches at the temple but at night at the Mount of Olives. On Wednesday Jesus informs his disciples that in two days during Passover, he will be crucified. Meanwhile, at the home of Caiaphas, the high priest, the chief priests and elders plot to seize Jesus by trickery and to kill him. They fear the people and do not want a riot during the period of the Passover feast. Then Judas Iscariot, one of Jesus' 12 disciples, acting under satan's influence, appears before them and offers to deliver Jesus to them. The leaders pay Judas 30 pieces of silver, and he begins to seek an opportunity to betray him.(Matt. 26:1-5, 14-16; Mk. 14:10-11; Lk. 22:3-6)

Thursday, Nisan 14

The Last Supper. On Thursday the disciples ask Jesus where he wishes to eat the Passover meal. He instructs them to enter the city where they will be met by a man carrying a pitcher of water who will take them to a large upper room. They do so and once in the room prepare the Passover. That evening Jesus and the 12 are in the upper room reclining about the table, and Jesus expresses his desire to observe the Passover with them before he suffers, because he will not eat it again until it is fulfilled in the kingdom of God.(Matt. 26:17-20; Mk. 14:12-17; Lk. 22:7-16)

Who Is the Greatest? The disciples are talking among themselves when suddenly a dispute arises as to which one of them is regarded as the greatest. Jesus admonishes them, saying that Gentile kings may be regarded as benefactors by their subjects, but not so with the disciples. The greatest should become as the younger and the leader as the servant. One who is served at the table is usually considered greater than the server. But among them it is Jesus who serves. The disciples have stood by him in his trials. Just as the Father has granted him a kingdom, he grants them that they may eat at his table in his kingdom and sit on thrones judging the 12 tribes of Israel.(Luke 22:24-30)

Jesus Washes the Disciples' Feet. Having loved his own who are in the world, Jesus loves them to the end. During the supper, Jesus rises from the table, takes off his outer garment, girds himself with a towel, pours water into a basin, and begins washing the disciples' feet, drying them with the towel. But Peter objects, "Lord, do you wash my feet?" Jesus explains that they may not realize what he is doing, but it will become clear later; that if he does not wash Peter's feet, Peter will have no part with him. Peter then requests that his hands and head also be washed. Jesus says, "He that is washed need not but to wash his feet and is completely clean, except one," referring to the one who would betray him. After washing their feet and replacing his garments, Jesus resumes his position at the table. He asks if they know what he had done. They call him Lord and Teacher. If he as their Lord and Teacher washes their feet, they ought to wash each other's feet. He has given them an example that they should do as he has done. While a servant is not greater than his master, one who receives those whom Jesus sends receives Jesus, and one who receives Jesus receives the one who sent him.(John 13:1-20)

Betrayal Predicted. While they are still eating, Jesus becomes troubled in spirit and says that one of them will betray him. Each one says, "Surely not I." They are deeply grieved and begin discussing who it might be. Reclining on Jesus' breast was the disciple Jesus loved (John). Peter asks him whom Jesus was talking about. John then asks Jesus who it is. He answers that it is the one for whom he will dip a bit of food. Jesus dips the morsel and gives it to Judas Iscariot who objects, saying, "Master, is it I?" Jesus replies, "You have said it."(Matt. 26:25) Judas still acting under satanic influence, leaves the supper when Jesus tells him that what he is to do should be done quickly. The others do not know why Judas left, supposing that as treasurer he has been dispatched to buy something or to make a donation to the poor.(Matt. 26:21-25; Mk. 14:18-21; Lk. 22:21-23; John 13:21-30)

The New Commandment. Jesus turns to the remaining 11 saying that he is now to be glorified in God and God in him; that he will be with them only a little while longer. Where he is going they cannot come. But a new commandment he gives to them: "that you love one another. As I have loved you, that you also love one another. By this, all will know that you are my disciples, if you have love one to another."(John 13:34-35)

Prediction of Denial. Peter asks where Jesus is going, and he answers that where he goes they cannot follow now, but they will later.(John 13:36) Jesus also tells Peter that satan has demanded the right to sift him like wheat, but that Jesus has prayed for him that his faith not fail; that when he regains his faith, he will strengthen his brothers. Peter replies that he is ready to follow Jesus to prison or to death.(Lk. 22:31-33) Jesus says, "A cock will not crow until you have denied me three times."(Matt. 26:34; Mk. 14:30; Lk. 22:34; John 13:37-38)

The Bread and the Cup. Taking some bread and giving thanks, Jesus breaks it and gives it to them, saying, "Take, eat; this is my body which is given for you. Do this in remembrance of me," and they all do so. Jesus then takes the cup and says, "This cup is poured out for you and for many for the remission of sins. It is the new testament (covenant) in my blood. I will drink no more of the fruit of the vine until that day that I drink it new in the kingdom of God."(Matt. 26:26-29; Mk. 14:22-25; Lk. 22:17-20; 1 Cor. 11:23-26)

The Upper Room Discourse; the Holy Spirit; Many Mansions. Jesus now gives the disciples further instruction. "Let not your heart be troubled. You believe in God. Believe also in me. In my Father's house are many mansions. If it were not so, I would have told you. I go to prepare a place for you. And if I go and prepare a place for you, I will come again and receive you to myself, that where I am you may be also. And where I go and the way you know."(John 14:1-4)   Thomas asks what he means, and Jesus says, "I am the way, the truth, and the life. No one comes to the Father but by me." Since they have known and seen Jesus, they also have known and seen the Father. In answer to a question by Philip, Jesus explains that he, Jesus, is in the Father, and the Father is in him. If one does not understand, he or she should be convinced by the works Jesus has done. He says, "In truth, I say to you, 'He that believes on me, the works that I do shall he do also; and greater than these shall he do because I go to my Father.' " Whatever they ask in his name, he will do it. If they love him, they will keep his commandments. "I will pray the Father, and he shall give you another comforter, that he may abide with you forever." The comforter is the Spirit of truth whom the world cannot know, but they will know, for he will dwell within them. Jesus will not leave them comfortless; he will come to them. Because Jesus lives, they will live also. He says, "At that day, you will know that I am in my Father, and you in me, and I in you." One who keeps Jesus' commandments loves Jesus and will be loved by the Father, and Jesus will love that person and manifest himself. In response to a question by Judas (not Iscariot), Jesus says, "If a man love me, he will keep my words, and my Father will love him, and we will come to him and make our abode with him." The comforter is the Holy Spirit whom the Father will send in Jesus' name. He will teach them all things and bring to their remembrance what Jesus has told them.(John 14:1-26)   He continues, "Peace I leave with you, my peace I give to you; not as the world gives do I give to you." He does not want them to be troubled. He is telling them beforehand so that when he goes they will continue to believe. He will not speak much more before the event, for the prince of the world (satan) is coming who has nothing in him.(John 14:27-31)

The Vine and the Branches. Jesus declares that he is the true vine and his Father is the gardener. Every branch that bears no fruit he takes away, and every branch which bears fruit he cleanses so that it may bear more fruit. Just as a branch can bear no fruit unless joined to the vine, they must abide in him. He is the vine; they are the branches. Without him they can do nothing. But if they abide in him, and his words abide in them, they need only ask and it shall be done. The bearing of fruit by disciples of Christ glorifies the Father. Love is the key, and he repeats his commandment that they love one another as he has loved them. He does not consider them servants but friends to whom he has made known everything his Father has told him. They did not choose Jesus; he chose them so that they will bring forth fruit that will last. They will experience the same persecution which Jesus has suffered. But those who would keep Jesus' words will keep theirs.(John 15:1-16:4)

Ask in Jesus' Name. It is to their advantage that he returns to the Father, for the Holy Spirit comes to convict the world concerning sin, righteousness, and judgment. The spirit of truth will be a guide to the truth and what is to come. They may weep and lament, and the world will be glad that Jesus is going, but the disciples' sorrow will be turned to joy. If they ask the Father for anything in his name, it will be granted. The disciples say they believe that he is of God. Jesus tells them that at the crucial time they will scatter, each to his own home, leaving him alone. (See also: Matt. 26:31; Mk. 14:27) But he is not alone, for the Father is with him. He says, "These things I have spoken to you that in me you might have peace. In the world you have tribulation, but be of good cheer; I have overcome the world."(John 16:5-33)

Jesus' High Priestly Prayer. Jesus lifts his eyes to heaven, praying to the Father. The hour has come that the Son be glorified that the Father might be glorified. For through the authority granted the Son to give eternal life, all will know the only true God and Jesus Christ whom he sent. Jesus has completed the work he was sent to do. "And now, O Father, glorify me with your own self with the glory which I had with you before the world was."(John 17:1-5) On behalf of his disciples, he acknowledges that they were given to him by the Father and declares that he has taught them all things. "And now I am no more in the world, but these are in the world, and I come to you, holy Father; keep through your own name those whom you have given me, that they may be one as we are . . . . I pray not that you should take them out of the world but that you should keep them from evil. They are not of this world even as I am not of this world. Sanctify them through your truth; your word is truth."(John 17:6-19)

Prayer for Believers. In his prayer Jesus now speaks for all believers. "Neither pray I for these alone, but for those also who shall believe in me through their word." He has given the disciples his glory that the Father has given him which is based upon love, for the Father has loved Jesus even before the foundation of the world. He prays that all believers be made perfect in one. Just as the Father is in Jesus and Jesus in the Father, believers are in both the Father and the Son, and the Father and the Son are in them. "And I have declared to them your name, and will declare it, that the love wherewith you have loved me may be in them, and I in them."(John 17:20-26)   [The reader will recall that with regard to all people, Jesus said, "For God so loved the world that he gave his only begotten son, that whoever believes in him shall not perish but have eternal life. For God sent not his son into the world to condemn the world but that the world through him might be saved."(John 3:16-17)]

Garden of Gethsemane. The upper room session is concluded with a hymn; then Jesus and the disciples cross over the ravine called Kidron to the Garden of Gethsemane located on the Mount of Olives, one-half mile from Jerusalem. Jesus instructs them that after he has been raised, they should go to Galilee where he will meet them. In the garden Jesus has the disciples sit while he takes Peter, James, and John a short distance away to pray. Jesus fervently prays, "Abba, my Father, all things are possible; if you are willing, let this cup pass from me and be removed; yet, not as I will, but as you will, that your will be done." At this, an angel appears and strengthens him. Jesus prays this prayer two more times, and after each prayer he finds the disciples asleep and wakens them, telling them to keep watching and praying that they not be subject to temptation. "The spirit is willing, but the flesh is weak." Knowing that he is being betrayed, he says, "Rise up, let us go; behold, he is at hand who does betray me."(Matt. 26:30-46; Mk. 14:26-42; Lk. 22:39-46; John 18:1)

The Arrest of Jesus. While Jesus is still speaking, Judas Iscariot arrives followed by a large crowd which includes men sent by the chief priests, elders, and Pharisees, along with a contingent of soldiers. Jesus asks whom they are seeking. They answer, "Jesus, of Nazareth." He says, "I am he." As he speaks, the crowd draws back, and all fall to the ground. Again they ask, and again Jesus identifies himself, saying that the others should be allowed to go. Judas approaches Jesus and, as a prearranged sign, kisses him. Jesus is seized. Peter who has a sword uses it against one Malchus, a servant of the high priest, cutting off his ear. Jesus tells Peter to put away his sword, for those who take the sword shall perish with the sword; that he could appeal to his Father who would put at his disposal more than 12 legions of angels. He touches Malchus' ear and heals it. Then, addressing the crowd, Jesus asks why they are out to seize him in this way, for they have seen him every day teaching in the temple and did not do so. Actually, he explains, this is happening that scripture might be fulfilled.(Matt. 26:47-56; Mk. 14:43-52; Lk. 22:47-53; John 18:2-12)

Trial of Jesus; First Hearing. During the rest of Thursday night and on Friday morning, Jesus is subjected to a trial consisting of six hearings. The first is at the home of Annas, the former high priest and father-in-law of Caiaphas, the present high priest. Jesus is taken there by those who have seized him. Peter and another disciple (probably John) follow. The rest of the disciples have fled. When asked, Peter denies that he is a disciple. Jesus is asked about his teaching. He answers that he has taught openly and asks why he is questioned this way. One of the officers strikes him for speaking so to a (former) high priest. Jesus responds that if he has spoken wrongly, to consider the wrong, but if rightly, why is he being struck? At this point Annas has Jesus taken to the home of Caiaphas.(John 18:13-24)

Second Hearing. The second proceeding is a hearing before Caiaphas, the whole council (Sanhedrin), and a group of scribes and elders. They endeavor to obtain testimony from witnesses in order to put Jesus to death. All of the witnesses' testimony is false and contradictory. Two men testify that Jesus had said he would destroy the temple and in three days build one not made with hands. But even their testimony on this point is inconsistent. Jesus is asked about their testimony, but he remains silent. Then Caiaphas demands to know if Jesus is the Christ (Messiah), the son of God. Jesus admits that he is and that hereafter they "shall see the son of man sitting at the right hand of power and coming in the clouds of heaven."(Ps. 110:1; Dan. 7:13)   Caiaphas believes that this is enough to prove Jesus guilty of blasphemy. The group decides that Jesus should be killed, and they blindfold him and begin to mistreat him, saying, "Prophesy to us, you Christ, who is he that struck you?" Out in the courtyard Peter registers more denials that he knows Jesus. Just then a cock crows, and Peter, remembering what Jesus told him, weeps bitterly.(Matt. 26:57-75; Mk. 14:53-72; Lk. 22:54-65; John 18:25-27)

Friday, Nisan 15

Third Hearing. The third hearing takes place Friday morning. Jesus is brought to the council chambers where he is again asked to tell the council whether he is the son of God. He admits that he is; whereupon the council orders him bound and taken to the headquarters of the Roman governor of Judea, Pontius Pilate. In the meantime, Judas Iscariot has learned that his action will lead to Jesus' death. He returns the 30 pieces of silver to the priests who are not at all concerned about his problem. Judas' remorse for what he has done is so strong that it leads him to suicide by hanging. With the money the priests buy a burial field for strangers, since they cannot put "blood-money" into the temple treasury. This action accords with the prophecy in Zech. 11:12-13.(Matt. 27:1-10; Mk. 15:1; Lk. 22:66-71)

Fourth Hearing. The fourth proceeding is before Pilate. The accusers lay the charges that Jesus is misleading the Jews, forbidding taxes to be paid to Caesar, and saying he is Christ, a king. Pilate asks why they do not punish him themselves. They answer that they are forbidden to put anyone to death. Pilate asks Jesus if he is king of the Jews. Jesus replies that Pilate has spoken correctly, but his kingdom is not of this world. He has come to bear witness to the truth. Pilate asks, "What is truth," but without waiting for an answer, he announces to the accusers that he finds no fault with Jesus. The chief priests and elders repeat their charges, so Pilate questions him again, but Jesus remains silent. Pilate heard someone say that Jesus is from Galilee which is in the jurisdiction of Herod Antipas who happens to be in Jerusalem. Pilate sends Jesus to Herod.(Matt. 27:11-14; Mk. 15:1-5; Lk. 23:1-7; John 18:28-38)

Fifth Hearing. The fifth proceeding is a hearing before Herod Antipas. He has been hoping to see Jesus perform a miracle. He questions him at some length, but Jesus does not answer. Again the priests and scribes are vigorously making accusations. Herod treats him with contempt, dresses him in a fancy robe, and returns him to Pilate. Because of this matter, Herod and Pilate become friends.(Lk. 23:8-12)

Sixth Hearing; Death Sentence. The sixth and last hearing is a continuation of the trial before Pilate. Many of the Jewish leaders are there, and Pilate tries to convince them that Jesus should be released under Pilate's policy to release one Jewish prisoner each year during Passover. But they and the crowd demand that Barabbas, a Jewish insurgent and murderer, be released and Jesus executed. While Pilate is pondering his decision, his wife sends word to him: "Have nothing to do with that just man, for I have suffered many things this day in a dream because of him." But the crowd continues clamoring for the release of Barabbas and the execution of Jesus. Pilate has Jesus whipped, and the soldiers put a crown of thorns on his head and dress him in a purple robe. They mock him and strike him with their hands. Pilate next presents Jesus to the crowd, saying, "Here is your man." The crowd yells, "Crucify him, crucify him!" Then Pilate says, "You take him and crucify him, for I find no fault in him." When they say that they have a law that he ought to die because he makes himself out to be the son of God, Pilate becomes fearful. He takes Jesus inside and questions him further. Doesn't Jesus know that he has the power to have him crucified?

Jesus answers that Pilate would have no authority unless it is given from above. For this reason, those who delivered him to Pilate have the greater sin. Then Pilate tries to release Jesus, but the accusers cry out that if he is released, Pilate is no friend of Caesar, for one who claims to be king speaks against Caesar. Since he is not getting any results and sees that a riot might occur, Pilate takes water and washes his hands before the crowd, saying that he is innocent of the blood of this just person. He orders the release of Barabbas and the crucifixion of Jesus.(Matt. 27:15-26; Mk. 15:6-15; Lk. 23:13-25; John 18:39-19:16)

The Way of the Cross. Jesus is turned over to the Roman soldiers who strip him and again dress him with the purple robe and the crown of thorns. They place a reed in his hand, and kneeling before him, they mock him with "Hail, King of the Jews." Then they spit on him and beat him with the reed. After this they put his own clothes back on him and take him out bearing his own cross. Their destination is an area called "Place of the Skull" (Greek, **Golgatha;** Latin, **Calvaria**). While on the way, they press into service one Simon of Cyrene to carry the cross behind Jesus. Many people follow, mourning for Jesus, and many women are weeping. He turns to the women and tells them not to weep for him but for themselves and their children. In addition to Jesus, two criminals are also being led to the place of crucifixion. When they arrive, the soldiers offer Jesus a drink of wine mixed with myrrh. After tasting the mixture, he refuses to drink it.(Matt. 27:27-34; Mk. 15:16-23; Lk. 23:26-33; John 19:17)

The Crucifixion. It is 9 a.m. when they put Jesus on the cross. The two criminals are also crucified, Jesus being placed between them. Jesus then says, "Father, forgive them, for they know not what they do." While the soldiers are keeping watch, they cast lots to divide his garments among them and gamble for his seamless woven tunic. This confiscation of Jesus' clothes fulfills Ps. 22:18, "They parted my raiment among them, and for my vesture they cast lots." Above Jesus' head is a sign, erected on order of Pontius Pilate. The sign bears this inscription in Greek, Latin, and Hebrew:

THIS IS JESUS OF NAZARETH
THE KING OF THE JEWS

Jesus' accusers go to Pilate and try to have the sign changed to read that Jesus only says he is king of the Jews. But Pilate answers, "What I have written, I have written."(Matt. 27:35-38; Mk. 15:24-28; Lk. 23:33-38; John 19:18-24)

Today in Paradise. People passing by the scene of the triple execution begin insulting Jesus. If Jesus is the son of God and the Christ (Messiah); if he trusts in God and could destroy, then rebuild the temple in three days; if he is king of Israel and has saved others, he should be able to save himself. Even the criminals on the other crosses join in the insults.(Matt. 27:39-44; Mk. 15:29-32; Lk. 23:35-37, 39)   But one of the robbers, having a change of heart, rebukes the other about their need to fear God. They deserve their punishment, but Jesus has done nothing wrong. He says to Jesus, "Lord, remember me when you have come into your kingdom." Jesus replies, "In truth, I say to you, today you shall be with me in paradise."(Lk. 23:39-43)

"Behold Your Mother." Standing by the cross of Jesus are his mother and her sister; Mary, the wife of Cleophus; and Mary Magdalene. There also is the disciple Jesus loved (John). To his mother Jesus says, "Woman, behold your son," and to the disciple, "Behold your mother." And from that time on the disciple took her as his own.(John 19:25-27)

"It Is Finished." At noon darkness falls over the land, and it stays dark until 3 p.m. After being on the cross for six hours, Jesus exclaims, "My God, my God, why have you forsaken me?"(Ps. 22:1)   Some think he is calling for Elijah. Jesus says that he is thirsty, and onlookers give him a drink by putting a sponge filled with sour wine to his lips with a reed, a branch of hyssop. Some are saying, "Let be, let us see whether Elijah comes to save him." Suddenly the people hear Jesus cry out, "Father into your hands I commend my spirit."(Ps. 31:5)   Then as he says, "It is finished," Jesus bows his head and breathes his last.(Matt. 27:45-50; Mk. 15:33-37; Lk. 23:44-46; John 19:28-30)

The Veil Is Torn. At that moment the veil of the temple is torn in two; the earth quakes, and rocks are torn apart. Tombs open, and saints who have been in the grave arise and appear to many in Jerusalem. When the centurion and guards see the earthquake and other phenomena, they become frightened and say, "Truly, this was the son of God." The centurion starts praising God, saying, "Certainly this was a righteous man." Many people begin to mourn. Men and women who came from Galilee with Jesus, including Mary Magdalene; Salome, the mother of James and John; and Mary, the mother of another James and Joseph, stand apart from the crowd watching.(Matt. 27:51-56; Mk. 15:38-41; Lk. 23:45-49)

His Side Is Pierced. Jewish officials ask that the legs of the condemned men be broken to hasten death, for they do not want the bodies on the crosses on the next day, the Sabbath. They do so to the two robbers but not Jesus' body, since he is already dead. One of the soldiers pierces Jesus' side with a spear, and blood and water come out. This is as prophesied in Ps. 34:20, "A bone of him shall not be broken"; and Zech. 12:10, "They shall look upon him whom they pierced."(John 19:31-37)

Jesus' Burial. As evening approaches, Joseph of Arimathea, a prominent member of the Jewish council and secret disciple of Jesus, receives permission from Pilate to take Jesus' body for burial. Joseph's action shows his courage, for he had voted against the council's action. He is a man of wealth and has his own tomb which was hewn out of rock in a garden he owns not far from Golgotha. Nicodemus, the Pharisee leader who had spoken with Jesus about being born again (John 3:1-21), also comes bringing a large amount of an embalming mixture of myrrh and aloes. The two men put Jesus' body in Joseph's tomb, prepare it with the spices, wrapping it with linen cloth. The Galilean women also come preparing spices and perfume for the burial. A large stone is rolled in front of the entrance.(Matt. 27:57-61; Mk. 15:42-47; Lk. 23:50-56; John 19:38-42)

Saturday, Nisan 16

Guards at the Tomb. The next day, Saturday, the Sabbath, they all rest according to the commandment.(Lk. 23:56)   Some of the Jewish priests and Pharisees have a meeting with Pilate and remind him that Jesus had said he would rise again after three days. Pilate tells them to do whatever is necessary to secure the grave. They then go to the grave, seal up the stone, and station a contingent of guards at the entrance.(Matt. 27:62-66)

Sunday, Nisan 17

He Is Risen. Early Sunday morning Mary Magdalene, Salome, Mary, the mother of James, and Joanna come to the grave. An angel has rolled away the stone and is sitting on it. The angel's appearance is dazzling, and his clothes white as snow. The guards see him and are afraid and become as dead men. Another angel is also present, and they tell the women that Jesus is not there. "He is risen. Come, see the place where they laid him, and go quickly, tell his disciples that he is risen from the dead; and, behold, he goes before you into Galilee; there you shall see him." They leave immediately with fear and joy and report to the disciples what has happened. They hear the news in disbelief. Peter and John go to the grave. After peering into the tomb and seeing only the cloth wrappings, they go in and take a closer look. They then believe that Jesus is gone, but not yet comprehending the significance of the event, they return to their homes. Outside the tomb, Mary Magdalene is weeping. She looks into the tomb and sees the two angels standing where the body had been. They ask her why she is weeping. She answers, "Because they have taken away my Lord, and I do not know where they have laid him." As she turns around, there is Jesus standing. Not recognizing him and supposing him to be the gardener, she asks where they have taken Jesus. Jesus says, "Mary!" She says, "Rabboni" (Jewish Aramaic for "teacher"). He says, "Do not touch me, for I have not yet ascended to my Father. But go to my brethren and tell them that I ascend to my Father, and your Father, and to my God and your God." Mary complies, telling the disciples that she has seen the Lord and what he said. Later Jesus appears to Mary and two others. He hails them and tells them to inform the disciples that he will meet them in Galilee. The women grasp his feet and worship him.(Matt. 28:1-10; Mk. 16:1-11; Lk. 24:1-12; John 20:1-18)

A False Story. In the meantime, some of the soldiers of the tomb guard report to the chief priests what has happened. They and the elders decide to give the soldiers a large sum of money if they will say that the disciples came at night and stole Jesus' body while they were asleep. If word gets back to the governor (Pilate), they will cover for them and keep them out of trouble. The soldiers take the money and proceed to spread the story.(Matt. 28:11-15)

Jesus Appears. On a road to Emmaus, a village about seven miles from Jerusalem, Jesus appears to two men, but they do not recognize him. They ask if he is aware of what has happened —how Jesus, a mighty prophet who was going to redeem Israel, was crucified. Now it is the third day. Some women report that they had seen angels who told them that he is still alive. Jesus asks the men whether it was not necessary for the Christ to suffer these things and enter into his glory; then he begins to teach them about himself as revealed in the scriptures. At their invitation, he remains with them, and when they recline at the table, he takes bread, blesses it, breaks it, and passes it to them. As they realize who he is, he vanishes. The men recount how they felt their hearts burning within when Jesus spoke to them. Then they return to Jerusalem and tell the 11 about their experience and how Jesus has really risen.(Mk. 16:12-13; Lk. 24:13-35)

Jesus Seen by Disciples; Doubting Thomas. Sunday evening Jesus comes and stands in the room in which 10 of the 11 disciples are assembled. At this they become frightened as seeing a spirit. Jesus assures them that they need not be troubled. He shows them his hands, his feet, and his side, saying, "A spirit does not have flesh and bones as you see me have." The reaction of the disciples is one of joy, yet dismay. Jesus asks for food and is given some broiled fish and honey which he proceeds to eat. Then he says to them, "As my Father has sent me, even so send I you. Receive the Holy Spirit. Whoever's sins you remit, they are remitted; whoever's sins you retain, they are retained." He explains that what is happening is in fulfillment of the law of Moses, the prophets, and the Psalms concerning him, and he opens their minds that they might understand the scripture.(Lk. 24:36-45; John 20:19-23)   Thomas, who was not with them when Jesus appeared, returns and is told that they have seen the Lord. Thomas says, "Except that I see in his hands the print of the nails, and put my finger into the print of the nails, and thrust my hand into his side, I will not believe." Eight days later when Thomas is present, Jesus comes and stands in their midst (even though the doors are shut) saying, "Peace be to you." To Thomas he says, "Reach here with your finger and touch my hands; reach with your hand and put it into my side; have faith and believe." Thomas answers, "My Lord and my God." Jesus says, "Thomas, because you have seen me, you have believed; blessed are they that have not seen me and yet believe."(John 20:24-31)

Feed My Sheep. The disciples now journey to Galilee and while waiting for their next meeting with Jesus, they decide to go fishing in the Sea of Galilee. After fishing all night from the boat, they have been unsuccessful. As day breaks, they see a man standing on the beach not realizing that it is Jesus. He calls out to them, "Children, have you any fish?" They answer, "No." Jesus says that if they will cast their nets on the right side of the boat, they will have a catch. They lower the nets and catch more fish than they are able to pull into the boat. John says to Peter, "It is the Lord." At this, Peter jumps into the water and swims to shore. The others follow in the boat dragging the net full of fish. There are 153 fish; yet the net is not broken. When they come ashore, they see that Jesus has been broiling fish over some coals and that there is also some bread. He invites them to eat, and after they finish breakfast, he speaks with them. He asks Peter three times whether Peter loves him, and each time Peter answers that Jesus must know that he loves him. After each answer, Jesus says, "Feed my sheep." Jesus then explains to him that when he, Peter, was young he girded himself and walked where he wished, but when he becomes old, he will be girded by another and carried where he does not want to go. In saying this, Jesus is indicating by what death Peter should glorify God. When Peter hears this, he asks about John. Jesus answers, "If I will that he tarry till I come, what is that to you? Follow me." Now Jesus did not say that John would not die; only that it is not Peter's concern if Jesus wills that John tarry until Jesus' return.(John 21:1-25)

Appearance on the Mountain; the Great Commission. Their next meeting is on a Galilean mountain designated by Jesus. He tells them that he has been given all authority in heaven and on earth. "Go, therefore, and teach the people of all nations, baptizing them in the name of the Father, and of the Son, and of the Holy Spirit, teaching them to observe all that I have commanded you. And, lo, I am with you always, until the end of the age."(Matt. 28:16-20)   He also indicates that signs will accompany those who have believed. In Jesus' name they will cast out demons, speak with new tongues, be protected against serpents, and if they drink any deadly poison, it will not harm them; and they will lay hands on the sick, and they shall recover.(Mk. 16:15-18)

The Ascension of Jesus. By prearrangement they return to Jerusalem, and Jesus continues his teaching of the disciples. He says that it is written that Christ should suffer and rise again from the dead on the third day; that repentance and remission of sins should be proclaimed in his name to all people beginning from Jerusalem. They are to stay in the city until they are clothed with power on high.(Lk. 24:45-48; Acts 1:4)   Then, it having been 40 days since his resurrection, Jesus leads them out as far as Bethany. He tells them that in a few days they are to be baptized with the Holy Spirit. They ask him whether this is the time when he will restore the kingdom to Israel. Jesus answers, "It is not for you to know the times or the seasons which the Father has put in his own power. You shall be witnesses for me both in Jerusalem and in all Judea, in Samaria, and in the remotest parts of the earth." After saying this, Jesus lifts his hands, blesses them, and parts from them to be received into heaven and to sit at the right hand of God. While they watch, Jesus is lifted up into a cloud and out of sight. As the disciples are looking skyward, two men clothed in white say to them, "Men of Galilee, why do you gaze into heaven? This same Jesus who is taken up from you into heaven shall return in like manner as you have seen him go into heaven." The disciples return to Jerusalem joyful. They go to the temple frequently, praising God. After Pentecost [see next chapter] they go out from Jerusalem and preach the gospel throughout the world, the Lord working with them, confirming the word with signs following.(Mk. 16:19-20; Lk. 24:49-53; Acts 1:3-12)   [NOTE: The apostle Paul lists (in addition to his own experience in Acts 9) postresurrection appearances of Jesus to Peter, to James, to all the disciples, and to 500 people at one time most of whom were still living in Paul's day.(1 Cor. 15:5-8)]

CHAPTER NINE
THE BOOK OF ACTS

The book of Acts was written by Luke about 64 A.D. It is referred to as the history of the first-century church; the acts of the apostles; or acts of the Holy Spirit. After the ascension of Jesus, the 11 remaining inner circle of disciples are known as the apostles. Jesus had commissioned these men as apostles and had delegated authority to them. (As the Father has sent me, so send I you.) While we see some action involving all the apostles in Acts, including Jesus' half-brother James, most of the action in the book revolves about two men, Peter and Paul. Peter is one of the original disciples; Paul becomes an apostle, sometimes called the thirteenth apostle, through his conversion experience in Acts 9. Paul was a highly educated man and had been a Pharisee as his father before him. He also had a trade, that of tentmaker. Peter's ministry is covered in chapters 1 - 12 and 15; Paul's adventures and ministry in chapters 7 - 9, 13 - 28. Acts also contains teachings in the form of sermons, discussions, and demonstrations of the power to perform miracles and healing. Paul was originally from Tarsus, a city on the southern coast of what is now Turkey. He was Jewish but also a Roman citizen by birth. He knew the Hebrew and Greek languages and undoubtedly also Aramaic, the common language of Palestine, and as a Roman citizen, Latin. Thoroughly schooled in Judaism as a student of Gamaliel and having a zeal which he brought to any project, he was a prime candidate for the type of apostleship necessary to extend Christian evangelism into Europe. As Paul said, he became all things to all men that he might save some.(1 Cor. 9:20-22)

Acts also shows an early resolution of the questions whether a non-Jew could become a Christian and whether a Christian was obligated to follow the practices of Judaism. The first question was resolved in Acts 10 and 11, the second in Acts 15. The gospel includes all people, and under the new covenant the practice of Judaism is not required.

First Christian Congregation. The book of Acts begins with the ascension of Jesus. Before he is taken up, he tells his followers to remain in Jerusalem until they are endued with power from on high through the Holy Spirit.(Acts 1:1-12) There they gather together in an upper room, 120 people including the 11 apostles,

Jesus' mother Mary, and his brothers. Peter takes charge of the meeting and declares that the first order of business is the filling of the position left vacant by the death of Judas Iscariot. After a discussion of qualifications, one Matthias is appointed as the twelfth apostle.(Acts 1:13-26)

Pentecost. Later, on the day of Pentecost, they are all present. ["Pentecost" is the Greek name given to a Jewish religious observance established in the Old Testament called the "Feast of Weeks or Ingathering," celebrating the harvest and God's goodness in providing a successful crop. The Greek word refers to the fact that this observance comes 50 days after Passover.] Suddenly there is a violent noise filling the whole house like a rushing wind, and tongues of fire appear coming to rest on each person. They are all filled with the Holy Spirit and begin speaking with other languages (tongues) as the Spirit gives them utterance. Many Jewish people from other nations are present in the city, and many who are nearby, hearing the noise, come to the house. They are amazed, because each hears his own language spoken. They ask how this could be, because those speaking are Galileans. Some are mocking and saying that they must be full of wine. But Peter stands before them and delivers his first sermon.(Acts 2:1-14)

Holy Spirit Prophecy Fulfilled. Peter explains that the people are not drunk, for it is only 9 a.m. What they have heard is a fulfillment of the prophecy in Joel 2:28-32, to the effect that God will pour out his Spirit on all mankind. Men and women, sons and daughters will receive the Spirit and prophesy. There will be wonders, and everyone who calls on the name of the Lord will be saved. Peter goes on to recount the ministry of Jesus who came from God, was murdered, but raised from the dead, as prophesied in Ps. 16:8-11, and is sitting at God's right hand. The Holy Spirit has come as Jesus promised, and Jesus is both Lord and Christ (Messiah).(Acts 2:15-36)

Three Thousand Baptized. At Peter's words, the people are conscience-stricken and ask what they should do. Peter answers, "Repent and be baptized, every one of you, in the name of Jesus Christ for the remission of sins, and you will receive the gift of the Holy Spirit. For the promise is for you and your children and to all that are far away, as many as the Lord our God shall call." He exhorts them further, concluding with, "Save yourselves from this crooked generation." As a result of the events of Pentecost and Peter's sermon, 3,000 people are baptized.(Acts 2:37-41)

House to House, Breaking Bread. The new Christians immediately begin devoting themselves to the teachings of the apostles, to fellowship, to the breaking of bread with one another, and prayer. They have a sense of awe, and many signs and wonders are performed by the apostles. They all stay in close contact and share what they have so that no one is in need. They continue daily with one accord at the temple and go from house to house breaking bread, taking their meals with gladness and singleness of heart, praising God. They have favor with all the people, and the Lord adds to the congregation daily many who are saved.(Acts 2:42-47)

Lame Man Healed. One day about 3 p.m., as Peter and John are in the temple, a 40-year-old man born lame begs them for money. Peter explains that he has no silver or gold to give him, but he will give him what he has. Looking at him intently, he says, "In the name of Jesus Christ of Nazareth, rise up and walk." Taking him by the hand, he lifts him, and immediately the man receives strength in his feet and ankles. Leaping up, he stands, then walks into the temple with them, praising God. Those who witness the event also praise God and come forward. Peter gives his second sermon, reviewing the recent well-known events concerning Jesus. He points to various scriptural declarations foretelling the coming of the Messiah as a fulfillment of the Abrahamic covenant, that through Abraham all people will be blessed. God has sent Jesus to bless them by turning them away from all their iniquities.(Acts 3:1-26)

Five Thousand Added. The temple officials, especially the Sadducees, are not happy with Peter and John, for they are teaching the people about resurrection through Jesus. The apostles are arrested and held overnight. But about 5,000 people have been added to the number of believers because of what Peter has said. The council convenes. Peter and John are brought before them and ordered not to preach Jesus any more, but they answer that they cannot but speak of the things which they have seen and heard. After threatening the apostles further, they release them. Peter and John return to their people rejoicing, praising God, and praying.(Acts 4:1-31)

Sharing Possessions. Their evangelistic mission continues. Many believers sell what they possess and turn the money over to the apostles to help the ministry and provide for those in need. A man named Joseph from the island of Cyprus donates the proceeds from the sale of some land. This man is a mainstay of the movement (later becoming an evangelist with Paul). The apostles refer to him as Barnabas which means "son of encouragement." About the same time, a man and his wife, Ananias and Sapphira, concoct a scheme whereby they will sell some land, make it

171

appear that they are giving all the proceeds to the congregation, but actually only donating some of the money, hoping that this will enhance their status and recognition in the Christian community. However, Peter learns of the actual amount they have received, sees through the scheme, and asks them why they have allowed satan to control them in this way. What they are doing is not lying to man but to the Holy Spirit and God. The confrontation with Peter and those present is so overwhelming and their consciences so stricken that they expire, Ananias first and his wife about three hours later when Peter discloses to her what he knows and what has happened to her husband.(Acts 5:1-11)

Apostles Freed from Jail. All of the apostles continue their work in the temple area, preaching, working miracles, and healing all who are brought to them. The high priest and Sadducees arrest the apostles and imprison them. But an angel opens the doors at night and lets them out. They are back at the temple the next morning teaching. When the high priest calls for them to be brought before the council, the guards find the prison doors still locked, but the apostles are not there. They then go to where the apostles are holding forth and escort them to the council. The high priest reminds them that they have been forbidden to preach Christ. They are filling Jerusalem with their teachings and trying to bring Jesus' blood upon them. But Peter and the apostles reply that they obey God rather than men. They are witnesses of Jesus whom God sent to be a saviour to Israel through repentance and the forgiveness of sins. This retort infuriates the council, and they purpose to have the apostles slain. But a Pharisee named Gamaliel, a doctor of the law, stands and reminds the group that there have been many false leaders arise who attracted followers for a time but whose efforts finally failed. Let these men alone, for if their work is only of men, it will fail. But if it is of God, it cannot be overthrown; lest the council find itself fighting God. The council agrees, has the apostles whipped, orders them not to speak in Jesus' name, and releases them. The apostles rejoice and continue to teach and preach Jesus Christ daily in the temple and house to house.(Acts 5:12-42)

The First Deacons. An internal problem faces the apostles when they learn that a dispute has arisen over the provision of food to needy widows. The Greek-Jewish-Christian group is claiming that the Hebrew-Jewish-Christian widows are being favored over their widows. The apostles appoint seven men selected by the congregation to be in charge of such day-to-day affairs so that the apostles can devote all their time to prayer and ministry of the word. Among "the seven" are Stephen and Philip.(Acts 6:1-6)

Martyrdom of Stephen. The number of Christians steadily increases, and even many priests are converted. The believers also take their message to the synagogues. One day men from a Greek-Jewish synagogue begin disputing with Stephen. Not able to withstand his arguments, they seize him and take him before the council, leveling a charge of blasphemy. The specific charge is that Stephen claims that Jesus will destroy the temple and change the customs authored by Moses. As the council looks upon Stephen, they see a face as of an angel. When the high priest asks him if the charge is true, Stephen gives them a review of Old Testament history. He then accuses them of resisting the Holy Spirit as their fathers did who persecuted the prophets; of failing to follow the law as given; and of killing the just one. They become angry, but he looks up to heaven and says, "I see the heavens opened and the son of man standing on the right hand of God." At this, they drive Stephen out of the city and kill him by stoning. Before he dies, Stephen prays, "Lord Jesus, receive my spirit. Lord, lay not this sin to their charge."(Acts 6:7 - 7:60)

Persecution and Dispersion. A witness to Stephen's martyrdom is one Saul who approves of what was done.(Acts 7:58; 8:1)   He is a young Pharisee born in Tarsus in Cilicia (a city on the coast of what is now Turkey). A Jew, he is also a Roman citizen. He has studied Judaism under Gamaliel and has a burning zeal for God.(Acts 8:1; 22:3, 27; 26:5)   He becomes a special agent for the council and engages in a campaign of persecution against the Christians in Jerusalem many of whom are imprisoned. Those who escape arrest go to other parts of Palestine. However, the apostles remain in Jerusalem.(Acts 8:3-4)

Conversion of Samaritans. While this persecution is going on in Jerusalem, Philip goes to the city of Samaria preaching, healing the sick, and exorcizing demons. Many men and women are baptized including a man named Simon who has been prominent as a practitioner of sorcery. When news of Philip's success reaches the apostles, they send Peter and John to Samaria. They lay hands on the believers, and they receive the Holy Spirit. Simon, desiring to have this gift, offers them money so that he might be able to lay on hands for the receiving of the Holy Spirit. Peter rebukes him saying that this gift cannot be bought and that Simon must repent and pray for forgiveness. Simon beseeches the apostles to pray for him. On their way back to Jerusalem, the apostles preach the gospel in many Samaritan villages.(Acts 8:5-25)

Philip and the Ethiopian Eunuch. Heeding the word of an angel who comes to him, Philip travels to Gaza, a desert area south of Jerusalem, where he meets a eunuch, an important official in Ethiopia, who has come to worship in Jerusalem. Philip approaches him as the man is seated in his chariot reading aloud from the book of Isaiah the passage describing the manner of death of the Messiah.(Isa. 53:7-8)   Philip asks him if he understands the passage, and the eunuch replies that he cannot unless someone explains it. Using that passage, Philip teaches him about Jesus. Traveling together, they come to some water, and at the eunuch's request Philip baptizes him after he has confessed that Jesus is the Son of God. Then the Spirit of the Lord takes Philip away, and the eunuch goes his way rejoicing. Philip is taken to Azotus, and he preaches in various cities until he reaches Caesarea where he sets up residence.(Acts 8:26-40; 21:8)

Conversion of Saul (Paul). Meanwhile, Saul of Tarsus has received a commission from the Jewish council to eradicate the Christians from Damascus (today the capital of Syria). As he nears Damascus, a light from heaven shines about him, and a voice says, "Saul, Saul, why are you persecuting me? I am Jesus whom you are persecuting; it is hard for you to kick against the pricks." Saul asks, "Lord, what would you have me do?" Jesus says, "Arise, and go into the city and you will be told what to do." Saul opens his eyes but is not able to see anything. His companions have heard the voice but have seen no one. They take Saul to the city. After three days, the Lord directs a believer named Ananias to go to Saul on the street called Straight and minister to him, for Saul has prayed and has seen a vision of Ananias coming and laying hands on him and of having his sight restored. Ananias objects that Saul is a persecutor of believers, but the Lord says, "Go your way, for he is a chosen vessel of mine, to bear my name before the Gentiles and kings and the children of Israel. For I will show him how great things he must suffer for my name's sake." Ananias does as directed. Saul receives his sight and is baptized. After spending several days with the Christians in Damascus, Saul begins preaching Christ in the synagogues, to the amazement of the people. Certain Jewish opponents in the city plot to kill him. To save Saul, the disciples have to lower him down the wall in a basket because the gates are being watched. He escapes and travels to Jerusalem to confer with the apostles.(Acts 9:1-26)

Saul Sent to Tarsus. Saul wants to join the group at Jerusalem, but they fear him and do not believe that he is a Christian. Barnabas befriends him and explains Saul's conversion and how he has preached boldly in Jesus' name. Saul is finally accepted and continues his preaching. When it is learned

174

that Saul's life is again in peril, the apostles send him back to his hometown of Tarsus. Then all the congregations in Palestine have peace and continue to grow.(Acts 9:26-31)

Peter's Ministry. Sometime later Peter embarks on a mission which takes him to many places in Judea. While visiting believers in Lydda, Peter heals a bedridden man. In Joppa (today, Tel Aviv-Jaffa), he raises Dorcas (also called Tabitha), the town's beloved seamstress, from death. This miracle also brings many into the fold.(Acts 9:32-42)

Peter and Cornelius. While Peter is staying at Joppa in the home of Simon the tanner, several miles away in Caesarea a Roman centurion named Cornelius has a vision. Cornelius is a convert to Judaism, a devout man, who along with all in his household, fears God, gives many donations to the people, and prays to God constantly. In the vision an angel of God tells Cornelius, "Your prayers and your alms have come before God as a memorial." He is instructed to send men to Simon's house in Joppa to see Peter who will instruct him further. As Cornelius' men near Joppa at about noon, Peter is on the roof, praying. Becoming hungry, he is about to go down for lunch when he falls into a trance. He sees a vision of heaven opening and a huge sheet descending filled with all sorts of animals. And a voice says, "Rise, Peter, kill and eat." Peter says, "Not so, Lord, for I have never eaten anything common or unclean." ["Common or unclean" indicates that Peter has seen animals on the sheet which under Mosaic law Jewish people were forbidden to eat.] The voice says, "What God has cleansed you do not call common." As Peter ponders what this all means, Cornelius' men arrive and explain their mission. The next day Peter travels to Caesarea with them and enters Cornelius' home where he, his family, and some friends are waiting. Cornelius kneels before Peter, but Peter instructs him to get up because he is just a man like Cornelius. Peter tells the group that under Jewish tradition, a Jew is not supposed to enter a Gentile's house, but God has told him not to call any man common or unclean. The gospel is for all people. God is no respecter of persons (i.e., does not respect one person more than another; considers everyone equally). Peter tells them of Jesus' ministry, death, and resurrection and how he commissioned the apostles to teach that through Jesus' name whoever believes in him shall receive remission of sins. While Peter is still speaking, the Holy Spirit falls upon all who have heard Peter's teaching, and they begin praising God and speaking in tongues. Peter says, "Who can deny these people water baptism who have received the Holy Spirit as we have also?" Peter remains for several days as a guest of the new believers.(Acts 9:43 - 10:48)

Jerusalem Council and the Gentile Question. Returning to Jerusalem, Peter is met by some intense questioning by some believers who still follow all of the Jewish law and traditions. They want to know why Peter entered a Gentile house and ate with them. Peter explains how he received the vision of the sheet and animals and how the Holy Spirit sent him to Cornelius' house. He outlines the happenings there, including the people's baptism and reception of the Holy Spirit. Peter's answer satisfies his questioners and they glorify God that Gentiles also have been granted repentance unto life.(Acts 11:1-18)

Barnabas Recruits Saul. One result of the earlier persecution of Christians was the spread of the gospel to areas such as Phoenicia (Lebanon), Cyrus, Cyrene (in north Africa), and Antioch (a large city in ancient Syria; now Antakya in southeast Turkey). When the apostles hear that there is a congregation at Antioch, Barnabas is sent to evangelize there, and many more converts are added. Then Barnabas travels to Tarsus, finds Saul and convinces him to accompany him to Antioch. [Saul (Paul) has been in Tarsus for 14 years.(Gal. 2:1)] For the next year Barnabas and Saul teach at Antioch. It is at Antioch that disciples of Christ are for the first time called "Christians." [Note: Before this the Christian movement was known as "The Way."] During the reign of Claudius Caesar there is a recession, and the Antioch congregation sends Barnabas and Saul to Jerusalem with a relief contribution for the congregation there.(Acts 11:19-30)

Martyrdom of James; Imprisonment of Peter. About that time Herod the king (Herod Agrippa I) is persecuting Christians. He has James, brother of John, killed with a sword and has Peter arrested to be tried after the Passover. But an angel of the Lord comes and releases Peter from prison. Peter goes to the home of Mary, the mother of John Mark, where many have gathered to pray for Peter's release. He knocks at the gate, and his knock is answered by a young woman named Rhoda. When she recognizes Peter's voice, she becomes so excited that she forgets to open the gate, runs inside, and announces that Peter is there. This information is received in disbelief, but when they open the door, they are able to see him. He explains what has happened and requests that they inform James (Jesus' half-brother) and others. Then Peter departs to another place.(Acts 12:1-17)

Death of Herod Agrippa I. When Herod calls for Peter's appearance before him, he learns of Peter's escape. The guards who Herod believes are responsible for Peter's escape are ordered executed. (A short time later Herod is also the victim of death.) He has been unhappy with the people of Tyre and Sidon (Lebanon). Their leaders in an attempt to restore good relations come to Caesarea to pay him honor. This action is prompted mainly by their dependence upon his country for their provisions. The opportunity is arranged through their friend Blastus who happens to be the king's chamberlain. A day is set, and at the appointed time Herod appears on his throne and delivers an oration to the visitors. They shout that his is the voice of a god, not a man. Herod accepts their adulation but does not give the true God the glory for his position, and for this reason an angel of the Lord smites him. Herod dies on the spot of an internal affliction (literally, "eaten of worms").(Acts 12:18-24)

Paul and Barnabas; First Missionary Journey. Meanwhile, Barnabas and Saul have completed their mission of taking the relief offering to the Jerusalem congregation, and they return to Antioch, taking John Mark with them. The three men join the many prophets and teachers who minister to the congregation at Antioch. Then one day the Holy Spirit speaks to them, saying that he has commissioned Saul and Barnabas for his work; that it is time for these men to be "separated," i.e., set apart, for a special mission. The people fast and pray, lay hands upon Saul and Barnabas, and send them forth. John Mark accompanies them. Their first evangelistic goal is to preach the gospel on the island of Cyprus. So they board a ship in Seleucia, the port city of Antioch, and sail to Cyprus. Beginning their ministry in the city of Salamis, they share the gospel in the island's synagogues. Finally they reach the city of Paphos on the west end of the island. The governor of Cyprus, a Roman proconsul named Sergius Paulus, calls for Saul and Barnabas to hear their message. When the men join the governor, they find that a magician called Elymas is with him. They explain the gospel message, but Elymas opposes them. [NOTE: At this point in Acts, Saul (Hebrew name) becomes known by his Roman name, Paul.(Acts 13:9)]   Paul, filled with the Holy Spirit, declares that Elymas will suffer temporary blindness and must cease perverting the way of the Lord. Darkness falls upon Elymas, and he is led away by the hand. Sergius Paulus is amazed at the teachings of Paul and Barnabas and the results of their encounter with Elymas. The Roman governor becomes a believer.(Acts 12:25 - 13:12)

To Asia Minor. From Cyprus the three evangelists sail to Perga. At this point John Mark leaves them and returns to Jerusalem. Paul and Barnabas go on to Antioch of Pisidia (in the Galatian region of what is now the south-central part of Turkey). In the synagogue on the Sabbath, the rabbis invite the evangelists to speak. Paul begins by recalling God's choosing of their fathers and their history. He mentions the Egyptian and wilderness experiences, Samuel the prophet, King Saul, and God's choice of David. He reminds them of the promise that a descendant of David would be a savior, that this promise has been fulfilled in Jesus. John the Baptist came to announce the coming of one whose shoes he was not worthy to loose. Now this word of salvation is being brought to them, children of Abraham and God-fearers (Gentile proselytes). Jesus was crucified by the rulers at Jerusalem and Pontius Pilate, but God raised him from the dead. His postresurrection appearances were witnessed by many. Paul and Barnabas are declaring to the people the glad tidings (good news, gospel) of how God has fulfilled his promise according to Ps. 2:7. "Thou art my son; this day have I begotten thee," and again, Ps. 16:10, "Thou shalt not suffer thy holy one to see corruption (bodily decay)." David saw corruption but not Jesus through whom is the forgiveness of sins available. All who believe are justified; whereas one cannot be justified only through the Mosaic law. Listeners should beware of disbelief, for as said in Hab. 1:5, despisers will wonder and perish even though a man brings them word of the work of God in their day.(Acts 13:13-42) Many of those present become followers, and Paul and Barnabas minister to them further. Some of the Gentiles request to hear them on the next Sabbath. On that day a great crowd is present, but there are also detractors who accuse the evangelists of blasphemy. Paul tells the opposition that the word was brought to them first, but since they judge themselves unworthy of eternal life, now the evangelists are going to the Gentiles. He quotes Isa. 49:6; "I have set you to be a light of the Gentiles, that you should be for salvation unto the ends of the earth." Many disciples result from Paul's preaching, receiving the word with joy, being filled with the Holy Spirit.(Acts 13:43-52)

Miracles in Lystra. But opposition grows in Antioch of Pisidia, and the evangelists are forced to leave, traveling southeast to Iconium, Lystra, and Derbe. Troublemakers follow and create confusion, but the evangelists are able to bring their message to enough people to form several Christian congregations. While in Lystra, Paul encounters a man who has not been able to walk since birth. Seeing that he is a man of faith, Paul says in a loud voice, "Stand upright on your feet." The man leaps up and walks. People native to the area (Lycaonians) are elated and believe Paul to be Mercury and Barnabas, Jupiter. A local priest of Jupiter brings garlands of flowers and oxen to sacrifice to Paul and Barnabas as gods. But they excitedly tell the people that they are merely human like themselves; that they should turn from paganism to the one true God who made heaven and earth and everything good. The opposition who have followed the evangelists from Antioch of Pisidia arouse the crowd, and they stone Paul. Presuming him to be dead, they drag him out of the city. As Paul's new disciples stand near him, he revives and returns to the city. The next day it's on to Derbe where he and Barnabas teach many. Then they return to Antioch of Pisidia by way of Lystra and Iconium encouraging the new Christians to hold fast and enter into the kingdom of God. They help the congregations choose elders and commend them to the Lord. On their way back to the coast, they preach throughout the area. They sail from Attalia near Perga and return to Antioch in Syria. They report the results of their mission and how God has opened the door of faith to the Gentiles.(Acts 13:50 - 14:28)

The Mosaic Law Question. Sometime after the return of Paul and Barnabas, certain Christians from Jerusalem arrive in Antioch and begin teaching that unless Christian men are circumcised they cannot be saved. Paul and Barnabas strongly disagree with them, and the contention reaches the point where they decide that the only way to settle the question is to take it to the apostles. In Jerusalem the matter is submitted to a meeting of the apostles and elders presided over by James, Jesus' half-brother. After both sides have presented their arguments, Peter addresses the group. He reminds those present how God had directed him to give the word of the gospel to the Gentiles; that there is no difference between people, for God purifies their hearts by faith. It does not behoove them to put a burden upon Gentile Christians which neither they themselves, nor their fathers, were able to bear. It is through the grace of the Lord Jesus Christ that they all will be saved. After hearing again from Paul and Barnabas, James makes a recommendation. He suggests that they remember what Simeon (familiar form of Simon, Peter's Hebrew given name) has said. It agrees with what God has said through the prophet Amos, that God would return and rebuild the tabernacle of David so that all, including all Gentiles, might seek after the Lord.(Amos 9:11, 12)   In James' judgment the thing to do is to write a letter to the Gentile-Christian congregations with a few helpful suggestions. This is agreed to by the apostles, the elders, and the entire congregation. In order to help Barnabas and Paul attest to the authenticity of the letter, Judas Barsabas and Silas are to accompany them back to Antioch. This is the letter:

> The apostles and the elders and brethren to those in Antioch and Syria and Cilicia, Brethren from among the nations, Greeting:

Inasmuch as we have heard that certain from among us, having gone out, troubled you by words upsetting your souls, saying be circumcised to keep the law, to whom we gave no command, it seemed good to us, having come to one accord, to send chosen men to you with our beloved Barnabas and Paul, men who have given up their lives for the name of our Lord Jesus Christ. We have sent, therefore, Judas and Silas to tell you also by word the same things. For it seemed good to the Holy Spirit and to us to lay upon you no further burden than these necessary things: to abstain from things sacrificed to idols, and from blood, and from what is strangled, and from fornication, from which if you keep yourselves, you will do well.

Farewell.

[Jesus had spoken out against fornication. The suggestions regarding blood and things strangled were health measures, and the warning against things sacrificed to idols involved their witness, for many food items were dedicated to pagan gods by Gentile growers and merchants before being taken to market. See Rom. 14:1-4; 14-21.] The four men deliver the letter to the whole Christian group at Antioch, and they rejoice when the letter is read to them. Judas and Silas stay on with them for awhile preaching and teaching and confirming the word. Judas returns to Jerusalem, but Silas remains with Paul and Barnabas in Antioch.(Acts 15:1-35)

Paul's Second Missionary Journey. Paul reveals to Barnabas his desire to visit the brethren in the cities of their missionary journey. Barnabas wants to take John Mark along, but Paul feels that he should not go because he left them during the previous mission. Their disagreement is sharp, and as a result Barnabas returns to Cyprus with Mark. Paul chooses Silas for his second journey. Retracing the previous route through Syria and Cilicia, they help to strengthen the congregations. In Derbe they meet Timothy, a young man whose mother is a Jewish-Christian and his father a Greek. In order to avoid problems with the local Jewish people, Timothy is circumcised at Paul's suggestion. [Paul is willing to take a practical, nondoctrinal approach in a local situation (1 Cor. 9:20), while vehemently arguing against arbitrary and legalistic requirements as we saw above. He would not suggest such a thing for a Gentile-Christian, as we see in Gal. 2:3.] Paul, Silas, and Timothy return to the cities, strengthening the congregations previously established and helping to form new ones. They then move north in the districts of Phrygia, Galatia, and Mysia. They start to go farther east in Asia Minor, but the Holy Spirit directs them otherwise, and they move westward to

Troas. [They have gone through the north and central portion of what is now Turkey. Troas was a port city opposite northern Greece, not far from the site of ancient Troy.] In a vision a Macedonian man appears to Paul, saying, "Come over to Macedonia and help us." Paul is convinced that the Lord intends that they should go into Macedonia (a province in Greece) and preach the gospel.(Acts 15:36 - 16:10) [NOTE: "We" sections in 16:10-14; 20:5 - 21:18; and 27:1 - 28:16 indicate that Luke joined Paul during the second journey, was with him later during part of the third journey and when he went to Rome. See also 2 Tim. 4:11.]

Paul's Ministry in Greece. The evangelists travel along the coast of the Aegean Sea by boat to Greece. After landing at Neapolis, their first stop is Philippi, about 10 miles inland, an important city and Roman colony. Going to a riverside to pray on the Sabbath, they encounter Lydia, a merchant of purple (dye or cloth), and some other women. Lydia is a God-fearer and listens intently to Paul's teaching. She and her whole household are baptized, and the evangelists remain as her guests. One day as they go to prayer, a young woman follows after them crying out, "These men are the servants of the most high God who show us the way of salvation." She repeats this for several days. The unfortunate girl is possessed by an evil spirit of divination and is being exploited by her masters. Finally Paul turns, saying, "I command you in the name of Jesus Christ to come out of her." And the spirit departs. Incensed that their source of profit is gone, the men have Paul and Silas brought before the Roman magistrates on a charge of teaching customs which a Roman is forbidden to follow. The evangelists are beaten and thrown into prison with their feet bound in stocks.(Acts 16:11-24)

Philippian Jailer's Conversion. At midnight while Paul and Silas are praying and singing praises to God, an earthquake shakes the prison, the doors fly open, and the prisoners are loosed from their bonds. The jailer awakens, takes in the scene, and is ready to kill himself, supposing that the prisoners have fled. Paul calls out to him not to harm himself, because they are all there. The jailer in a state of shock beseeches Paul to tell him how to be saved. He is told, "Believe on the Lord Jesus Christ, and you will be saved, you and your household." After further teaching, the jailer and all in his house are baptized. He washes the wounds suffered by Paul and Silas and gives them something to eat. The next day the magistrates send word that they are to be released, but Paul will have none of that, saying that they are Romans and have been beaten without due process. The magistrates, now fearful because they are Romans, come and bring them out of prison requesting that they leave the area. Paul and Silas say their farewells to Lydia and the other Christians at Philippi and move south to Thessalonica.(Acts 16:25 - 17:1)

Thessalonians and Bereans. In Thessalonica and nearby Berea, Paul, Silas, and Timothy have a great deal of success, making converts of both men and women. The Bereans are particularly receptive, searching the scriptures daily to verify what the evangelists are saying. However, there is opposition also, so much so that the brethren send Paul to Athens while Silas and Timothy remain in Berea for a time, joining Paul later.(Acts 17:1-15)

In Athens. While waiting for his companions, Paul preaches in the synagogues and marketplaces of Athens. Athenians and others who visit Athens are interested in philosophy and are always ready to talk about or to hear the newest ideas. Some followers of the philosophies of Epicureus and the Stoics, thinking Paul to be a mere chatterer, take him to the Areopagus on Mars Hill (a place of discussion in the city) to speak of his strange doctrine. Paul begins his Mars Hill sermon by referring to something familiar to his listeners. He has seen that they are religious and has noticed that they have an altar in the city with the inscription, "TO THE UNKNOWN GOD." Paul is there to tell them all about the God whom they have been worshiping in ignorance. The God who made heaven and earth does not live in a temple made with hands. Nor does he want worship in the form of things made with hands, for since he made everything, he is not in need of things. He has created all beings, and humanity is all of one blood, God having provided appointed times and limits of habitation. Those who seek God are assured that he is not far away, for we live, move, and have our being in him, as many Greek poets have said. Since we are God's offspring, we should not think of him in terms of any image made by any human art or device. It is time to stop overlooking ignorance about God; it is time for everyone to repent. For God has set a day in which he is about to judge the world in righteousness, by a man whom he has proved by raising him from the dead. When the Athenians hear of the resurrection of the dead, some mock Paul; some want to hear more; and some are convinced and become believers, including two people of note, namely, Dionysius and a woman named Damaris.(Acts 17:16-34)

Paul in Corinth. Paul's next stop is Corinth, a few miles south of Athens, where Silas and Timothy rejoin him. In Corinth Paul's teaching convinces many Jewish and Greek people to become Christians. But there are also detractors who oppose him. He stops preaching in the synagogue, telling them that he now goes to the Gentiles. Crispus, the head of the synagogue, becomes a believer, and they continue in the house of Justus, another convert whose residence is near the synagogue. In a vision the Lord assures Paul that there are many God-fearing people in Corinth, and he will be able to minister there unharmed. The opposition makes an unsuccessful try at getting the Roman consul, Gallio, to judge Paul, but since no Roman law is involved, the matter is thrown out of court. For the next one and a half years Paul remains at Corinth spreading the word. When Paul finally departs, he is accompanied by Priscilla and Aquila, a Roman-Jewish couple he met when he first came to Corinth. They are in Corinth because of the persecution of the Jewish people in Rome by the emperor, Claudius. Priscilla and Aquila are tentmakers, as is Paul, and after their conversion to Christianity, Paul lives and works with them. Their destination now is Ephesus, a city in Asia Minor located a few miles inland from the Aegean coast. Leaving them there, Paul returns to Antioch via Caesarea and Jerusalem.(Acts 18:1-22)

Paul's Third Missionary Journey. Paul begins his third missionary journey by going from Antioch to the Christian groups in Galatia and Phrygia. Meanwhile in Ephesus, Priscilla and Aquila become acquainted with Apollos, a Jewish man from Alexandria, Egypt, who is very eloquent in preaching about Christ. However, they discover that he knows only the type of baptism practiced by John the Baptist. They are able to advance his Christian education, and he moves on to Corinth being highly recommended to the believers there by the Ephesian congregation.(Acts 18:23-28)

Paul in Ephesus. On arriving in Ephesus, Paul meets 12 men who are believers but know only the baptism of John. When Paul asks if they have received the Holy Spirit, they say that they never heard of it. Paul explains. They accept, Paul lays hands on them, and they receive the Holy Spirit and begin speaking in tongues and prophesying. Paul continues to teach in the synagogue for about three months, then moves to the school of one Tyrannus. There he holds forth for about two years. As a result of his teaching, all in Asia Minor hear the word of the Lord Jesus Christ, both the Jewish and Gentile people. He is able also to perform many special miracles and healings. Then one day some traveling exorcists come to Ephesus. They try to cast a demon out of a man by saying, "We adjure you by Jesus whom Paul preaches." But the evil spirit within the man says, "Jesus I know, and Paul I know, but who are you?" Suddenly the man attacks the exorcists, and they flee, naked and wounded. On hearing this, a great fear comes upon the people, and the name of Jesus is magnified. Numbers of people confess and become believers. Many who have practiced curious magical arts bring their books on magic and burn them publicly. And the word of God continues to spread powerfully.(Acts 19:1-20)

The Silversmith Controversy. Paul now feels the spirit motivating him to return to Greece, then on to Jerusalem, and he also feels compelled to go to Rome. First he sends Timothy and Erastus to Greece. But another crisis arises in Ephesus. A silversmith named Demetrius, who is one of many making money selling silver shrines of the pagan goddess Diana, calls a meeting of the craftsmen. [The Greek goddess Artemis, called Diana by the Romans, had been especially revered in Ephesus for centuries. Ephesus was a large cosmopolitan city in Paul's day, as excavations have revealed.] Demetrius tells his fellow craftsmen that Paul's preaching that there are no gods made with hands is hurting business. Their revered goddess is being put into disrepute. They then foment an angry crowd of people who rush to the city's amphitheater, seizing two of Paul's companions in travel. Paul wants to enter, but disciples hold him back. Alexander, a Jewish leader, is dragged into the crowd, and when the word of his presence gets around, the crowd raises a din, praising Diana for two hours. The city clerk finally takes charge, and when the crowd quiets down, he tells those present that there is no need for such a demonstration. Diana's place is so well established, no one is able to detract from her greatness. They have seized men who have done no harm. If Demetrius has a case, he should resort to the proper officials or at a proper assembly. If they do not disperse, they are in danger of being called into question (by Roman rulers). With this he dismisses the assembly.(Acts 19:24-41)

A Rescue from Death. When this uproar ends, Paul leaves for Greece where he stays for three months. When he is ready to leave for Syria, he learns that people are laying in wait for him; so he changes plans, returning to Troas via Macedonia. Among those with him are Timothy, Tychicus, and Trophimus. In Troas, as Paul is teaching a group in a third-story room, a young man named Eutychus, who has fallen asleep because of the late hour and the long session, falls from the window in which he is sitting and is found dead. Paul rushes down and embraces him, saying, "Trouble not yourselves, for his life is in him." Eutychus, revived, returns, and they break bread, continuing their discussion until morning.(Acts 20:1-12)

Paul's Farewell to the Ephesians. Going down the coast from Troas by boat, Paul stops off at Miletus, a port city near Ephesus. Paul sends a request for the elders of the Ephesian congregation to meet him there, for he wishes to be in Jerusalem for Pentecost. Paul tells them that he does not know what will befall him in the future, but the Holy Spirit has told him that he will suffer affliction as his ministry continues. He says, "None of these things move me; neither do I count my life dear to myself so that I might finish with joy my course and ministry which I have received from the Lord to testify of the gospel of the grace of God." They will see him no more. They should take heed to minister to their flock, for merciless people may try to persuade them of other doctrines and draw people away. He reminds them also to support those who are ministering to the people and also to support the weak, remembering the words of Christ, "It is more blessed to give than to receive." They say their farewells tearfully embracing Paul and kissing him, sorrowing because they will see him no more.(Acts 20:13-38)

Return to Jerusalem. Paul and his companions then sail to Caesarea with stopovers and meetings with believers at Tyre and Ptolemais. In Caesarea they are guests of Philip the evangelist. (Philip has four daughters who prophesy.) One day a prophet named Agabus arrives. Taking Paul's belt he puts it around his own hands and feet and tells Paul that whoever owns that belt will be bound and delivered to the Gentiles. Paul's friends try to persuade Paul not to go to Jerusalem, but he is determined. They go on to Jerusalem where they stay in the home of Mnason of Cyprus, one of the early disciples.(Acts 21:1-16)

Paul's Arrest. The next day Paul reports to James and the elders. They praise the Lord on hearing of his work among the Gentiles. However, they see a problem, for many of the Jewish-Christians still follow the practices of the Mosaic law and Jewish customs. This group believes that Paul's teaching that Gentile-Christians need not be circumcised amounts to a forsaking of Moses. James and the elders ask Paul to make an appearance at the temple as sponsor of four men who have taken a vow and are ready for their haircuts and purification at the temple. [NOTE: This is the Nazarite vow, a voluntary setting of oneself apart to worship God. It involves abstinence from wine and strong drink and letting the hair grow until whatever period of worship the Nazarite has set is over. The head is then shaved, and the Nazarite goes through a purification ceremony signifying the vow's completion. Paul had previously taken such a vow, getting his hair cut in Cenchrea, Greece.(Acts 18:18) This vow is described in the Old Testament, and the word "Nazarite" is not connected with or used in reference to "Nazareth" or "Nazarene."(See Nu. 6:1-21; Judges 13:5; 1 Sam. 1:11; Lk. 1:15.)] Paul agrees and enters the temple with the men. There are in the temple at the time some Jewish men from Asia who had seen Paul in town with Trophimus, an Ephesian. When they now see Paul in the temple with the Nazarites, they jump to the conclusion that he has brought Gentiles into the temple in violation of Jewish law. They set up a cry that Paul has polluted the temple. Paul is seized, but the commander of the Roman garrison near the temple comes with soldiers and rescues Paul from the beating he is getting. The commander cannot tell what is going on, and to quiet the mob he has Paul taken to the Roman barracks. Paul explains that he is a Jew from Tarsus which is not an insignificant city, and he wishes to speak to the people. The commander is relieved somewhat, because he thought Paul might be a certain Egyptian insurgent. Paul is allowed to speak, and standing on the steps he addresses the crowd in Hebrew. He identifies himself and tells them the details of his conversion experience on the road to Damascus and how the Lord spoke to him, commissioning him to be an evangelist to the Gentiles for "the just one." At this point the crowd begins to shout that Paul deserves to be killed. They cast off clothing and throw dust into the air. The Roman commander quickly takes Paul inside giving instructions that he is to be scourged and questioned. As he is about to be beaten, Paul lets it be known that this is no way to treat a Roman citizen who has had no trial. The commander is impressed that Paul is a free-born citizen, for the commander paid a large amount of money for his own citizenship.(Acts 21:17 - 22:29)

Before the Council. The next day the commander brings in the Jewish council to find out what the grievance is against Paul. Paul speaks to the group saying that he has lived in all good conscience. The high priest, Ananias, orders Paul to be struck on the mouth. Paul responds, "God shall smite you, whited wall. Do you judge me after the law and command me to be struck contrary to the law?" Those near him say, "Do you revile God's high priest?" Paul answers, "I did not know that he was the high priest; for it is written, 'You shall not speak evil of the ruler of your people.' "[Paul's statements might be taken as a reference to the manner in which high priests were being selected in those days.] Paul, knowing that some on the council are Sadducees who do not believe in resurrection and that some are Pharisees who do, says, "Men and brethren, I am a Pharisee, the son of a Pharisee. I am being called into question because of the hope and the resurrection of the dead." This touches off a dispute between the two groups. Finally the Pharisees say that they see no evil in Paul, and if a spirit or angel has spoken to him, they should not fight against God. This ends the confrontation, and the commander has Paul taken away for his safety. That night the Lord stands by Paul saying, "Be of good cheer, Paul, for you have testified of me in Jerusalem; so must you bear witness also at Rome."(Acts 22:29 - 23:11)

The Ambush Conspiracy. Paul has a nephew, his sister's son, living in Jerusalem. The nephew comes to see him and reveals what he has heard of a plot to kill him. Forty men have vowed to ambush him and have convinced some of the council to be parties to the conspiracy. They are to ask that Paul be brought to the council chamber, and on the way Paul will be attacked and slain. This information is given to the Roman commander. That evening about 9 p.m. the commander sends Paul, guarded by 470 soldiers, to Caesarea, to Felix, the Roman governor of Judea. The commander also dispatches this letter:

Claudius Lysias, to the most excellent governor, Felix, greeting.

This man was taken from the Jews and would have been killed by them. Then I came with an army and rescued him, having understood that he is a Roman. And when I endeavored to discover the reason for their accusations, I brought him forth to their council. I saw that they accused him under their law but of nothing worthy of death or imprisonment. When I learned that the Jews laid wait for the man, I sent him straightway to you and directed his accusers to tell you what they have against him.

Farewell.

When Paul and the letter are delivered to Felix, he questions Paul about where he is from, then orders him kept in the judgment hall built by Herod.(Acts 23:12-35)

Paul's Imprisonment in Caesarea. Five days later the high priest and council arrive. Paul is brought before them, and the council, speaking through their lawyer, one Tertullus, charges Paul with inciting sedition as a ringleader of a sect called the Nazarenes and with profaning the temple. He also complains about the action of Claudius Lysias in taking Paul from them. Felix then lets Paul speak. Paul says that they cannot prove a thing against him. He has only been in Jerusalem for 12 days. He hasn't argued with anyone. He only came to Jerusalem to bring alms and offerings to his people and was in the temple only to accomplish purification ceremonies. He admits that he confesses "the way" (Christianity), believing all things written in the law and the prophets. He believes in the resurrection of the dead, both of the just and the unjust which many of them also believe. Felix, knowing something about "the way," tells the group that he will decide the matter when Claudius Lysias arrives. However, he never decides the matter and keeps Paul there for the last two years of his tenure as governor. He allows Paul to have a great deal of liberty and permits him to have friends in at will. Paul explains the gospel to Felix and his wife, Drusilla, who is a Jewess. [Drusilla's great-grandmother, one of the wives of Herod I, was Jewish, a Hasmonean.] Felix hopes to get a bribe to release Paul, but not getting one, he keeps him prisoner. Felix finds occasion to converse with him frequently.(Acts 24:1-27)

Paul's Appeal to Caesar. Festus takes over the governorship of Judea and after three days travels from Caesarea to Jerusalem to confer with the high priest and council. They renew their contentions about Paul, hoping to get Festus to bring Paul to Jerusalem so that he can be ambushed along the way. But Festus invites them to come to his headquarters in Caesarea. Paul again is brought before them to answer their charges, and again Paul declares his innocence of any wrongdoing. Festus, wanting to grant a favor to the high priest and council, proposes that Paul agree to a hearing in Jerusalem presided over by the governor. Paul responds that he is now in the right place for any judgment to be issued from Caesar's judgment seat. If he is innocent of their charges, he should not be turned over to them. Then, exercising his right as a Roman citizen, he says, "I appeal to Caesar." Festus confers with his own council, then declares, "To Caesar you have appealed; to Caesar you will go."(Acts 24:27 - 25:12)

Hearing before Agrippa and Bernice. A few days later Agrippa the king and Bernice arrive to pay their respects to the governor. [Agrippa here is Herod Agrippa II, son of Herod Agrippa I whose sudden death is described in Acts 12. Agrippa II and Bernice are brother and sister.] Festus describes the previous events regarding Paul and explains that under Roman law an accused must be given the right to present a defense. For that reason he refuses to turn Paul over to the Jewish council. Since Paul has appealed to Rome, Festus has detained him in order to send him to Rome for a hearing before the emperor. Agrippa says that he also would like to hear what Paul has to say. Festus replies that he shall hear him the next day. At the appointed time the hearing is held in a large hall attended by a great deal of pomp and ceremony. There are military commanders present and also prominent citizens of Caesarea. Festus opens the proceedings by reviewing the situation up to this point. He says that he has found nothing Paul has done to be deserving of death, but since Paul has appealed to Rome, he will be sent there. However, the governor must send a statement of the charges against Paul to the emperor. Hopefully, this examination will provide something for him to write. At this point Agrippa informs Paul that he may speak.(Acts 25:13 - 26:1)

Paul Recounts His Conversion. Paul takes this opportunity to expound the gospel and particularly to use the knowledge which these members of the Herod family have about Judaism as a base for some of his points. Paul says that his manner of living from his youth and his prior status as a Pharisee are well known. But he is now on trial for the hope which God has conveyed through their forefathers, the hope of the Messiah and the resurrection. Why should it be thought incredible that God raises the dead? Paul himself once defied the name of Jesus of Nazareth. Exercizing authority granted by the chief priests, he persecuted and jailed many Christians. But he voted against condemning them to death. While on his way to Damascus to ferret out more Christians, he saw a light from heaven which shined about him, brighter than the sun. Paul says, "I heard a voice speaking to me in the Hebrew tongue, 'Saul, Saul, why are you persecuting me? It is hard for you to kick against the pricks.' And I said, 'Who are you, Lord?' And he said, 'I am Jesus whom you are persecuting, But rise and stand on your feet, for I have appeared to you for this purpose: to make you a minister and a witness both of these things which you have seen and of those things in which I will appear to you, delivering you from the people and from the Gentiles to whom I am now sending you — to open their eyes, to turn them from darkness to light, from the power of satan to God, that they may receive forgiveness of sins and inheritance among them who are sanctified by faith that is in me.' "(Acts 26:1-18)

Paul Explains His Ministry. Paul tells Agrippa that he was not disobedient to the heavenly vision. He has gone throughout many lands in Judea and to Gentiles giving them the message of repentance and of living good lives demonstrating their repentance. But even though Paul has been in danger of death, he continues to witness to all, both great and small, saying only what the prophets and Moses said would come: that Christ would suffer and would be the first to rise from the dead and show light to the world. Suddenly Festus exclaims that Paul's great learning has made him mad. Paul replies that he is not mad but is seriously speaking truth. Agrippa must know this, for these things have not taken place in secret. Does the king not believe in the prophets? Paul is sure that he does. To this Agrippa says, "You have almost persuaded me to become a Christian." Paul says, "I wish to God both almost and all the way, and that you and all those hearing me today will become as I am except for my imprisonment." Then Agrippa, Festus, Bernice, and others seated with them leave the hall saying to one another that Paul is not deserving of imprisonment let alone death. Agrippa remarks to Festus that Paul could be freed if he had not appealed to Caesar.(Acts 26:19-32)

Paul Sent to Rome. On the day set for Paul's departure to Italy, Paul and other prisoners are turned over to a centurion named Julius, of the imperial contingent. On board ship Paul is given liberty to commune with friends and refresh himself. They sail north to Sidon, then past Cyprus northwest to Myra, a port city on the Asia Minor coast. There they change to a grain ship bound for Italy. There are now 276 passengers on board.(Acts 27:37)   Encountering heavy winds, they barely make it to Fair Havens, a bay near Lasea on the south coast of the island of Crete. Being the fall season, the winds in this region make sailing dangerous. After they have languished in the bay area for a long time, Paul advises the centurion against continuing the voyage. But Julius believes the captain who says that they can at least make it to Phoenix, another and safer area on the Cretan coast. When it is deemed safe to leave, they head out. But suddenly they find themselves caught in a violent wind prevalent in those waters at this time of the year and named Euroclydon (or Euraquilo, northeastern). They run with the wind for awhile but finally have to strike the sails and jettison cargo to stay afloat. Everyone fasts to save what little food is left. On the third day of the storm Paul encourages them, revealing that the Lord has spoken to him through an angel, telling him that Paul must be brought to Rome; that all lives will be saved; but they will be cast onto a certain island.(Acts 27:1-26)

Shipwreck on the Island of Malta. On the fourteenth night out, after having been driven into and out of the Adriatic Sea, the sailors believe that they must be near land. They take a depth measurement and find it to be 20 fathoms, then 15 fathoms. They drop four anchors, fearing being cast onto rocks, and some try to lower a lifeboat. Paul informs the centurion that unless they stay on the ship they will be lost. The soldiers then cut the ropes, and the lifeboat falls into the sea. Paul recommends eating something for strength and health, for no harm is to befall them. So saying, he takes some bread, gives thanks, and begins eating. This cheers the other passengers, and they all take nourishment. They then cast out the remaining cargo. Visible ahead is the shoreline of a place unknown to them. A likely spot for landing appears to be near the mouth of a river, and they lift the anchors, hoist the mainsail, and make for shore. But the ship runs aground where two currents meet, the back part of the ship being broken off by violent waves. The soldiers prepare to kill the prisoners lest they escape. The centurion, desiring to save Paul, orders them to let the prisoners swim to shore if they can. All eventually end up in the water on boards or pieces of the ship, and all come safely to land. Later they discover that they are on the island of Malta. The people living there are very friendly and welcome them.(Acts 27:27 - 28:2)

The Road to Rome. A fire is made for them because of the rain and cold, and when Paul lays a bundle of kindling on the fire, a viper snake suddenly emerges from the pile and fastens its teeth into his hand. The island people seeing the snake hanging on his hand believe that Paul must be a murderer and that although he has escaped the sea, justice is requiring his life. But Paul merely shakes the snake off into the fire. When they see that he is not swollen or dead, they believe that he is a god. The chief citizen of the island, one Publius, extends them hospitality. The survivors remain on Malta for three months. During that time Paul heals Publius' father of a physical ailment and also many others who come for healing. Finally they are able to get passage on an Alexandrian ship bound for Italy. Their trip takes them to Syracuse, Sicily, then to Rhegium on the toe of Italy, and finally to Puteoli near Naples. There they find brethren with whom they stay for seven days. As they travel the road to Rome, the brethren hear of them, and as far as Appi Forum (40 miles south of Rome) and Three Taverns (or Three Shops; 33 miles from Rome) they come out to meet Paul and the others. Their greetings give Paul a great deal of encouragement, and he gives thanks to God.(Acts 28:2-15)

Paul in Rome. On their arrival in Rome, the centurion turns Paul over to the captain of the guard. Paul is permitted to live by himself with a soldier guarding him. After three days, leading Jews come to see Paul at his request. He explains how he happens to be a prisoner in Rome; that he wants to speak to them because for the hope of Israel he is now imprisoned. They answer that they have received no letters from Judea concerning Paul, and no one they know has spoken against him; that they do wish to hear about "the sect" because there is so much talk against it. A day is set for their return, and on that day many come to hear him. Paul explains to them the kingdom of God, giving persuasive arguments about Jesus from the law and the prophets of the Old Testament. The session lasts from morning until evening. Some believe what Paul has said, and some do not. There is no agreement among the group, and after Paul quotes to them the words of Isa. 6:9-10, they begin to leave. What Paul has said to them is this:

> Go to this people and say, "Hearing, you shall hear and in no way understand, and seeing, you will see and in no way perceive. For the heart of the people has grown fat; and their ears are dull of hearing, and their eyes they have closed lest they should see with their eyes and hear with their ears, and with their hearts they should understand and should be converted, and I should heal them."

Paul tells them that the salvation of God is being sent to the Gentiles, and that they will hear it. As the listeners depart, they continue to debate among themselves. Thereafter, Paul dwells in his own rented quarters, under guard, for two years, receiving all who come to him, preaching the kingdom of God, and teaching those things which concern the Lord Jesus Christ, with all confidence, no one forbidding him.(Acts 28:16-31)

CHAPTER TEN

THE EPISTLES AND REVELATION

In this chapter we set forth in digest form a review of the Epistles and the book of Revelation. "Epistle" is another word for "letter." The Epistles were written by Paul, Peter, John, James, and Jude to the first-century Christians to explain and interpret the gospel of Jesus; to warn against backsliding and the false doctrines of deceivers; and to encourage believers under persecution. In the Epistles we also find answers to specific questions or problems which arose in the congregations. Thus we see early application of Christian principles to various types of situations.

History tells us that the Christians were persecuted during the reigns of many Roman emperors — Caligula (A.D. 37-41); Claudius (A.D. 41-54); Nero (A.D. 54-68); Vespasian (A.D. 69-79); Titus (A.D. 79-81); and Domitian (A.D. 81-96). The Jews were also persecuted, and for a time, Christians were considered as a sect of Judaism. Vespasian and Titus were responsible for destroying the temple in Jerusalem in A.D. 70. In A.D. 135 the Roman emperor Hadrian put down a Jewish revolt and forbade Jews from living in Jerusalem after the city was rebuilt. Gradually the enforcement of this edict was relaxed. Christians continued under varying degrees of persecution until A.D. 312 when the emperor Constantine declared the entire Roman empire to be Christian.

As we noted in the book of Acts, Paul started Christian congregations in Asia Minor and in Greece. The church at Rome was apparently begun by others. Some scholars speculate the possibility that some of those present in Jerusalem at Pentecost (Acts 2) returned to Rome to form groups such as those mentioned in Rom. 16.(See also Acts 28:14-15.) Paul maintained his contact with these congregations through visits and through his letters. Some letters were written in Paul's own handwriting (Gal. 6:11; 2 Thess. 3:17); sometimes he was assisted by others who performed secretarial services.(Rom. 16:22; 1 Cor. 1:1; 2 Cor. 1:1) The epistles of James, Peter, John, and Jude were referred to as "General Epistles" by the early church, possibly to differentiate them from those of Paul. This designation does not appear in most modern versions. According to early church tradition, James and Jude were half-brothers of Jesus, and Peter and John were two of the original apostles.

THE LETTERS OF PAUL

LETTER TO THE ROMANS

Greetings to the Roman Christians. Paul, as an apostle appointed by Jesus, greets the Roman Christians saying, "First, I thank my God through Jesus Christ for you all, that your faith is spoken of throughout the whole world." He desires to see them and is ready to preach the gospel to them in Rome. He is not ashamed of the gospel of Christ, because it is the power of salvation to everyone who believes, "to the Jew first and also to the Greek (Gentiles)."(Rom. 1:1-16)

All Know God. In the gospel the righteousness of God is revealed "from faith to faith." The just shall live by faith.(Hab. 2:4) God is known by all, for he has manifested himself to them. "For the invisible things of him from the creation of the world are clearly seen, being understood by the things that are made, his eternal power and Godhead; so that they are without excuse; for when they knew God they did not praise him as God, nor were they thankful, but became conceited in their imaginations, and their foolish heart was darkened. Professing themselves to be wise, they became fools." Mankind has been guilty of every conceivable kind of evil including idolatry, perversion, homosexuality, murder, slander, gossip, and hardness of heart, taking pleasure in committing such acts.(Rom. 1:17-32)

Salvation by Faith through Grace. The Jew has the advantage of the Mosaic law and God's revelations in scripture. Both Jew and Gentile know right from wrong through what is written on their hearts — their consciences. It is not enough to hear divine principles; only those who follow divine principles in their actions are justified before God. Not everyone who calls himself a Jew is a Jew. A man may call himself a Jew because he is circumcised. But if he knowing the law does not live according to the law, his circumcision counts for nothing. A Jew is a person who is one inwardly, in his heart, praising God rather than men. Jews can be proud that to them were entrusted the words of God, but the word is of little effect if not acted upon in belief. By the same token, man is not justified (made right with God) by following law without faith in God. The law came only to show what sin is. Since all have sinned by virtue of a fleshly nature, all, whether Jew or Gentile, may be justified freely by God's grace through the redemption afforded by Jesus Christ. Faith in God through Christ results in the remission of sin. Following the Mosaic law is not necessary for faith, but faith establishes the law. Abraham provides a good example for this point, for before the law was given to Moses, Abraham's faith was counted to him for righteousness. This occurred before God made circumcision the sign of the Abrahamic and Mosaic covenants. Faith is the confidence and trust that God is able to do and will do what he promises to do. Our faith is imputed to us for righteousness through belief in the gospel of Jesus who was delivered for our offenses and raised again for our justification.(Rom. 2 - 4)

Reconciliation with God. God has shown his love for us by sending Jesus at the right time, for Christ died for the ungodly. Jesus provides the means whereby those in enmity with God can be reconciled to him. Having faith through Christ makes it possible to endure anything, for perseverance results in strong character and hope which does not disappoint, because the love of God is poured out into our hearts by the Holy Spirit. Just as sin came into the world through one man (Adam), through the obedience of one (Christ) many will be made righteous.(Rom. 5)

Baptism into Christ. Those baptized into Christ in effect died with him on the cross. Like him, they are raised spiritually from the dead and are spiritually united with him. The believer's old self has been crucified, and he or she now walks in the newness of life. Rather than being slaves to sin as before, believers are slaves to God and righteousness. The wages of sin is spiritual death, but the free gift of God is eternal life in Christ. Just as a widow may validly remarry, believers have been freed from the Mosaic law and have become married to Jesus who is raised from the dead that we might bring forth fruit unto God. The Mosaic law taught what sin is in a very precise way. The law is spiritual, but we, being of the flesh (i.e., prone to follow sinful passion), have a kind of law in our members compelling us to do evil even though we wish to do good. While we delight in the law of God in the inner self, we experience a battle within ourselves between good and evil. How are we to be set free from this feeling of wretchedness and struggle? On the one hand, we serve the law of God, but on the other with our flesh, the law of sin.(Rom. 6 - 7)

Sons and Daughters of God. There is no condemnation for those in Christ Jesus, for the law of the spirit of life in him has set believers free from the law of sin and death. Christ is in the believer, and the Holy Spirit helps him or her to control the flesh and walk in fellowship with God. In fact, believers become adopted sons and daughters of God so that they can call to him as "Abba, Father" (Daddy or Papa), bearing that close relationship as heirs with Jesus. Also, the Holy Spirit helps us in prayer, and he intercedes for us with groanings too deep for words. God causes all things to work together for good to those who love God, who are called according to his purpose. According to God's foreknowledge, he has predestined that his adopted children be justified and glorified. "If God is for us, who can be against us? . . . [N]either death, nor life, nor angels, nor principalities, nor powers, nor things present, nor things to come, nor height, nor depth, nor any other creature shall be able to separate us from the love of God, which is in Christ Jesus our Lord."(Rom. 8)

To the Jew First. Paul expresses his concern for his Jewish brethren, for he is "an Israelite, of the seed of Abraham, the tribe of Benjamin." He reviews the Abrahamic covenant and the words of the prophets showing that Israel knew that God would take action to bring Gentiles within the fold. God said that he would lay a "stumbling stone" in Zion (the Messiah), and the Jews have stumbled over the stumbling stone. The Jews do have a zeal for God but have missed the significance of the coming of Christ. There is no real difference between Jews and Gentiles, for the same God is Lord of all. For whoever calls upon the name of the Lord shall be saved. Faith comes by hearing and heeding the word of God. God has not forgotten his covenant people, and even though Paul is an apostle to the Gentiles, Christians must realize that their salvation has come through Israel acting as God's instrument. Israelites, as natural branches of the olive tree, have cut themselves off through unbelief, and Christians, as new wild branches, have been grafted in among the natural branches. But the day will come when the natural branches will be grafted back into their own olive tree. Therefore, it should be that Christians show consideration for the Jewish people who will be reconciled when they heed Isaiah's words that "whoever believes on him (the Messiah) shall not be ashamed."(Rom. 9 - 11; Isa. 28:16)

Being a Living Sacrifice. Paul now turns his attention to Christian conduct. One should not be conformed to the ways of the world but be transformed by the renewing of the mind and demonstrate that which is according to God's perfect will. Paul exhorts believers to present themselves as "a living sacrifice, holy, acceptable to God," which is their "intelligent service." Within the flock there are people with a variety of talents and spiritual gifts, including service, teaching, exhortation, giving, leadership, showing mercy, prayer, hospitality in helping others, having compassion. These talents and gifts should be used for the benefit of all, including the less fortunate. And all things should be done diligently, cheerfully, and lovingly with a fervent spirit and without hypocrisy and personal pride. Evil cannot be overcome by evil but only by good.(Rom. 12)

Submission to Authorities Above. Everyone should submit to authorities above whom God has appointed, for all authority stems from God. No one suffers from doing good but from doing evil. Therefore, render to all their due whether it involves tribute, custom, fear, or honor. But in all things one should demonstrate love, for love fulfills the law. This is possible by putting on Jesus Christ, making no provision for the lusts of the flesh.(Rom. 13)

Helping Others. A Christian helps and edifies his weaker brother and his neighbor and does not sit in judgment upon him. Everyone must give account of himself or herself to God. One should not get critical over trivial things like food and drink or engage in doubtful disputations. The kingdom of God is not food and drink but is righteousness, peace, and joy in the Holy Spirit. Let all find unity with each other just as Christ has received each one to the glory of God.(Rom. 14 - 15:13)

A Personal Note. Paul is persuaded that the Roman Christians are full of goodness, filled with knowledge, and able to admonish one another. He has written boldly through the grace of God, for he (Paul) is a minister of Jesus Christ to the Gentiles. He plans to visit Rome and eventually travel to Spain, but first he must take a contribution from the Greek congregations to Jerusalem to aid the brethren there. He greets several of the Roman brethren and groups, especially Priscilla and Aquila who, he says, risked "their own necks" to save his life. In his concluding remarks Paul commends them to God through the grace of "our Lord Jesus Christ."(Rom. 15:14 - 16:27)

FIRST LETTER TO THE CORINTHIANS

Living the Spiritual Life; Eliminating Divisions. Paul greets the congregation at Corinth in Greece who are set apart in Christ Jesus and who constantly call upon his name. While Corinthian Christians are not lacking in any gift, there are certain problems which have come to Paul's attention, and he shares his thoughts with them. He wishes there to be no divisions among the brethren. Some of them are saying "I am of Paul"; or "I am of Apollos"; or "I am of Cephas (Peter)"; or "I of Christ." "Is Christ divided? Was Paul crucified for you? Or were you baptized in the name of Paul?" Paul is glad that he only baptized a few of them, lest anyone say he baptized in his own name; that he is called to preach, not to baptize. They need wisdom in this matter. It may be that unbelievers find the gospel to be foolishness, but God has chosen the foolish things, the weak things, to confound the wise or mighty things of the world. The Corinthian Christians are in Christ Jesus who is to them wisdom, righteousness, sanctification, and redemption. Paul did not come to them as great in speech or oratory. He spoke to them of the gospel only through the Holy Spirit who searches all things, the "deep things of God." And it is the Holy Spirit who teaches spiritual wisdom as contrasted to the wisdom of the natural man. A truly spiritual person has the mind of Christ and has good judgment in all things. But the Corinthians are still "babes in Christ" and require very specific instruction. Paul and Apollos have ministered to them as servants of God. Paul says, "I have planted; Apollos watered, but God gave the increase. So, then, neither is he who plants anything, neither he who waters; but God gives the increase." In this God's ministers are one with Christ. One may lay a foundation; another may build on it, but the only true foundation is Jesus Christ. And everyone's work built upon that foundation will be manifest as if tested by fire. It may be that people's work will be like gold, silver, precious stones or like wood, hay, or stubble. If one's work lasts, he or she will receive a reward. If it does not last, as burned in fire, he or she may suffer loss though personally saved. Corinthians should also know that each of them is a temple of God, and the temple is holy. Paul concludes this point by saying, "Therefore let no man glory in men, for all things are yours, whether Paul, or Apollos, or Cephas, or the world, or life, or death, or things present, or things to come; all are yours. And you are Christ's, and Christ is God's." Apostles and ministers may be branded as fools or a spectacle. They may be persecuted, reviled, and defamed, but God is their judge.(1 Cor. 1 - 4)

A Case of Immorality. Paul has heard that certain of the flock have been guilty of a high degree of immorality. The group should cleanse itself of such people. "A little leaven (yeast) leavens the whole lump (dough)." This leaven of impurity should be purged and new leaven of sincerity and truth brought in.(1 Cor. 5) [Paul means purging the brother or sister through loving instruction and forgiveness, per his later letter.(2 Cor. 2:6-11; see also Gal. 6:1-2)]

Going to Court. Paul has heard that some members of the Corinthian congregation have resorted to the civil courts to settle disputes with other members. In so doing, they are forcing their Christian brothers to be judged by unbelievers. Instead of relying on the civil law, they should submit their problems to others of the faith or simply suffer the loss. Do they not know that the saints will judge the world and the angels?(1 Cor. 6:1-8; compare Matt. 18:15-17)

Taking Care of One's Body. In the matter of things affecting their own bodies, the brethren should use great care, for the body of a believer is a temple of the Holy Spirit, bought for a price, a member of Jesus Christ. The body is for the Lord, and the Lord is for the body. Even in things lawful, as with food and drink, it is not always expedient, lest a person come under the power of it. Fornication is a sin against one's own body.(1 Cor. 6:9-20)

Husband and Wife. Regarding relationships between men and women, it is better that a man have his own wife and a woman her own husband so that there will be no fornication. A husband and wife should render to each other due benevolence, for they have the power over each other's bodies. One should not deny the other unless it is by agreement for a time. Paul believes that remaining unmarried to serve the Lord is the highest calling, but that is his personal opinion, not a commandment from God. If a single person, a widow, or a widower finds that passion could lead him or her to an affair, then marriage is certainly the appropriate relationship. Married persons are bound by their vows. And where a believer is married to an unbeliever, it is better to remain married so that the unbeliever can be brought within the faith and for the children's benefit. But if the unbeliever leaves, a brother or sister is not under bondage in such a case, for God has called us to peace.(1 Cor. 7; see also: 1 Pet. 3:1-7; Eph. 5:22-33)

Food and Drink, a Matter of Conscience. As to things offered to idols, the Christian has knowledge of the one true God but should be careful in his or her contacts with others not to act pridefully, for it is through love that another is helped and taught. Thus a Christian is not bound by arbitrary rules regarding food and drink, but his or her witness should involve being considerate of others, for a weaker brother might be misled. For example, one would not go to an idol's temple for dinner, and if a host has revealed that the food being served was sacrificed to idols, the Christian should not partake. It's a matter of understanding and conscience so that a weaker brother or sister will not be caused to stumble.(1 Cor. 8; 10:28)

Support of the Clergy. An apostle or minister called of God to preach the gospel has the duty to do so without expecting a special reward other than the joy and satisfaction from following this calling. But since they also have human needs, these needs should be met by the people whom they serve. A pastor of a flock should be able to gain support from the gospel which is preached without having to work at another job. In any event, one called by God to preach the gospel is obligated regardless of circumstances.

Paul is an apostle, but he has never asked anyone for a contribution for himself, lest he abuse his privilege.(1 Cor. 9:1-18)

Paul, All Things to All People. In his ministry he has made himself a servant of all. To the Jews, he became a Jew; to the Gentiles, a Gentile; to the weak, as weak; as all things to all people that he might by all means save some. In this he has kept his body under subjection, in training so to speak, that he might win the race of life. In the same way, Christians, being temperate in all things, run the race to receive a crown of victory which is incorruptible.(1 Cor. 9:19-27)

Protection from Temptation. Temptations confront the believer on every side. That which befell the children led by Moses was revealed for example and admonition. But God is faithful and will not allow a believer to be tempted beyond his or her ability to resist and will provide the means to escape temptation. Every action should be done to the glory of God that no one be offended, and thereby many may be saved, both Jew and Gentile.(1 Cor. 10)

Worship Services. When believers gather together in worship services, Paul would prefer the men to be bareheaded and the women's heads covered. But if anyone disagrees, it is merely a matter of custom. That which is important is that Paul has heard that there is dissension at their meetings and that they bring their meals to their services and do not properly partake of communion. The way to observe the Lord's Supper is in accordance with what Paul received from the Lord: that on the night when he was betrayed, he took bread and broke it saying, "Take, eat; this is my body which is broken for you. This do in remembrance of me." He also took the cup, saying, "This cup is the new covenant in my blood. This do, as often as you drink it, in remembrance of me." This commemorates the Lord's death until he comes. One who participates in an unworthy manner may find that he or she is forfeiting protection against sickness or even death.(1 Cor. 11)

Spiritual Gifts. A believer calls upon Jesus as Lord by virtue of the Holy Spirit. The Holy Spirit endows believers with certain spiritual gifts. These gifts may not be the same for everyone, but every believer receives a manifestation of the Holy Spirit for the benefit of all. These gifts include word of wisdom, word of knowledge, faith, healing, working of miracles, prophecy, discernment of spirits, varieties of tongues, and interpretation of tongues. While gifts may be diverse, it is the same God and the same Spirit.(1 Cor. 12:1-11)

The Gifts and the Body of Christ. Christians are baptized into one body — Christ. Just as the human body has many members with different functions, so also has the body of Christ. Every part of the human body is essential to the working of the body as a whole, and in the same way, every member of the body of Christ is important. If one suffers, all suffer. If one is honored, all rejoice. God has chosen some to be apostles, some prophets, some teachers, some with the gift of miracles, others with the gifts of healing, helps, government, or diversities of tongues. Everyone may not have all these gifts, but each one should seek the best gifts.(1 Cor. 12:12-31)

The Gift of Love. More important than all these gifts is the gift of love. A person may be able to prophesy, to know and understand all mysteries, to move mountains, may give to the poor, and offer his body as a sacrifice; it profits nothing without love. Love has patience, is kind, is not envious, is not vain or prideful, does not act improperly, is not greedy, is not easily provoked, does not consider evil, rejoices in truth rather than unrighteousness. Love covers all things, hopes all things, endures all things, and love never fails. Now we only have partial knowledge, like looking through a dark glass. But when the perfect comes, we will see clearly. There are now faith, hope, and love. The greatest of these is love.(1 Cor. 13)

On the Gift of Tongues. Paul urges that Christians desire spiritual gifts. As between the gift of prophecy and the gift of tongues, prophecy is better, because it involves speaking the word for the enlightenment of others. Speaking in tongues only edifies the speaker unless there is an interpretation for the benefit of others. Paul speaks in tongues more than any Corinthian, but in the congregation he would rather speak five words of under- standing to teach others than 10,000 words in an unknown tongue. God is not a God of disorder but of peace. Therefore, a worship service should be orderly. If there are some who have something to share, such as a psalm, a teaching, a tongue, a revelation, or interpretation, they should be permitted to express themselves, each in his or her turn. Talking during a service should be curtailed, and if a woman wants to ask her husband something, she should wait until they get home. Paul concludes this topic by saying, "Wherefore, brethren, covet to prophesy, and forbid not to speak with tongues. Let all things be done decently and in order."(1 Cor. 14)

The Gospel and Resurrection. Paul next reviews the gospel message. Christ died for our sins, was buried, and rose again on the third day. He was seen after his resurrection by Cephas

(Peter), the 12, by 500 others at the same time (most of whom were still alive when Paul wrote), then by James and the apostles and last of all by Paul (on the road to Damascus). Since Christ was resurrected, it is error to say that there is no resurrection. In Adam all have died (spiritually), but in Christ all shall be made alive. Christ puts all enemies under his feet, and the last enemy to be destroyed is death. When all things are subjected to him, then "shall the Son also himself be subject to him who put all things under him, that God may be all in all." Someone may ask, "How are the dead raised up? And with what body do they come?" Paul answers that it is known that seed is not planted without knowing what it will produce; that a seed dies that a new plant may grow. Each part of creation has its own body, its own form, whether it is human, animal, fish, or bird, whether celestial or terrestrial. And the glory of each is distinctive to it. So also is the resurrection of the dead. Each person has a natural body, but he or she is raised a spiritual being, with a spiritual body. "There is a natural body, and there is a spiritual body." The first man, Adam, was formed with a natural body first, but it was activated by the infusion of the spirit. The last Adam (Christ) became a life-giving spirit. Flesh and blood cannot inherit the kingdom of God, for something perishable cannot inherit that which is imperishable. Thus resurrection results in the person's spiritual body being raised in glory and power and bearing the image of the heavenly. Paul says, "Behold, I show you a mystery. We shall not all sleep, but we shall all be changed, in a moment, in the twinkling of an eye, at the last trumpet; for the trumpet shall sound, and the dead shall be raised imperishable. Death is swallowed up in victory and its sting eliminated." The sting of death is sin, but through Christ sin can be conquered. Steadfastness in the work of the Lord will assure that one's labor is not in vain in the Lord.(1 Cor. 15) [NOTE: In Rom. 6:3-11 Paul says that believers are baptized into Jesus' death and resurrection; that rendering the old self dead results in freedom from sin, a new life, and victory over death. CROSS-REFERENCES: In Matt. 22:30 Jesus says, "For in the resurrection they neither marry, nor are given in marriage, but are as the angels of God in heaven." (See also: 1 Thess. 4:13 -5:11; 2 Cor. 5:17)]

A Personal Note. Paul plans on visiting the Corinthians in the near future and asks that they take up a collection for the saints at Jerusalem on the first day of every week so that there will be no need for collections when he comes. They may select someone to carry the gift to Jerusalem. If Timothy comes to them in the meantime, they are to accept him, because he is doing the Lord's work. Apollos will be along later. Paul rejoices that the

Corinthians have sent three men to visit him. He concludes with his love and a closing greeting from himself and Priscilla and Aquila, saying "Maranatha" (Lord come!).(1 Cor. 16)

SECOND LETTER TO THE CORINTHIANS

Reconciliation in Christ. Paul writes again to the Corinthians, saying that he has encountered problems which have delayed his visit to them. He understands that his previous letter made them sorrowful, and that was not his intent. He wrote out of love to correct certain problems, not to lord it over them.(See also 2 Cor. 7.)   He is merely a fellow worker for their joy, for they are standing firm in their faith. If there are any who were disciplined by the majority, they should be brought within the fold by forgiveness. Whom they forgive, Paul forgives. Their triumph is in Christ, and God receives them as a sweet aroma. Does Paul need letters of commendation to or from Corinthian brethren? They actually are his letter written on his heart, a letter of Christ not written with ink or on stone tablets but on tablets of human hearts. The servants of God through Christ are servants of a new covenant of the spirit which gives life. Whereas Moses wore a veil because of the glory which shone on his face, believers through Christ behold with unveiled face the glory of the Lord as in a mirror, "being changed into the same image from glory to glory, as by the Spirit of the Lord."(2 Cor. 1 - 3)

Inner Strength. Christians may meet opposition on every side. The god of this world (satan) has blinded the minds of unbelievers, lest the light of the gospel should shine upon them. Believers may be troubled but are not distressed; perplexed but not in despair; persecuted but not forsaken; cast down but not destroyed, always having the Lord Jesus within themselves so that Jesus' life may be shown and seen through them. The outward body may perish, but the "inward" person is "renewed day by day." We look not at the things which are seen but at the things which are not seen, for "the things which are seen are temporal, but the things which are not seen are eternal."(2 Cor. 4)

All Things New. The spiritual self is temporarily housed in the body, and were it to be dissolved, a believer has a building of God not made with hands, eternal in the heavens. We can be "confident that while we are at home in the body, we are absent from the Lord (for we walk by faith, not by sight). We are . . . willing, rather, to be absent from the body and to be present with the Lord." There is a judgment with Christ as judge. And he died for all that they might know him spiritually. Anyone who is in Christ is a new creature. "Old things have passed away. Behold, all things are become new." Through Jesus Christ, God has "reconciled the world to himself, not imputing their trespasses to them" and has committed to his workers the word of reconciliation as ambassadors of Christ who, while he himself was sinless, was in effect made sin (on the cross) that all might be made the righteousness of God in him.(2 Cor. 5)

Remaining Steadfast. Paul beseeches the Corinthians to keep steadfast in the faith as not having received the grace of God in vain; to be patient ministers in truth and love through the Holy Spirit in spite of all adversity. They need to be very careful in their relationships with unbelievers so that they may cleanse themselves and work toward holiness in fear of God. Paul repeats his apology for the tone of his previous letter but does not retreat from the statement of principle which he set forth in it for their own good.(2 Cor. 6 - 7)

Helping the Less Fortunate. The churches of Macedonia have been very generous in their giving, even in times of poverty, for the benefit of others. Paul would that the Corinthians abound in this grace also; that they assist their less fortunate brethren in the faith, just as the other congregations would come to their aid in time of need. They should give from whatever they have but not feel an obligation to produce a donation if they are unable to do so. Since they have been blessed materially, Paul is confident that they will share from their bounty as a ministry to others. The idea is to equalize things among them so that if any suffers a loss or a need to be met, help will be available. And so shall the fund be administered.(See: Ex. 16:18)   They should give from the heart, not grudgingly or of necessity, for God loves a cheerful giver. He who sows sparingly will reap sparingly. He who sows bountifully will reap bountifully. Paul quotes from Ps. 112:9: "He has dispersed abroad; he has given to the poor; his righteousness remains forever." Such service to the needy is both a ministry and a means to thank God for his many blessings.(2 Cor. 8 - 9)

Paul's Endurance for the Gospel. Paul talks about his work as an apostle. This assignment was given him by the Lord to build people up. He realizes that his letters are more authoritarian than his speech when he is with them. But his duty is to do only one thing — to preach the gospel to them and to people in the outer reaches. He wants them to be aware that false teachers might infiltrate their ranks, just as satan disguises himself as an angel of light. He, Paul, will continue to be diligent in order to bring the truth to them. He recounts some of the things he has been through in order to carry out his ministry. He was beaten, imprisoned, stoned, shipwrecked, in danger from robbers and even some false brethren. He has experienced hardship, sleepless nights, hunger and thirst, cold and exposure, along with his concern for all the congregations. In Damascus he escaped harm only by being let down the wall in a basket.(2 Cor. 10 - 11)

Weak but Strong. Paul has received revelations and visions from the Lord, including one which revealed Paradise and words too great for expression. Because of this, he was given a "thorn in the flesh" which was a messenger of satan to buffet him — to keep him from exalting himself. Paul asked the Lord three times that it might depart from him, and the Lord told him, "My grace is sufficient for you, for power is perfected in weakness." Thus Paul is content with weaknesses and tribulations in Christ's service, for when he is weak, then he is strong. When Paul comes to Corinth, it will be for the third time. He wants them to know that it was through weakness of the body that Christ was crucified, yet he lives because of the power of God. And believers who are weak with Jesus are mighty with him because of the power of God directed to them. They need to test themselves as to whether Jesus is in them, that is, being free of the strife which previously prevailed there. He wishes them peace, joy, and comfort, ending his letter with: "The grace of the Lord Jesus Christ and the love of God, and the fellowship of the Holy Spirit be with you all."(2 Cor. 12 - 13)

LETTER TO THE GALATIANS

Faith, the Law, Fruit of the Spirit. Paul writes to the congregations in Galatia (now Turkey). He has learned that many of them have listened to Judaizers who have come among them claiming that a Christian is bound to observe the Mosaic law. Paul's attitude is clear from the first part of his letter. "I marvel that you are so soon removed from him who called you into the grace of Christ to another gospel which is not another; but there are some who trouble you and would pervert the gospel of Christ." To strengthen his point, he reminds them that he is an apostle chosen by the Lord himself. Further, he has not had to rely upon men; Paul's knowledge of the gospel is based upon direct revelation from Jesus Christ. He did go to Jerusalem for a short time and stay with Peter for 15 days, and he talked with James, the Lord's brother, but he did not confer with the other apostles. He did not go to Jerusalem again until he went there with Barnabas and Titus 14 years later. The apostles approved of Paul's ministry to the Gentiles (the other apostles continuing their ministries to the Jewish people). Also Titus, a Greek, was not required to be circumcised. There were people who tried to bring them "into bondage," but they did not listen to them. James,

Peter, and John approved of Paul's views and sent Paul and Titus off with the right hand of fellowship with a reminder to help the poor, which Paul was eager to do. Later when Peter was visiting Antioch, Paul even rebuked him for seeming to give preference to some Judaizers who came there to advance their doctrine. Paul said to Peter, "If you being a Jew live as a Gentile, and not as the Jews, why compel the Gentiles to live as Jews?" Justification does not come from the Mosaic law; it comes by faith in God through faith in Jesus Christ. If righteousness comes through the law, then Jesus died for nothing.(Gal. 1 - 2)

Faith in God's Promises. To the Galatians Paul says, "O, foolish Galatians, who has bewitched you, that you do not obey the truth, before whose eyes Jesus Christ has been openly set forth as crucified among you?" Have they received the Holy Spirit by the law or by faith? Abraham believed God and it was counted to him as righteousness (long before the law was given to Moses). It is not the law which is vital, it is the covenant, God's promises. If that is true, what is the law's function? It was merely a device (pedagogue or schoolmaster) to teach and control conduct until the arrival of a mediator from the seed of Abraham. Paul says, "For as many of you as have been baptized into Christ have put on Christ. There is neither Jew nor Greek; there is neither bond nor free; there is neither male nor female; for you are all one in Christ Jesus. And if you are Christ's, then are you Abraham's seed and heirs according to the promise."(Gal. 3)

Heirs with Christ. A child may be an heir of his or her father, but until maturity the child is in a position not much different from that of a servant even though potentially the "lord of all." Just as a human father adopts (recognizes) a child as an heir, so also does God adopt believers as spiritual heirs through his son and heir, Jesus Christ. Thus believers have a close relationship with God whereby in their hearts they cry out to God, "Abba, Father." If one is in this blessed position, why would he or she want to get caught up in trivia like the observation of certain days, months, times, and years? If they are free, as was Sarah through whom the promise was made, they certainly do not want to be reduced to the bondage typified by Hagar, Sarah's bond-woman.(Gal. 4)

Fruit of the Spirit. Reliance on Mosaic law means that the whole law must be observed. Actually, the law is fulfilled in one sentence: "You shall love your neighbor as yourself."(Lev. 19:18) Therefore, walk in the spirit and fulfill not the lusts of the flesh which are contrary to the spirit. Beware of strife, for it can destroy. Works of the flesh include immorality, idolatry, sorcery (witchcraft), anger, strife, and drunkenness. But the fruit of the spirit is love, joy, peace, patience, gentleness, goodness, faith, kindness, and self-control.(Gal. 5)

Helping Others. If someone is doing the wrong thing, a spiritual brother or sister should help restore that person in the spirit of gentleness and kindness, being careful not to be tempted. Believers should bear one another's burden as fulfillment of the law of Christ so that the brother or sister may mature to bear his or her own burden. Those who receive instruction in the word toward this result should then share all good things with the one who is their teacher. We reap what we sow; therefore, believers will take advantage of every opportunity to help others, especially their brothers and sisters in "the household of faith." Paul concludes his letter, observing that his writing is large, being written in his own hand. He gives glory to God, testifying that he bears on his body the marks of the Lord Jesus. "Brethren, the grace of our Lord Jesus Christ be with your spirit. Amen."(Gal. 6)

LETTER TO THE EPHESIANS

Spiritual Unity. Paul writes to the congregation at Ephesus assuring them that he thinks of them often, giving thanks for them and mentioning them in his prayers. He has heard of their great faith and love and wishes to impart to them some important principles for their spiritual growth and revelation in their relationship with God through Jesus. They, being among the elect by virtue of their trust in God through Christ, have been sealed with the Holy Spirit of promise. The believer's hope rests in the power of God directed to all which he demonstrated in raising Christ from the dead and setting him at his own right hand in heavenly places, far above any other power, authority, or dominion in any age, and making him head of the assembly of believers which is the body of Christ. God through his grace and mercy has saved them, has brought them out of their former life of transgression, and has seated them spiritually in the heavenly places with Christ. This salvation is not a result of works without faith, it is a gift received by the believer through his or her faith and by the grace of God. For the faithful are his workmanship created in Jesus Christ in order to do those good works which God has prepared for them to accomplish. Believers, once having been sinners, are now reconciled to God through the blood of Jesus Christ and are fellow citizens in the household of God. They are a holy temple built upon a foundation of the apostles and prophets, Jesus Christ himself being the chief cornerstone, bound together through the Holy Spirit.(Eph. 1 - 2)

Power of the Spirit. Paul is a prisoner of Christ to teach understanding of the mysteries of God, the unsearchable riches of Christ, to make people realize the fellowship of the mystery which from the beginning of the world was hid in God who created all things by Jesus Christ, and in order that the wisdom of God might be made known through this great assembly of believers to rulers and authorities in heavenly places. Paul prays that God will grant believers through his riches in glory to be strengthened with power through his Spirit in the inner man; that Christ may dwell in their hearts through faith, being rooted and grounded in love; that they may know the love of Christ which surpasses all knowledge and be filled with the fullness of God.(Eph. 3)

Strength in Joint Effort. Believers are exhorted to walk worthy of their calling, being patient with one another in love. There is one body, unified in God the Father, Christ, and the Holy Spirit. To each believer is given a gift of Christ. Some are apostles, some prophets, some evangelists, some pastors and teachers for the perfecting of believers as mature comrades in Christ. In this way they will be able to avoid the false doctrines of deceivers. Through Christ's love and the joint effort of every member of the body of Christ, each being a member of the others, the whole congregation is edified and made strong. A Christian is a new person, putting off the old self, putting on a new identity, renewing the spirit of the mind, no longer given to anger or lying, but acting in love and truth and giving no place to the devil. Paul says, "And grieve not the Holy Spirit of God, whereby you are sealed for the day of redemption. Let all bitterness and wrath and anger and clamor and evil speaking be put away from you, with all malice. And be you kind to one another, tenderhearted, forgiving one another, even as God for Christ's sake has forgiven you."(Eph. 4)

Be Filled with the Holy Spirit. Followers of God walk in love as Christ loves and has given himself as an offering and sacrifice to God as a sweet-smelling savor. They should avoid the filthiness of sin and use their time wisely according to the will of God, for the days (of the world) are evil. "Be not drunk with wine wherein is excess; but be filled with the Spirit, speaking to yourselves in psalms and hymns and spiritual songs, singing and making melody in your heart to the Lord, giving thanks always for all things to God and the Father in the name of our Lord Jesus Christ, submitting yourselves one to another as God-fearers in Christ." Christ is the head of the family of believers, and in the same way the husband is the head of the household. With this position goes the responsibility to love and cherish his wife as

Christ cherishes his congregation which he will present to himself as washed clean with the water of the word. Husbands should love their wives as their own bodies, for no one hates his own flesh but nourishes and cherishes it as Christ does the body of believers. Wives likewise should recognize the leadership of the husband and give him respect.(Eph. 5)

Provoke Not to Anger. Children should obey their parents and honor their fathers and mothers. Fathers are not to provoke their children to anger but are to bring them up according to Christian principles and discipline. Workers should be obedient to their employers and diligent in their work, but more so be workers of Christ with good will, rendering service as to God and not as to men, knowing that God will provide. Employers should likewise act, knowing that they have a superior in heaven who shows no partiality.(Eph. 6:1-9)

Put on the Armor of God. Each one may be strong in the Lord by putting on the full armor of God (literally, a "panoply," a complete suit of armor) being then able to stand firm against the schemes ("fiery darts") of the devil. We do not contend with flesh and blood. Our battle is in the spiritual realm, against spiritual powers of evil and wickedness in heavenly places. The armor of God which permits us to stand firm includes the girding of truth, the breastplate of righteousness, the footwear of the gospel of peace, the shield of faith, the helmet of salvation, the sword of the spirit which is the word of God, with continual prayer and petition in the Spirit, persevering in prayer for all the saints (believers). Paul asks for prayers for himself and his ministry that he, an ambassador in chains, may speak boldly to make known the mystery of the gospel. Paul wishes the Ephesians peace, love, and faith from God the Father and the Lord Jesus Christ, and the same to all who love Jesus in sincerity.(Eph. 6:10-24)

LETTER TO THE PHILIPPIANS

A Love Letter; Preachers of Christ. Paul writes from Rome, where he is under guard, to the Christian congregation at Philippi, Greece. He has a great amount of affection for the Philippians, not only because this was the first congregation which he formed in Europe but also because they have encouraged him and helped him financially of their own volition.(Phil. 4:10-23) Even though he is a prisoner, he and those with him have been able to share the gospel so that it is known throughout the praetorian guard and elsewhere. There are those preaching the gospel out of love and with consideration of Paul's views. But there are also those who are preaching Christ who are envious of Paul and who are personally ambitious. He is not concerned about them; he rejoices over the fact that Christ is being proclaimed, whether under pretense or truth. Paul believes that the spread of the gospel, along with the prayers of the Philippians, will assure his release. He is not worried about his own situation, saying, "For me to live is Christ, and to die is gain." He would rather depart and be with Christ, but he knows that the body of believers needs him at this time, and he hopes to see them again and share their joy.(Phil. 1)

True Humility. Paul exhorts the Philippians to continue steadfast in love and humility. Christ showed what true humility is, for though he was in the form of God and equal with God, he left his high estate and became a bond-servant made in the likeness of men. He humbled himself on the cross, and God highly exalted him and gave him a name which is above every name, that at the name of Jesus every knee should bow, in heaven, on earth, and under the earth. And every tongue should confess that Jesus Christ is Lord to the glory of God the Father. Christians need to work out their own salvation with fear and trembling, for God works in them to accomplish his good pleasure. All things should be done without contention, for the Philippians are shining lights in the world and in a crooked and perverse generation.(Phil. 2)

Pressing toward the Mark. In a reflective mood Paul recounts that he is a Hebrew, circumcised on the eighth day, and once a Pharisee who persecuted Christians. But that is past, and while he has lost worldly things, he considers that as refuse that he may win Christ; that he may know him, the power of his resurrection, and the fellowship of his sufferings. Paul has not yet attained perfection, but he is pressing on toward the mark for the prize of the high calling of God in Jesus Christ. The Philippians should take care against backsliding, looking to the day when they will be transformed into conformity with the body of Christ's glory by the exertion of the power that he has to subject all things to himself.(Phil. 3)

Rejoice in the Lord. Paul praises the Philippians for their joyful steadfastness in the Lord. He mentions the women who labored with him for the gospel's sake in Philippi. Paul says, "Rejoice in the Lord always; again, I say, 'Rejoice!' Let your moderation be known to all men. The Lord is at hand. Do not worry about anything, but in everything by prayer and supplication with thanksgiving let your requests be made known to God. And the peace of God which passes all understanding shall keep your hearts and minds through Jesus Christ. Finally, brethren, whatever things are true, whatever things are honest, whatever things are just, whatever things are pure, whatever things are lovely, whatever things are of good report, if there is any virtue, if there is any praise, think on these things." Paul thanks them for their generosity. They have been the only ones to keep in touch with him throughout his ministry and the only ones who have made sure that he has help in a material way, even though he has never asked for anything, for he knows how to be content in poverty and in plenty. He says, "I can do all things through him who strengthens me." Paul is confident that his God will bless the Philippians and supply all their needs "according to his riches in glory by Christ Jesus." Paul closes his letter, "The grace of our Lord Jesus Christ be with you all. Amen."(Phil. 4)

LETTER TO THE COLOSSIANS

Christ and Creation. Paul writes to the Christian community in the city of Colossae located in Asia Minor. He has received word of their great faith and spiritual growth and wants to impart to them insights which will increase their wisdom and spiritual understanding. He encourages them to give thanks to God the Father who "has delivered us from the power of darkness and has translated us into the kingdom of his beloved son in whom we have redemption through his blood, the forgiveness of sins; who is the image of the invisible God, the firstborn of every creature, for by him were all things created that are in heaven and on earth, visible and invisible. Whether they be thrones or dominions, rulers or authorities, all things were created by him and for him, and by him all things consist." Christ is the head of the body of believers. Further, through him the Father reconciles all things to himself through the blood on the cross. Paul as a minister to the Gentiles strives to bring them into the fold so that everyone may be presented complete (perfect) in Christ.(Col. 1)

The Gospel and the New Self. Paul realizes that there are now many believers who have never seen him, and he writes so that all may understand the true gospel and be able to judge and withstand false teaching — so that they may walk with the Lord "having been rooted and built up in him and established in the faith" which they have been taught. Rather than to concentrate on man-made ordinances which say, "Touch not; taste not; handle not," they need to lay stress on principles by which they control the inner self.(Col. 2) It is more important to control inordinate passion, immorality, and greed, for these comprise idolatry; and to put aside anger, slander, and abusive language. The new self will exhibit compassion, kindness, humility, gentleness, patience, helping and forgiving others as the Lord has forgiven them. The peace of Christ will rule their hearts, and they can express their joy in psalms and hymns, spiritual songs, singing with thankfulness to God. Whatever a believer does should be done in the name of the Lord Jesus giving thanks through him to God the Father. It is also important that these attributes be evident and exercised in family relationships.(Col. 3)

The Gospel; Seasoning with Salt. People in leadership positions should operate justly and fairly, knowing that they have a superior in heaven. All should be diligent in prayer and pray also for Paul that he might be able to continue explaining the mystery of Christ even though he (Paul) is a prisoner. Christians should also conduct themselves wisely with everyone, making time together quality time, letting their speech be gracious, "seasoned with salt," so that they may know how to answer every person. All of Paul's helpers who are with him, including Luke the beloved physician, send greetings. Paul desires that this letter be read by all the Colossians and shared with the believers at Laodicea. Paul ends his letter, "This greeting is written by me, Paul, with my own hand. Remember my bonds. Grace be with you. Amen."(Col. 4)

FIRST LETTER TO THE THESSALONIANS

A Shining Example. Paul writes to the Christians at Thessalonica, Greece. He gives thanks for them, because in their affliction they have remained steadfast in the joy of the Holy Spirit and are known for their faith throughout Greece and even beyond. The Thessalonians are very dear to Paul, and he longs to see them, but satan has been a hindrance.(1 Thess. 1 - 2)

A Christian Witness to the World. Paul has had some concern about them because of the persecution they have been subjected to, but he is now relieved and happy because Timothy has brought a good report. He prays that they will even increase and abound in love not only to each other but also to everyone else, just as Paul loves them, so that the Lord Jesus may establish their hearts in holiness before God the Father at the coming of the Lord with all his saints. He exhorts them to continue their good work, abstaining from any kind of immoral conduct so that each one may know how to mature in sanctification and honor; to lead quiet and industrious lives, meeting their own needs, as good examples to non-Christians.(1 Thess. 3 - 4:1-12)

Meeting the Lord in the Air. As to the concern of the Thessalonians about their departed brothers and sisters ("those who are asleep"), Paul encourages them not to be sorrowful, as are people who have no hope. God will bring them to himself. Paul says, "We, the living who remain to the coming of the Lord shall not precede those who are asleep. For the Lord himself shall descend from heaven with a commanding shout, with the voice of an archangel and the trumpet of God, and the dead in Christ shall rise first; then we the living who remain, together with them, shall be caught away in the clouds to meet the Lord in the air; and so shall we always be with the Lord. So encourage one another with these words." There is no need to talk of times and seasons, for they know that the day of the Lord comes as a thief in the night. They as staunch believers, people of the day and shining lights, can rely on their faith, for God has appointed them to gain salvation through the Lord Jesus Christ who "died for us, that whether we may watch or we may sleep, we may live together with him. Wherefore, encourage one another and build up one another, even as you are doing."(1 Thess. 4:13 - 5:11)

Quench Not the Spirit. Paul encourages the Thessalonians to keep in mind several points. Don't render evil for evil. Always rejoice. Pray without ceasing. Give God through Christ Jesus thanks for everything. Do not quench the Spirit. Do not despise the expression of prophecies. Prove all things. Hold to what is good. Abstain from even the appearance of evil. In closing, Paul asks for their prayers, telling them to greet everyone with a holy kiss and asking that the epistle be read to all. "The grace of our Lord Jesus Christ be with you. Amen."(1 Thess. 5:12-28)

SECOND LETTER TO THE THESSALONIANS

Safety in Christ. Paul has received word that the Thessalonians have been given some erroneous information by others since his first letter, and he wishes to set the record straight. He assures them that he writes out of his great love and esteem for them, but they will profit from a reminder of things he taught them when he was with them. He realizes that they are still being persecuted, but they know that God will protect them and judge the persecutors.(2 Thess. 1)

The Gathering of the Saints. About the "day of Christ" and the gathering of the saints to himself, Paul says that first the apostasy is revealed, that is, the man of sin, the son of perdition who upon the urging of satan, exalts himself as if equal with God, deceitfully performing false signs and wonders and causing many to commit lawless acts. The "restrainer" is working now until all is revealed. The lawless ones, those who do not believe truth and delight in unrighteousness, will suffer judgment. But the Thessalonians need not be troubled about this, for they have the truth, and God out of his love for them has provided for their salvation, sanctification, and obtaining of the glory of Jesus Christ. Thus they have been provided eternal consolation and good hope through grace. They may comfort their hearts and strengthen themselves through good word and work.(2 Thess. 2)

No Work, No Food. The Lord is faithful, will protect them from evil, and direct their hearts into the love of God and the patience of Christ. Now Paul has heard that there are some who are not working and are acting like busybodies. They should discipline themselves, get to work, and earn their own food. The rule for Christians is that if one will not work, he should not be fed. Paul showed them the example by working hard for whatever he received. They should not be weary in doing good. If a brother does not heed instruction, count him not as an enemy, but admonish him as a brother. Paul ends his letter, "The grace of our Lord Jesus Christ be with you all. Amen."(2 Thess. 3)

FIRST LETTER TO TIMOTHY

Instructions to Evangelists and Pastors. One and Two Timothy and Titus have been called the Pastoral Epistles since they deal with the work of pastors. Also Paul gives instructions on various activities within a local body of believers. In 1 Timothy, Paul greets Timothy as his "own son in the faith" and speaks out against false teachers who concentrate on myths, legalisms, and endless genealogies. The true gospel message is love, a pure heart, a good conscience, and sincere faith; that Christ came to save sinners. These things Paul is sharing so that Timothy can "war a good warfare."(1 Tim. 1)   Regarding prayer, intercessory prayer and thanksgiving should be offered for all people, including kings and others in authority, for Christ wills that everyone be saved through the knowledge of the truth. There is one God and one mediator between man and God, the man Christ Jesus. Paul desires that people pray, "lifting up holy hands, without wrath and doubting." He urges that women dress modestly, profess godliness, and perform good works. He prefers that they not teach or exercise positions of authority over men, reminding them of their high calling as mothers.(1 Tim. 2)

Elders and Deacons. An overseer (bishop, elder, presbyter) should be blameless, married, vigilant, sober, discreet, hospitable, able to teach, not greedy, gentle, not contentious, not loving money, one who manages his household well, and has his children under control. He should be a mature Christian of good report among non-Christians. Similar qualifications should be applied to others who serve the local body (such as deacons).

These things are written so that one may know how to behave in the house of God which is the assembly of the living God, the pillar and base of the truth.(1 Tim. 3)

Truth versus False Doctrines. In the future some believers may be drawn away by false doctrines conceived through evil spirits, such as dietary rules and rules against marriage. Every creature of God is good, and all food is meant for use with thanksgiving and prayer. Timothy is encouraged to use his gift of teaching which he received through prophecy and the laying on of hands by the elders. He should not be self-conscious about his youth and should set a good example for everyone so that those who hear him may be saved.(1 Tim. 4)

Honor Senior Citizens. Older men and women should be honored, the younger considered as brothers and sisters. Widows should be helped by their families, and it is preferable that younger widows remarry. But if a widow has no one to help, her welfare is an obligation of her fellow Christians, especially if she is 60 years old or older and dedicated to performing Christian good works. Elders (bishops) who rule well, particularly those who labor in the word and teaching, are worthy of double honor and the support of the people. On a personal note, Paul advises Timothy to take a little wine for the sake of his stomach problem and other infirmities.(1 Tim. 5)

Nothing In, Nothing Out. Employees and employers should have mutual consideration for each other. One should not consider religion as a way to get rich. Godliness with contentment are the real riches, the believer being content if adequately fed and clothed. "For we brought nothing into this world, and it is certain we can carry nothing out." The "love of money is the root of all evil." Of course, there are believers who have material wealth. They should not be conceited or set their hope on the uncertainty of riches but upon God who supplies all things. Their instruction should be to do good, to be rich in good works, to be ready to share with a generous heart, storing up for themselves the treasure of a good foundation for their eternal lives. Paul entreats Timothy to continue in the gospel of the true sovereign, Jesus, King of kings and Lord of lords. In closing, Paul says, "O, Timothy, keep that which is committed to your trust, avoiding pointless and empty babblings and oppositions of falsely-named knowledge which some have professed concerning the faith but have missed the mark. Grace be with you. Amen."(1 Tim. 6)

SECOND LETTER TO TIMOTHY

Fighting the Good Fight, Finishing the Course, Keeping the Faith. In his second letter to Timothy, Paul greets him as his "beloved son." He has a great desire to see him, remembering former times and how Timothy's grandmother, Lois, and his mother, Eunice, had such strong faith which they imparted to Timothy. Paul encourages Timothy to carry out his calling as an evangelist without fear, saying, "For God has not given us the spirit of fear, but of power, and of love and of a sound mind." Some have turned away from Paul in his hour of trial, but there are some who have remained steadfast such as Onesiphorus who has become a good minister. Timothy is to train others to be teachers of the gospel who center on the gospel message, not striving with others about words. He is to endure the difficulties he will encounter as a soldier of Jesus Christ and as a farmer who is partaker of the first fruits. His work will involve continued study of God's word, "straightly cutting the word of truth;" avoiding useless theories which do not honor God; teaching so as to produce "vessels of gold," that is, vessels of honor set apart for the master's use and suitable for every good work; patiently working with difficult people that they might repent, acknowledge the truth, and rescue themselves from the snares of the devil.(2 Tim. 1 - 2)

All Scripture Inspired. Timothy will encounter deceivers who appear to be believers but who deny the power of the gospel, using it to personal advantage, "ever learning but never able to come to the knowledge of the truth," whose erroneous teachings will be exposed, just as was the falsity of Jannes and Jambres, the magicians who opposed Moses. Paul instructs Timothy to continue in the things which Paul has taught him about the gospel, remembering "that from a child you have known the holy scriptures which are able to make you wise for salvation through faith which is in Christ Jesus. All scripture is God-inspired and profitable for teaching, for conviction, for correction, for instruction in righteousness that the man of God may be complete, fully-fitted (ready and able) for every good work."(2 Tim. 3)

The Crown of Righteousness. Paul charges Timothy before God and Jesus, who will judge the living and the dead, to teach and preach the word "in season and out of season" with patience and encouragement. As for himself, Paul is now being "poured out," and the time of his release has come. He has fought the good fight, has finished the course, has kept the faith. There is ready for him a "crown of righteousness" which the Lord will present to him "in that day," not only to him but also to all who "love his appearing." Many who were with Paul have left; only Luke is with him. Trophimus got sick and is at Miletus. Paul requests that Timothy come to him before winter and bring Mark with him, also his cloak and his books, especially the parchments. He asks to be remembered to Priscilla and Aquila and the others and ends his letter, "The Lord Jesus Christ be with your spirit. Grace be with you. Amen."(2 Tim. 4)

LETTER TO TITUS

Christ, the Blessed Hope. Paul begins his letter to Titus with an acknowledgement of God's truth, the hope of eternal life with God which he promised before the world began. Paul greets Titus as his "own son according to common faith." He has some instructions for Titus since he has appointed him as an evangelist and organizer of Christian affairs in Crete. He outlines for Titus the qualifications for elders (bishops) who will also need to be persuasive preachers and teachers to combat the teachings of Judaizers and the natural resistance of the people of Crete. Titus is to be a good example and impart sound teaching, including the principles that the older men should be sensible, temperate and sound in faith, love, and patience; that the older women in the same way should act in holiness without making false accusations, not given to much wine, being teachers of good things, training young women in responsibility, loving their husbands and children; that workers be faithful, honest, and obedient to their employers. These admonitions are important, for the grace of God which brings salvation has appeared to everyone, teaching all to live a moral life in this world and to look for that blessed hope and glorious appearing of God and the savior, Jesus Christ. Jesus gave himself for all in order to redeem them from iniquity and purify to himself a "peculiar people" who are zealous to do good works.(Titus 1 - 2)

The Christian's Public Conduct. Public witness is important also and includes being law-abiding, not speaking evil to anyone, being gentle and not brawlers. Let the believers keep in mind that they once did the baser things and were saved by God's mercy, by the "washing or regeneration," and renewing by the Holy Spirit whom he has poured out upon them richly through the savior, Jesus Christ; that justified by grace, believers might be made heirs according to the hope of eternal life. One should shun foolish controversies, genealogies, strife, and disputes about the law, for they are unprofitable and pointless. Paul requests that Titus meet him in Nicopolis and bring Zenas the lawyer and Apollos. "All who are with me greet you. Greet those who love us in the faith. Grace be with you all. Amen."(Titus 3)

LETTER TO PHILEMON

A Matter of Conscience. Paul writes to Philemon, one of the more well-to-do Christians in Colossae in whose home an assembly of Christians meets. He counts Philemon as a brother in Christ, and it is with joy that he contemplates all that Philemon has done for others. Now Paul wishes to speak on behalf of Onesimus (Col. 4:9) who is helping Paul, for Paul realizes that Onesimus is bound to Philemon either as a slave or a bond-servant. Paul is sending Onesimus back to straighten things out in the hope that Philemon will not only forgive him but further release him from his obligation and accept him as a beloved brother, as Paul so considers him, receiving him in the same way he would receive Paul.(See also: Eph. 6:9; Col. 4:1.)   If Onesimus has wronged Philemon or owes him anything, he may put it on Paul's account, and he will repay it; but Philemon may remember that he owes his very self to Paul. Paul is confident that Philemon will respond favorably and knows that he will do even more than is requested. Paul tells of his plan to visit him in the future and gives greeting to others. "The grace of our Lord Jesus Christ be with your spirit. Amen."

LETTER TO THE HEBREWS

Jesus Christ, High Priest, Mediator of the New Covenant. Hebrews begins, "God, who at different times and in many ways spoke in time past to the fathers by the prophets, has in these last days spoken to us by his son whom he has appointed heir of all things, by whom also he made the worlds, who being the brightness of his glory and the express image of his person, and upholding all things by the word of his power, when he himself purged our sins, sat down on the right hand of the majesty on high, being so much better than the angels, since he has by inheritance obtained a more excellent name than they. For to which of the angels did he say at any time, 'Thou art my son; this day have I begotten thee.' "?(Ps. 2:7) Thus the basic proposition of Hebrews is set, which is further demonstrated by appeal to many Old Testament passages including prophecies about the Messiah, the new covenant, and Old Testament heroes of faith. As in the passage just quoted, the watchword is "better." Every aspect of Christ and the new covenant is better than what went before. And it is so good that believers need to guard against backsliding, lest they forfeit the blessings which they can attain through the gospel. Jesus was made a little lower than the angels for a time that he might suffer death for all people as their brother so that they may attain sanctification and have protection against the schemes of satan.(Heb. 1 - 2)

Jesus, the High Priest. Jesus, as the high priest of the Christian body of believers, is "worthy of more glory than Moses." Remember, the children of Israel who came out of Egypt could not enter into God's rest because of unbelief. God said, "So I swore in my wrath, they shall not enter into my rest."(Ps. 95:11) Christians should be steadfast in their faith so as to enter into that rest, heeding God's word. "For the word of God is vital, and powerful, and sharper than any two-edged sword, piercing even to the dividing apart of soul and spirit, and of the joints and marrow, and is a discerner of the thoughts and intents of the heart." Let all know that Jesus is not a high priest who cannot be touched. He was tested as we are, yet without sin. "Let us therefore come boldly to the throne of grace, that we may obtain mercy and find grace to help in time of need."(Heb. 3 - 4)

Christian Maturity. There are many Christians who have become inattentive and need to become alert. For while they should be teachers, they are still in need of basic instruction themselves (milk rather than meat). In order to mature, to be able to digest "meat," they must train themselves to be able to discern both good and evil. Christ's teachings on repentance from dead works, faith in God, baptism, laying on of hands, resurrection of the dead, and eternal judgment are basic. Let the believer go on from a knowledge of these truths to complete maturity. Those who have been enlightened and have been partakers of the Holy Spirit, the word of God and spiritual power, and then have fallen away run the risk of losing their expectancy. This needs to be said, but Paul is confident that his people will not be slothful and will diligently seek God's promises by following the example of their more mature brothers and sisters in Christ. Further, God will not forget their past efforts for the faith, their "work and labor of love" in ministering to others. The promises were given to Abraham and confirmed by God's oath. God cannot lie. And since he could swear by none greater, he certified his own declaration. These promises set before us a blessed hope which is the anchor of the soul. This hope is realized in Jesus who is a high priest forever after the order of Melchizedek.(Heb. 5 - 6; Ps. 110:4)

A High Priesthood; a Better Covenant. Melchizedek was a king of Salem whose name means "king of righteousness," and the word "salem" means that he was "king of peace." Abraham, who was God's chosen man and the ancestor of Moses, Aaron, and the Levitical priests, paid homage and a tenth of his spoils of battle to Melchizedek.(Gen. 14:18-20) Therefore, a priesthood after his order is a higher priesthood than that under the Mosaic law. Since Jesus was of the tribe of Judah and not Levi, his priesthood is independent and supersedes the priesthood of Aaron's descendants. And whereas priests under the Mosaic law were men having the same passions and weaknesses as those whom they represented before the altar, and whereas their priesthood ended when they died, Christ was appointed by oath as a high priest forever. Now this high priest, who intercedes for us, sits at God's right hand, with a more excellent ministry as mediator of a better covenant and better promises. The new covenant is that prophesied in Jeremiah 31:31-34. God will write his laws on the hearts and minds of the people, and everyone will know the Lord. God will be merciful about past unrighteousness and will no longer remember their sins and iniquities. When the new covenant is set, the first becomes old and is superseded.(Heb. 7 - 8)

Christ Died Once for All. Worship, confession of sin, and forgiveness under the first covenant involved all of the regulations and activities at the tabernacle, including animal sacrifices, representation by the priests, and the once-a-year day of atonement when the high priest went into the holy of holies. However, all these things could not purge the conscience of sin to make the people perfect, but they were merely a forerunner of things to come. Christ's sacrifice was more effective, because his blood sealed the new covenant: "I will put my laws in their hearts and in their minds will I write them." He is the testator of the new covenant as a testament, the executor of his own will. He is also mediator of the covenant as a contract. Under the new covenant, "as it is appointed to men once to die," Christ, having been offered once to bear the sins of many, shall appear the second time to those who await him, apart from sin, for salvation. God had no pleasure in the former sacrifices, and he revealed this through prophecy.(Ps. 40:6-8) But Jesus' one sacrifice is effective now and forever. Where there is a remission of sins, there is no need for any further sacrifices. One who lives by Jesus in effect enters boldly into the holy of holies with him in a new living way. Thus one should hold fast the profession of faith without wavering, for he who promised is faithful. Such faith is shown through encouraging others to operate in love and good works and through gathering together to exhort and edify one another. Anyone who denies Christ is subject to God's judgment. While it is a fearful thing to fall into the hands of the living God, these Christians having been through many tribulations and persecutions in the past will remember to have patience, that after they have done the will of God they will receive the promise, for he that shall come will come and will not tarry. They should not retreat from their faith in the salvation of their souls.(Heb. 9 - 10)

The Hall of Faith. "Now faith is the substance of things hoped for, the evidence (assurance) of things not seen." It is by faith that the Old Testament heroes of God accomplished their deeds, including Abel, Enoch, Noah, Abraham and Sarah, Isaac, Jacob, Joseph, Moses, those who took Jericho, Rahab, Gideon, Barak, Samson, Jephthah, David, Samuel, and the prophets. They accomplished great things in God's service, often suffering hardship and violence that they might obtain a better resurrection. They were stoned, sawn asunder, tempted, slain, wandering in sheepskins and goatskins, destitute, afflicted, tormented. The world was not worthy of them. They wandered in deserts and mountains and in dens and caves of the earth. "And these all, having given witness to their faith, did not receive the promise, God having foreseen something better for us, that not apart from us they should be made perfect."(Heb. 11)

Jesus, Perfecter of Faith. There being such a "great cloud of witnesses," believers should lay aside every weight and temptation and persevere in the race set before them, looking to Jesus, the perfecter of faith, who endured the cross for the joy set before him and is now seated at the right hand of God. They can endure much, remembering that God the Father disciplines and instructs just as natural parents do, and they have all endured that.(Prov. 3:11) Subjecting oneself to the heavenly Father results in being a partaker of his holiness and the peaceable fruit of right-standing with him. Slack hands and feeble knees should be strengthened, walking a straight path resulting in healing. Care should be taken not to reject so valuable a birthright in the manner of Esau but to heed the voice of Jesus the mediator, for believers have come to Mount Zion, to the city of the living God, the heavenly Jerusalem with a company of countless angels. Believers have received a kingdom which cannot be moved and should serve God with grace, reverence, and godly fear, "for our God is a consuming fire."(Heb. 12)

Good Deeds, Sacrifices Pleasing to God. Brotherly love should continue showing hospitality to strangers, for thereby some have entertained angels without realizing it. Marriage is honorable and the bed undefiled, but God judges immorality. Contentment in all circumstances is possible, for God provides.(Ps. 27:1, 118:6) Jesus Christ is the same yesterday, today, and forever. The offering of the "sacrifice of praise to God continually," doing good, and sharing are sacrifices pleasing to God. There should be cooperation with those in leadership positions so that they may continue with joy as watchmen for the souls of the faithful. Paul closes with a request for prayer. Timothy has been set free, and if he comes, Paul will be able to come on a visit. "Salute all your leaders and all the saints. Those from Italy salute you. Grace be with you all. Amen."(Heb. 13)

EPISTLES OF JAMES, PETER, JOHN, AND JUDE

THE LETTER OF JAMES

Christian Faith and Action. James writes to the Christians throughout the empire ("12 tribes which are in the dispersion"; see Acts 8:4). He speaks of enduring trials and temptations patiently and joyfully that they may be "perfect and complete, lacking in nothing." If a believer is in need of more wisdom to endure, he or she may ask God in faith, "nothing wavering." God gives generously and without reproach. But a double-minded person who asks in doubt and unbelief will get nothing. Poor and rich alike should be humble before God. Temptations do not come from God. He cannot be tempted by evil, and he tempts no one. Temptations are experienced only because of the human propensity to lust. God has blessed believers, and they should remember to be doers of the word and not hearers only. This involves being "quick to hear, slow to speak, and slow to anger." They operate under the "law of liberty," but if any of them claims to be religious and cannot bridle his tongue, his religion is worthless. The pure and undefiled religion is to visit orphans and widows and keep oneself unspotted from the world.(Jas. 1)

Showing Faith by Action. Living by the law of liberty means living by the royal law of love. Showing favoritism to the rich over the poor is a violation of that law. Mercy triumphs over judgment, and one who shows no mercy will be judged without mercy. What good is it if someone claims to be a Christian yet has no works? If a brother or sister is without food and clothing and a Christian says for them to go in peace and to be warmed and filled but does not provide what is needed, what good is that? "So also faith, if it has no works, is dead by itself. But someone will say, 'You have faith and I have works.' Show me your faith without works, and from my works I will show you my faith." One may believe that there is one God, but the demons also believe and tremble. Faith is proved and demonstrated by doing the will of God in the manner of Abraham and Rahab. So just as the body is dead without the spirit, faith without works is dead.(Jas. 2)

Corralling the Tongue. The greatest enemy of anyone is his or her own tongue, for it forms our speech. Out of the same mouth comes both blessing and cursing. The tongue is little, but just as a bridle controls a horse, a rudder directs a ship, or a small fire starts a large fire, the tongue can control and affect the whole person. The wise person who seeks perfection will bridle his or her tongue so as to give offense to no one. This can only be done with God's help. Controlling the tongue will eliminate envy and strife, thus bringing about peace and harmony.(Jas. 3)

Asking Not; Asking Amiss. Many are losing the "war" with themselves because of giving in to the temptations of the world. Yet they desire the things of God. They have not because they ask not, or they ask but receive not because they ask amiss, preferring to continue in their worldly life. But God is good and will allow them to cleanse themselves. If they submit themselves to him in humility, if they come near to him, he will draw close to them. They can resist the devil, and he will flee. There is only one lawgiver and one judge; therefore, no one else is qualified to judge anyone. Closeness to God involves seeking his will as to all activities, even in one's job or business, doing what one knows to be good, keeping in mind that mortal life is like a vapor; it does not last long.(Jas. 4)

Prayer Accomplishes Much. Speaking to the rich again, James points out the limited value of wealth and asks for an examination of conscience on how they obtained it. James then speaks on having patience since the "coming of the Lord is drawing near." One should not groan against others, for "the judge stands at the door." Job was patient, and the Lord was merciful to him. If anyone among the believers is afflicted, he or she should pray. If any are merry, they should sing psalms. If any is sick, let him or her call for the elders of their congregation so that they can pray, anointing him or her with oil. The prayer of faith will raise up the sick person, and any sins will be forgiven. Confession of sins and prayers for each other are beneficial for healing, for the effectual prayer of a righteous person can accomplish a great deal, as Elijah demonstrated. If any believer strays from the truth, another who is able to turn him or her back to the truth will save a soul from death and cover a multitude of sins.(Jas. 5)

THE FIRST LETTER OF PETER

A People for God's Own Possession. Peter writes to the Christians scattered throughout Asia Minor. He refers to them as the elect, sanctified into an incorruptible inheritance through the resurrected Jesus Christ. Peter knows of their trials and tribulations. He compares their faith to gold tested by fire and their love for and joy in Jesus Christ as inexpressible and full of glory. Their obtaining of salvation through their faith was foretold by the prophets who were in effect serving Christians rather than themselves. Christians have been taught by preachers of the gospel and the Holy Spirit things into which angels long to look. They have been redeemed by the precious blood of the lamb, Jesus Christ, who was foreknown before the foundation of the world. He has been revealed "in these last times" for their sakes, they having purified their souls in having love for one another. They have been born again of incorruptible seed by the word of God which lives forever.(1 Pet. 1; Isa. 40:6-8)

From Darkness to Light. Born-again Christians are living stones building up a spiritual house, a holy priesthood offering spiritual sacrifices acceptable to God through Jesus Christ. He is the chief cornerstone of Zion, the stumbling stone which the builders rejected.(Isa. 8:14, 28:16; Ps. 118:22)   Those who reject Christ stumble on the word. But Christians are a chosen people, a kingly priesthood, a holy nation, a people for God's own possession called from darkness into his marvelous light. Once they were not a people, but now they are the people of God who have obtained mercy.(Hos. 1:10)   Peter beseeches the people to remain steadfast, to be law-abiding citizens, and servants of God. If they should suffer, they should remember the sufferings of Christ for them. Christ "bore our sins in his own body on the tree (cross), that we being dead to sins may live to righteousness, for by his wounds you were healed."(Isa. 53:4-5)   They were once sheep going astray but have now returned to the shepherd and overseer of their souls.(1 Pet. 2; Isa. 53:6)

Wives and Husbands. Peter also has some advice for wives and husbands. It behooves a wife to be submissive to the husband's leadership, and if the husband is not a believer, he might be won to Christ without a word through her chaste and respectful conduct. Rather than ornaments and dresses, that which is most precious to God is the gentle and quiet spirit of the inner person. A husband, likewise, should live with his wife with knowledge and understanding, protecting her as one would a weaker vessel, honoring her as a joint heir of the grace of life, so that his prayers will not be cut off. As for believers generally, Peter asks them to be mindful of each other, not rendering evil for evil, but rather blessing so as to inherit a blessing.(Ps. 34:12-18)   No one should be harmed for doing good. But if a believer suffers for Christ while doing good, it is better in God's eyes than suffering for doing evil. Christ the just suffered for the sins of the unjust, being put to death in the flesh but made alive in the Spirit. By the Spirit he preached to the spirits in prison of those who had been disobedient in the days of Noah while the ark was being built to save eight people. They were saved through the water which prefigured baptism into the resurrection of Jesus Christ.(1 Pet. 3)

Holding Fast to the Gospel. Those who have allied themselves with Christ should not again take part in the immoral acts of worldly people who think it strange that Christians will not join them in their excesses and who speak evil of them. They will be judged, both the living and the dead. It is for this reason that the gospel was preached to those who are dead that they might be judged accordingly as people in the flesh, but live to God in the spirit. Peter again encourages these Christians under persecution to hold fast for the faith and keep their witness pure. Judgment begins with the saved, and if they barely make it, what will happen to the ungodly?(1 Pet. 4)

Feeding the Flock. Speaking to the elders as an elder who witnessed the sufferings of Christ and is a partaker of the glory to be revealed, Peter encourages them to feed the flock of God willingly, not for money primarily, but eagerly, not lording it over them, but being good examples for them. "And when the Chief Shepherd shall appear, you will receive a crown of glory which does not fade away."(See John 21:15-17)   Younger people should be humble and follow the elders' instruction, putting away pride. All should humble themselves to God so that he might exalt them at the proper time, casting their cares upon him, because he cares for them. "Be sober, be vigilant, because your adversary the devil, as a roaring lion, walks about seeking whom he may devour; so resist him, being steadfast in the faith, knowing that the same afflictions suffered by your brethren are also in the world." Peter says that he has written briefly through Silvanus; that the believers at Babylon greet them as does "Mark my son. Greet one another with a kiss of love. Peace be with you all that are in Christ Jesus. Amen."(1 Pet. 5)

THE SECOND LETTER OF PETER

Remembrance Stirred Up. Peter writes to the members of the flock to stir up their remembrance, because he knows that shortly he must put off his earthly tabernacle, just as Jesus had shown him (John 21:18-19), and he wants them to have this message after his death. He writes as Simon Peter, an apostle of Jesus Christ. He is not relating cleverly devised fables in telling them of the power and coming of Jesus. He was an eyewitness of his majesty. He was there when God the Father said, "This is my beloved son in whom I am well pleased." He was with Jesus when he was on the holy mountain. They should also take heed of the sure word of prophecy, knowing that it was not a matter of human interpretation, "but holy men of God spoke as they were moved by the Holy Spirit."(2 Pet. 1)

False Prophets. There were false prophets before, and there will be false teachers among Christians. They will be judged just as God did not spare the rebellious angels but cast them into the abyss (Tartarus) in chains of darkness reserved for judgment. Nor did he spare the ancient world in the time of Noah or the cities of Sodom and Gomorrah. He spared Lot, a righteous man, as an example of how God knows how to deliver the godly out of temptation and reserve the ungodly for punishment in a day of judgment. These false teachers are deceivers, blemishes in the midst of believers, and followers of the ways of Balaam the false prophet. They promise liberty but bring people into a bondage of corruption. As to those who once escaped the pollutions of the world, if they again become entangled and overcome by such pollution, they are in worse condition than they were before. They are like a dog which returns to his own vomit (Prov. 26:11) or a pig which after being washed returns to wallowing in the mud.(2 Pet. 2)

New Heavens and a New Earth. This is Peter's second letter in which he is stirring up their minds, urging them to remember the words of the prophets and the apostles. There will be scoffers in the last days walking according to their own lusts and questioning the promise of Christ's coming. The heavens and the earth are being preserved for fire, being kept to a day of judgment and destruction of ungodly people. As to time, one day with the Lord is as a thousand years, and a thousand years as one day. The Lord is not slow; he is patient, not wishing anyone to perish, but rather desiring that all come to repentance. The day of the Lord will come as a thief in the night. The heavens will pass away with a great noise, and the earth will be burned up. But according to God's promise, there will be new heavens and a new earth wherein righteousness dwells. Seeing that this is true, the Christian should be diligent, being found by God in peace, without spot and blameless. The patience of the Lord should be considered as salvation. The beloved brother, Paul, has also written of these things in his epistles in which there are some things difficult to understand and which unlearned and unstable people distort, as they do the other scriptures, to their own destruction. In closing, Peter warns against backsliding and says, "But grow in grace and the knowledge of our Lord and savior Jesus Christ. To him be glory both now and to the day of eternity. Amen."(2 Pet. 3)

THE FIRST LETTER OF JOHN

God Is Love. John writes as an intimate eyewitness of Jesus and his ministry. "That which was from the beginning which we have heard, which we have seen with our eyes, which we have looked upon, and our hands have handled of the word of life; and the life was manifested, and we have seen and bear witness and show you that eternal life which was with the Father and was manifested to us; that which we have seen and heard we report to you that you may also have fellowship with the Father and with his son Jesus Christ. And these things we write to you that your joy may be full."

God Is Light. First, know that God is light. One cannot truthfully say that he or she has fellowship with God and walks in darkness. People who walk in the light have fellowship with each other, and the blood of Jesus Christ his son cleanses them from all sin. Those who deny that they have sin deceive themselves and make out God as a liar. If a believer confesses his sin, God is faithful and just to forgive him and cleanse him from all unrighteousness. But John writes to urge believers not to sin and to remember that they have an advocate with the Father, Jesus, who is the propitiation for the sins of the whole world. To know him is to keep his word, particularly the new commandment of love. If one claims to be following his word or to be in the light and yet hates his brother, that one is blind and walking in darkness.(1 John 1 - 2:11)

Many Antichrists. John writes so that young and old who have the word will hold to it and be blessed with the forgiveness of their sins. One cannot love the world and love God. "For all that is in the world, the lust of the flesh, the lust of the eyes, and pride (boasting) of life, is not of the Father but of the world." Concerning false doctrine, John says, "Little children, it is the last time, and as you have heard that antichrist shall come, even now there are many antichrists; therefore, you know that it is the last time." These antichrists are false teachers who try to seduce believers with false teaching about Jesus. Those to whom John writes know the truth which he has taught them. "But the anointing which you have received of him abides in you, and you do not need any man to teach you; but as the same anointing teaches you all things and is truth, and is no lie, and as it has been taught, you shall abide in him." They should continue to abide in Jesus until he appears, for one who acts righteously is born of him.(1 John 2:12-29)

Passing from Death to Life. The Father has shown his love by calling the faithful the children of God, but the world does not recognize this, because it does not recognize God. One who practices righteousness is righteous just as God is righteous. He who commits sin is of the devil. God manifested himself in the Son that he might negate the works of the devil. A person who is truly born of God cannot sin. Whoever does not do righteousness is not of God, and neither is anyone who does not love others. The message from the beginning has been to love one another. Those who love others have passed from death to life, but he who does not love his brother abides in death and is the same as a murderer. A Christian should lay down his life for a brother, just as Jesus laid down his life for us. Love is not just a matter of speaking words; it is action. If someone has worldly goods, sees a brother in need, yet closes his heart toward him, how does the love of God dwell in him? Love is shown through deeds done according to truth. We know when we have failed to act in love, and so does God, for he knows all things. Those who know that they are doing deeds of love also know that whatever they ask they receive from him, because they are keeping his commandment to believe on the name of God's son, Jesus Christ, and love one another. People who do this in faith know that he abides in them through the Holy Spirit which he has given.(1 John 3)

Love Casts Out Fear. Not every spirit is of God, and people need to know the difference. There are many false prophets in the world. Every spirit who confesses that Jesus Christ has come in the flesh is of God. Every spirit who does not confess this is not of God but "is that of the antichrist, which you heard that it comes, and it is already in the world." John gives this assurance: "You are of God, little children, and have overcome them, because greater is he that is in you than he that is in the world." Those of the world speak of the world, and the world listens. Those of God hear the truth. Those not of God do not listen. By this we know the difference between the spirit of truth and the spirit of error. John exhorts the faithful to continue in love. "Beloved, let us love one another, for love is of God. And everyone who loves is born of God and knows God. He who loves not knows not God, for God is love." While no one has seen God at any time, he dwells in those who love one another as he loves, and his love is perfected in them. His love is manifest through giving the world Jesus Christ, his only begotten son, the propitiation of sin, that those who believe might live through him and have boldness in the day of judgment that as he is so are they in this world. Perfect love casts out fear; so if anyone has fear, that person is not perfect in love. "We love him because he first loved us." If anyone says he loves God but hates his brother, he is a liar. If he cannot love his brother whom he has seen, how can he love God whom he has not seen? He who loves God loves his brother also.(1 John 4)

Ask and Receive. Whoever believes that Jesus is the Christ (Messiah) and the Son of God is born of God. The believer shows love for God by keeping his commandments. This is not burdensome, for whoever is born of God overcomes the world. This is the believer's victory that overcomes the world, their faith. Jesus is he who came by the water and the blood, the Holy Spirit bearing witness. These three agree in one. God has given eternal life in his son to those who believe in him. "He that has the Son has life; he that has not the Son of God has not life." John writes this epistle to assure believers that they have eternal life in Christ. "And this is the confidence that we have in him, that if we ask anything according to his will, he hears us. And if we know that he hears us, whatever we ask, we know that we have the requests that we ask of him." If a believer sees a brother sin, intercessory prayer for him will be effective, and God will give him life. Whoever is born of God does not sin and is diligent in the faith. As a result, the wicked one does not touch that person. The whole world lies in wickedness, but the believer knows that he or she is of God; that the son of God has come giving understanding of eternal life in him. John closes with an admonition, "Little children, guard yourselves from idols. Amen."(1 John 5)

THE SECOND LETTER OF JOHN

Chosen Lady. John the elder writes to "the elect lady and her children." He rejoices that some of her children are now walking in the truth and shares two thoughts with her. The first is a reminder to walk after the commandment of love, the love for one another. The second is to beware of deceivers who do not acknowledge that Jesus came in the flesh. "This is the deceiver and the antichrist." Such a deceiver is not worthy of their hospitality and should not be encouraged lest one be considered a partaker of his evil deeds. One who abides in Christ's teachings has both the Father and the Son and safeguards the reward for which he or she has labored. John has more to say but will share it "face to face" on his next visit. "The children of your elect sister greet you. Amen."

THE THIRD LETTER OF JOHN

Christian Hospitality. John the elder writes to Gaius who is beloved in the truth, expressing his wish that Gaius prosper and be in good health just as his soul prospers. John is joyful, for he has heard how Gaius is active in the faith and how he receives traveling Christians, even though strangers to him, and helps them on their way. His love has been testified to in the congregation. Those who show hospitality in this way become fellow helpers in the advancement of the truth. John wrote to another congregation, but Diotrephes who wishes to be first would not accept it and spoke against John. This man does not receive the brethren and orders people who would show them hospitality out of the assembly. John will take care of that matter when he visits them. Demetrius is doing well in the truth, as John himself has witnessed. There is more to say, but it can wait until John comes and they can speak face to face. "Peace be with you. The friends salute you. Greet the friends by name."

THE LETTER OF JUDE

Building Up the Faith. "Jude, the servant of Jesus Christ and brother of James, to those who are sanctified by God the Father, called and preserved in Jesus Christ." Jude warns of the need to contend earnestly for the faith, because certain men have "crept in unawares" and are denying God and Jesus Christ. He compares such men to satan, the fallen angels, the people of Sodom and Gomorrah, Cain, and Balaam, the false prophet of the Old Testament, and Korah who led the rebellion against Moses. They are spots in the believers' love feasts, clouds without water, trees with withered fruit, raging waves foaming out shame, wandering stars destined for eternal darkness. They are murmurers and complainers who walk after their own lusts, speaking great words, seeking admiration for their own advantage. The apostles warned that there would be mockers in the last time who do not have the Spirit. Such people will be judged for their ungodly deeds. To the believers Jude says, "Keep yourselves in the love of God, looking for the mercy of our Lord Jesus Christ to eternal life. And on some have compassion making a difference. And others save with fear, pulling them out of the fire, hating even the garment spotted by the flesh. Now to him who is able to keep you from falling and to present you faultless before the presence of his glory with great joy, to the only wise God our savior, be glory and majesty, dominion and power, now and ever. Amen."

REVELATION

THE REVELATION TO JOHN

The Apocalypse. The book of Revelation describes a vision which came to John the apostle while he was on the isle of Patmos, a small island off the coast of Asia Minor and presently under the dominion of Greece. The occurrences in the vision are highly symbolic in nature as are the visions related in the books of Daniel and Ezekiel. The 22 chapters of Revelation fall into four basic categories of subject matter.

Chapter 1 - 3 is a message from the risen Jesus to seven churches or congregations of varying degrees of adherence to Christian principles. Blessings to be bestowed on "overcomers" are described and warnings of chastisement given to evildoers who do not repent of their evil deeds.

Chapters 4 and 5 depict a scene of and around the throne of God in heaven and Jesus, the Lamb of God.

Chapters 6 - 20 picture horrendous events taking place in heaven and on a symbolic earth leading up to and including a great battle between God's forces and the evil forces of satan led by the "beast" and the "false prophet." God's army under the command of Jesus triumphs. The evil forces are defeated and cast into the Lake of Fire forever.

Chapters 21 and 22 describe the New Jerusalem, a beautiful and heavenly city where peace and joy abound. What John saw in his vision is to be imparted to the churches.

There is a great deal of interest today in what the book of Revelation might mean in terms of predictive history of future political and spiritual events. Many theories abound. It is not our purpose here to interpret along any particular line of theory; our effort is to relate the high points of the book in its own terms.

The Vision. "The revelation of Jesus Christ which God gave to him to show to his servants things which must soon come to pass which he sent and signified by his angel to his servant John who testified of the word of God and the testimony of Jesus Christ and of all things which he saw. Blessed is he who reads and those who hear the words of this prophecy and keep the things written in it, for the time is near."(Rev. 1:1-3)

Thus John brings the word from Jesus who will come with clouds and be seen by everyone, including those who pierced him, and they will mourn because of him. John is a fellow believer and companion in tribulation who while on the isle of Patmos for the word of God and testimony of Jesus and while in the Spirit on the Lord's day, hears a great voice like a trumpet saying, "I am the Alpha and Omega [first and last letters of the Greek alphabet; similar to saying, "I am the A and Z"], the first and last, and what you see write in a book and send it to the seven congregations which are in Asia, to Ephesus, to Smyrna, to Pergamum, to

Thyatira, to Sardis, to Philadelphia, and to Laodicea." Then
John sees seven candlesticks and a man wearing a long white
garment and a golden belt. His hair is white, and his eyes are as a
flame of fire. His feet are like polished brass and his voice as the
sound of many waters. In his mouth is a "two-edged sword" and
in his right hand, seven stars. His countenance shines like the
sun. John falls down before him, but the man says, "Fear not. I
am the Alpha and Omega, the first and the last. I am he who was
dead but lives; I am alive forever, amen, and have the keys of
hades and of death. Write the things which are and the things
which shall be hereafter: the mystery of the seven stars which you
saw in my right hand and the seven golden candlesticks. The
seven stars are the angels of the seven congregations, and the
seven candlesticks which you saw are the seven congregations."(Rev. 1)

The Message to the Seven Congregations. The Lord then
gives instructions on what John should write to each of these
Christian congregations. Five of them have backsliding problems. Two of them, Smyrna and Philadelphia, are holding fast
and are good examples. The problems outlined by Jesus are these:

Ephesus: In the main steadfast, but now have left their "first
love." They need to have a reawakening.

Pergamum: They hold fast the word but tolerate some in their
group given to idolatry and fornication; also, some hold to the
erroneous doctrines of the Nicolaitans.

Thyatira: They have good works, love, faith, and patience but
tolerate a self-ordained prophetess who misleads many into
idolatry and fornication.

Sardis: They have established a good reputation but are
actually a dead group spiritually, although there are a few
worthy exceptions.

Laodicea: "Lukewarm" is the word for these Christians; they
are neither hot nor cold, and the Lord will spew them out of
his mouth. They think they are something because they are
wealthy; whereas spiritually they are destitute.

Each of these congregations is told to repent or the Lord will come
quickly to discipline them with his righteousness by removing
their candlestick; by fighting evil with the sword of his mouth. He
says, "As many as I love, I reprove and discipline. Be zealous,
therefore, and repent."(See Heb. 12:6; Prov. 3:11)

The attributes of the congregations at Smyrna and Philadelphia:

Smyrna: This group is poor in material things but rich spiritually, for they are steadfast in the face of persecution. Satan may cause tribulation, but faithfulness to the death will assure them a crown of life.

Philadelphia: This congregation is faithful in every way. The Lord has an open door for them which cannot be shut. They have endured patiently and will be protected from the hour of temptation or trial to come upon the world.

Rewards for Overcomers. As to each of the seven congregations, the Lord gives an insight into the rewards to be granted to "overcomers" who are steadfast in the faith. An "overcomer" can be assured of these blessings:

To eat of the tree of life in the midst of the paradise of God.

To escape the second death.

To eat of the hidden manna and receive a white stone with a new name written on it which only the recipient will know.

To receive power over many nations.

To receive the morning star.

To be clothed in white.

To have his or her name kept in the book of life.

To have his or her name confessed by Jesus before his Father and his angels.

To be made a pillar in the temple of God.

To have written upon him or her the name of God and the name of the new heavenly city, the new Jerusalem.

To sit with Jesus on his throne, even as he has overcome and is seated with his Father on his throne.

For everyone, he says, "Behold, I stand at the door and knock. If anyone hears my voice and opens the door, I will come in to him, and will sup with him, and he with me. . . . He that has an ear, let him hear what the spirit says to the congregations."(Rev. 2 - 3)

God's Throne. After these instructions, John while still in the Spirit receives a vision of a throne set in heaven. One is seated on the throne having the appearance of agate-like stone. There is a rainbow around the stone like an emerald. Twenty-four elders dressed in white, having golden crowns are seated about the throne. From the throne there is lightning and thundering. The floor is like a sea of crystal glass. Four living creatures are before the throne with wings and many eyes. All are giving glory, honor, and thanks to the one who sits on the throne, who lives forever. The elders bow before him, cast their crowns before the throne and say, "You are worthy, O Lord, to receive glory and honor and power, for you have created all things and for your pleasure they are and were created."(Rev. 4)

The Book with Seven Seals. In the right hand of God is a book which is sealed with seven seals (as a letter or document might be sealed with sealing wax). An angel loudly proclaims, "Who is worthy to open the book and remove the seals?" John weeps at the knowledge that no human is worthy to open this book. But an elder assures him that one of Judah and the root of David is worthy and will open the book and remove the seals. In the midst of the elders stands a lamb with the appearance of having been slain, having seven horns and seven eyes, representing the seven spirits of God sent forth to all the earth. The Lamb takes the book, and the four creatures and the elders fall down before him, each one having harps and golden vials (or bowls) full of incense which are the prayers of the saints. They sing a new song, "Worthy are you to take the book and break its seals, for you were slain and did purchase for God with your blood those from every tribe, tongue, people, and nation, and you have made them to be kings and priests to our God, and they will reign upon the earth." Then John sees that there are millions of angels, creatures, and elders surrounding the throne, and they are all saying with a loud voice, "Worthy is the Lamb that was slain to receive power, and riches, and wisdom, and might, and honor, and glory, and blessing." And he hears, as it were, all creation saying, "Blessing and honor and glory and power be to him that sits on the throne and to the Lamb for ever and ever."(Rev. 5)

The Lamb of God Removes the Seals. Next John sees the Lamb remove one of the seals from the book, and a white horse and rider appear, the rider having a bow and a crown and going forth to conquer. The second seal is removed, and there is a red horse whose rider has a sword and the power to take peace from the earth. Removal of the third seal brings forth a black horse whose rider has a set of scales in his hand. One of the four creatures says, "A measure of wheat for a penny, and three measures of barley for a penny, and see that you do not hurt the oil and the wine." The fourth seal is opened, and there is a pale horse with a rider named Death. Hades follows after him, and authority is given over a fourth of the earth to kill by sword, by hunger, by death, and by the beasts of the earth. The fifth seal is broken, and John sees beneath the altar the souls of those martyred for the sake of the word of God and for their testimony. They cry out, asking when their deaths will be avenged. Each one receives a white robe, and they are told to rest until they and others have been fulfilled. The sixth seal is opened followed by a great earthquake. The sun darkens. The moon becomes red. The stars fall from heaven to earth. Everyone on earth, including kings, the great and the rich, hide in rocks and caves to hide from the wrath of God and the Lamb.(Rev. 6)   Then John has a vision of four angels standing at the four corners of the earth holding back the wind. Another angel cries out not to hurt the earth or the sea or the trees until the servants of God are sealed with seals placed on their foreheads. Then are sealed 144,000, that is, 12,000 from each of the 12 tribes of Israel. And about the throne are multitudes wearing white robes. An elder tells John that these are those who came out of the great tribulation, their robes washed white in the blood of the Lamb. God and the Lamb care for them and wipe away every tear.(Rev. 7)

The Last Seal; Seven Trumpets. The seventh seal is removed from the book by the Lamb, and there is silence in heaven for about half an hour. Seven angels stand before God, and each is given a trumpet. Another angel offers up incense, that is, the prayers of the saints, from a golden censer. Then the censer is filled with fire which is thrown to the earth, and there are voices, thunderings, lightnings, and earthquakes. As each angel blows his trumpet, a different event is brought before John.

First trumpet: Hail, fire, and blood cast upon the earth burning up one-third of the trees and all the grass.

Second trumpet: A burning mountain is cast into the sea, and one-third of the sea becomes blood and one-third of the sea life and one-third of the ships are destroyed.

Third trumpet: A great star named Wormwood falls from heaven, and one-third of the waters become wormwood (poisonous), and many die from it.

Fourth trumpet: A third part of the sun, moon, and stars is darkened. An angel flying through heaven warns of the trumpets yet to sound.(Rev. 8)

Fifth trumpet: A star falls into a bottomless pit, and locusts come forth from the pit to torment those who do not have the seal of God on their foreheads. These locusts are like horses with human faces having a lion's teeth and wearing gold crowns. They have breastplates and scorpion tails. Their leader, Abaddon (Greek, Apollyon), is the angel of the bottomless pit.

Sixth trumpet: Four angels bound in the Euphrates River are let loose; they are prepared to kill one-third of the people. And there appears an army of 200,000 men with lions' heads on horseback. This army goes forth and kills one-third of the population, but those people not killed refuse to repent of their gross immoralities and crimes.(Rev. 9)   Another angel comes to John carrying a small book. John is ordered not to write anything until all is revealed in the days of the seventh angel. Instead, John is told to eat the small book, which he does. As predicted by the angel, it tastes sweet as honey, but in his stomach, it is bitter. It is then revealed to John that he will prophesy again before many people, nations, and kings.(Rev. 10)   He is given a measuring rod and told to measure the temple. He is not to measure the court of the Gentiles, because they will tread upon the holy city for 42 months. But two witnesses will preach for 1260 days. These witnesses have great authority, but the beast from the bottomless pit will kill them, and their bodies will lie in the street of the great city called spiritually Sodom and Egypt where the Lord was crucified. All peoples and nations will see their bodies for three and a half days. Then God will revitalize them and return them to heaven. Those witnessing this will fear. There will be a great earthquake destroying a tenth of the city and killing 7,000 men. The rest will fear and give glory to God.(Rev. 11:1-14)

Seventh trumpet: Great voices give praise to God and his Christ. The 24 elders worship God, giving thanks and prophesying that the time has come that the dead be judged, rewards given to the prophets and saints, and those destroyed who are destroying the earth. Then the temple of God is opened and the Ark of the Covenant can be seen.(Rev. 11:15-19)   A great sign appears in heaven, a woman clothed with the sun, the moon at her feet, and a crown of 12 stars on her head. She is travailing with child. Another great sign appears in heaven, a huge red dragon with seven crowned heads and 10 horns. His tail sweeps a third of the stars down to earth. The dragon stands before the woman to devour her child as soon as it is born. A man-child is born who is to rule all nations with a rod of iron, and he is taken up to God and his throne. The woman flees from the dragon to a place prepared by God where she will be nourished for 1260 days. Then there is war in heaven. Michael and his angels cast out the dragon, "that old serpent, called the devil and satan who deceives the whole world." He is cast to earth, and his angels are cast out with him. Then a loud voice from heaven declares that salvation has come, the kingdom of God and the power of his Christ, for the accuser of the brethren has been cast down. They overcome by the blood of the Lamb and by the word of their testimony. The devil comes to the people of the earth with great wrath, for he has but a short time. But the dragon continues to persecute the woman. She is given wings of an eagle to fly where she can be nourished "for a time, and times, and a half of time." The great serpent issues a flood from his mouth to drown her, but the earth opens her mouth and swallows the flood. The dragon is angry and goes to make war on those of her children who keep the commandments of God and hold to the teachings of Jesus Christ.(Rev. 12)

Two Beasts and the Dragon. As John is standing by the seashore, he sees a beast with seven heads and 10 horns rise from the sea. On each head is the name "blasphemy." His body is that of a leopard, his feet those of a bear, his mouth that of a lion. The dragon gives the beast his power and authority, which is his for 42 months. One of the heads has been wounded but healed. The world is amazed at the beast and follows him. People worship the dragon which gave the power to the beast, and they also worship the beast who blasphemes God and wars against the saints and overcomes them. Everyone whose name is not in the book of life will worship him. Thus the perseverance of the saints lies in their faith. Then another beast comes out of the earth having two horns like a lamb. He performs great signs and deceives the people of the earth. He forces everyone to worship the beast with the wounded head and even makes an idol which looks like the first beast. He is also able to give the idol life and the ability to speak. Anyone who does not worship the image is killed. He causes everyone to have a mark on his or her forehead or hand, and anyone without the mark, or the name of the beast, or the number 666, the number of the beast, cannot buy or sell.(Rev. 13)

A Warning against Taking the Mark of the Beast. But then John sees a Lamb on Mount Zion with 144,000 having his Father's name on their foreheads. A voice like many harps playing comes from heaven, and they are singing a new song which only the 144,000 redeemed from the earth could learn. These are virgin men, the first fruits for God and the Lamb. They have no guile and are without fault before God. An angel is seen flying through heaven preaching fear of God and imminent judgment. Another angel is saying, "Babylon is fallen, is fallen, because she made all nations drink of the wine of fornication." A third angel follows, saying that if anyone worships the beast and the idol and receives the mark of the beast, he or she will suffer greatly. But the saints who keep the commandments of God and the faith of Jesus will persevere. A voice is heard saying to John, "Write, 'Blessed are the dead who die in the Lord hereafter. Yes, says the spirit, that they may rest from their labors, and their works do follow them.' " Then John sees a white cloud upon which is seated one like the son of man with a golden crown and a sharp sickle. He and angels with sickles thrust them into the earth and reap a harvest of grapes which are cast into the great winepress of the wrath of God. The winepress is trodden outside the city, and blood comes forth as high as a horse's bridle for 200 miles.(Rev. 14)

Seven Vials of Wrath. Another sign is seen in heaven, seven angels having the seven last plagues in which the wrath of God is finished. And on the sea of glass are those who have triumphed over the beast, his image, and his work. They sing a song of Moses and of the Lamb, extolling almighty God as king of all nations; his righteous acts are revealed; he will be worshiped by all. The angels are given seven golden vials (or bowls) full of the wrath of God.(Rev. 15)   A voice is heard from the temple directing the angels to pour out the vials of wrath upon the earth.

First vial: Sores upon those having the mark of the beast and those who worship his image.

Second vial: The sea becomes blood, and every creature in the sea dies.

Third vial: The rivers become blood signifying judgment on those who killed the saints and the prophets.

Fourth vial: Poured out on the sun and burning those who do not repent even after being burned.

Fifth vial: Poured out on the seat of the beast causing darkness, and they gnaw their tongues because of pain but do not repent of their deeds.

Sixth vial: Poured out on the river Euphrates, drying it up so that kings from the east may be prepared. Three unclean spirits like frogs come out of the mouths of the dragon, the beast, and the false prophet. These evil spirits go forth to gather kings of the earth into the battle of the great day of God Almighty who says, "Behold, I come as a thief. Blessed is he that watches and keeps his garments, lest he walk naked and men see his shame." And he gathered them together into a place called Armageddon (or Har-Magedon, NASB).

Seventh vial: Poured into the air. A voice from the temple proclaims, "It is done." There are lightning flashes, thunder, and a tremendous earthquake. The "great city" is divided into three parts, the cities of the nations fall; wrath falls upon Babylon; islands flee and mountains disappear; huge hail-stones fall on blasphemous men.(Rev. 16)

The Great Harlot Is Judged. One of the angels carries John away in the Spirit to show him the judgment upon the great harlot who sits upon many waters, with whom kings committed fornication and by whom inhabitants of earth become drunk with the wine of her fornication. John sees a woman seated on a scarlet beast with seven heads and 10 horns, full of names of blasphemy. The woman is richly arrayed in scarlet and purple, gold and jewels, and holds a golden cup full of abominations. On her forehead is a name: "MYSTERY, BABYLON THE GREAT, THE MOTHER OF HARLOTS, AND ABOMINATIONS OF THE EARTH." She is drunk with the blood of saints and martyrs of Jesus. The beast carrying the woman will come out of the bottomless pit and is destined for destruction. Those whose names are not in the book of life will wonder about the beast. Its seven heads represent seven mountains on which the woman sits and seven kings, five of whom have fallen. One is, and one will come and remain a little while. The beast is an eighth king who will be destroyed. The 10 horns represent 10 kings without kingdoms who receive authority with the beast for one hour. But they all give the authority to the beast. These make war with the Lamb who will defeat them, for he is Lord of lords and King of kings. He will be accompanied by the faithful. The waters upon which the woman was seated are multitudes of people. The 10 horns hate the harlot and will eat her flesh and burn her. They will be fulfilling God's will and accordingly will give their kingdoms to the beast until the words of God are fulfilled. The woman represents "that great city which reigns over the kings of the earth."(Rev. 17)

Babylon Is Fallen. As John's vision continues, another angel comes down from heaven with great power, lighting the earth with his glory, and proclaiming, "Babylon the great is fallen, is fallen, and is become the habitation of devils and the hold of every foul spirit." No one will partake of her merchandise, her fineries, or abundance. There is great lamentation by those who did business with her and revelled in her pleasures. There may now be rejoicing by heaven, the prophets, and apostles, because God has avenged them against her. Babylon, in whom is found the blood of prophets, saints, and martyrs on the earth, is finished.(Rev. 18)

Rejoicing in Heaven; the Beast, the False Prophet, the Lake of Fire. Then John hears a great voice of many people in heaven rejoicing, giving honor and glory to God for his judgment upon the great harlot. The 24 elders and the four creatures fall down and worship God on his throne. A mighty voice proclaims the marriage of the Lamb whose bride has made herself ready, arrayed in fine linen, clean and white, the fine linen of the righteousness of the saints. John is directed by a saint to write, "Blessed are they who are called to the marriage supper of the Lamb." John falls at his feet to worship him, but he says, "Not that. I am your fellow servant and of your brethren that have the testimony of Jesus. Worship God, for the testimony of Jesus is the spirit of prophecy." At this, heaven opens and reveals Jesus mounted on a white horse leading the heavenly armies clothed in white and riding white horses. His name is "The Word of God." He has a sharp sword which proceeds from his mouth to smite the nations over whom he will rule with a rod of iron; he who treads the winepress of the fierceness and wrath of almighty God. On his garment a name is written: "KING OF KINGS AND LORD OF LORDS." The beast and kings of the earth with their armies are gathered for battle. But the forces of the one on the white horse overcome them. The beast and the false prophet, who had deceived those with the mark of the beast and those who worshiped the idol, are cast into the lake of fire. The rest are slain by the sword of him who sits on the white horse.(Rev. 19)

Dragon Sealed in Bottomless Pit; Jesus Defeats Forces of Evil. In his vision John sees an angel descend from heaven having the key to the bottomless pit and a great chain. He lays hold of the dragon, that old serpent the devil and satan, binds him for a thousand years, casts him into the bottomless pit, and seals him there. He shall not deceive the nations until the time when he will be released for a little season. John sees thrones, and judgment is given to those who sit upon them; he sees the souls of those who were beheaded for the witness of Jesus and the word of God, those who refused to worship the beast or his image or to take his mark, and they live and reign with Christ for a thousand years. The rest of the dead do not live again until the thousand years are finished. This is the first resurrection. They are priests of God and Christ and are to reign with him for a thousand years. At the end of this period, satan will be released to deceive the nations, that is, Gog and Magog, to gather them for battle against the saints and the beloved city. But God will destroy them with fire from heaven, and the devil will be cast into the lake of fire, along with the beast and false prophet. Then John has a vision of a great white throne, and the dead, great and small, are standing before God. The books are open, along with the book of life, and the dead are judged of the things written in the books concerning their works. The sea gives up the dead in it. Death and Hades are cast into the lake of fire. This is the second death. Whoever is not in the book of life is cast into the lake of fire.(Rev. 20)

New Heaven, New Earth, New Jerusalem, All Things New. An angel carries John in the Spirit to a high mountain, and he sees a new heaven and a new earth, for the first have passed away, and there is no more sea. A new Jerusalem comes down from God as a bride adorned for her husband. A great voice says that God will dwell with his people and be their God. He will wipe away every tear, and there will be no more death, pain, or sorrow, for the former things have passed away. He who is seated on the throne says, "Behold, I make all things new. Write, for these words are true and faithful. It is done. I am Alpha and Omega, the beginning and the end, the first and the last. I will give to him who thirsts of the fountain of the water of life freely. He who overcomes shall inherit all things. I will be his God, and he shall be my son. But the fearful and unbelieving and the abominable and murderers and the immoral and sorcerers and idolaters and all liars shall have their part in the lake which burns with fire and brimstone, which is the second death." After this, John is carried away in the Spirit by the angel to show him the new Jerusalem. It is a large, walled city with 12 gates of pearl. The streets are made of golden glass, and all the buildings and walls are made of jewels and precious stones. It has no temple, because the Lord God Almighty and the Lamb are the temple. Their glory provides perpetual light. It is forever open to those who are saved, those whose names are written in the Lamb's book of life. But nothing which would defile can enter the city.(Rev. 21)

The River of Life, the Tree of Life; Even So, Come, Lord Jesus. From the throne of God and the Lamb flows a pure river of the water of life, clear as crystal. A tree of life grows in the middle of the street, and it bears 12 kinds of fruit, yielding a crop every month. The leaves are for healing the people. There is no more curse. God's servants will see his face, and they shall bear his name on their foreheads; they shall reign with him forever. The angel speaks to John, saying that the words are true; that the Lord has sent his angel to show his servants the things which must shortly be done, for the Lord has said, "Behold, I come quickly. Blessed is he who keeps the words of the prophecy of this book." And John is not to seal the book, because the time is at hand. The Lord has said also that he comes to give everyone rewards according to deeds. Thus blessed are those who do his commandments, for they have the right to the tree of life and may enter into the gates of the city. Outside are the immoral, the wicked, the sorcerers, the murderers, and those who practice lying. And the Lord says, "I, Jesus, have sent my angel to testify to you these things in the congregations. I am the root and offspring of David and the bright and morning star." John writes, "And the Spirit and the bride say, 'Come.' And let him who thirsts come. And whoever will, let him take the water of life freely." If anyone adds or takes away anything from this book, that person will suffer discipline. "He who testifies says, 'Surely I come quickly.' Amen. Even so, come, Lord Jesus. The grace of our Lord Jesus Christ be with you all. Amen."(Rev. 22)

CHART **H**

PERIOD OF NEW TESTAMENT WRITING
IN RELATION TO NEW TESTAMENT HISTORY

(Not to scale)

A.D. 95

A.D. 95

Post New
Testament
Period
Early
"Church
Fathers"

Revelation
Vision of
John
(A.D. 95)

Growth of
Christian
Congrega-
tions
Persecution
(A.D. 64-95)

Period of Writing
of 27
New Testament Books
(A.D. 47-95)

Holy Spirit
Apostles
Evangelism
Journeys of
Peter & Paul
Governors
Felix & Festus
Herod
Agrippa
(A.D. 30-64)

Jesus' Death
on the Cross
Resurrection
Post Resurrec-
tion Teaching
(A.D. 30)

A.D. 47

Public Ministry
of Jesus
John the Baptist
Disciples
Apostles
Pontius Pilate
Sanhedrin
Herod
Antipas
(A.D. 27-30)

Birth of
Jesus
Christ
(6 B.C.)

Intertesta-
mental
Period
Augustus
Caesar
Herod I

243

FURTHER READING AND STUDY

A renowned preacher of the 13th century, Bernard of Clairvaux, once remarked that there were even then so many books about the Bible that he much preferred to just read the Bible. Today thousands of books on biblical subjects are available in bookstores and libraries. But as Bernard said, there is no substitute for reading the Bible itself. The reader may ask how one should approach the reading or study of scripture. Where or how do you start? Some say to start at the beginning with the book of Genesis; others say to start with John's Gospel; still others, with Matthew's Gospel. We would say that now, having read what is in this book, the reader has an overall view of the thrust and progression of the biblical message and is in a position to begin reading or study at any point the reader may wish. The 10 chapters can serve as an outline for a planned program or as a key for occasional reading. While we are on this subject, let's think about some of the motivations one may have in going to the Good Book.

1. **Devotional reading** for personal communion with God, for spiritual awareness and comprehension of self-worth, for peace and consolation. In seminary our professors frequently reminded us students not to be so caught up in our biblical studies that we overlooked our own devotional reading and meditation.

2. **Study reading** to gain understanding of the Bible and its principles. This could include studies of particular books of the Bible, persons of the Bible, or other topical approaches. This type of study can be done individually or in a group.

3. **Problem-solving reading,** seeking answers for problems or questions arising from daily life, including both personal and interpersonal situations, personal goals, health, and healing; this type of reading and study is used in counseling and involves correlating passages dealing with the type of problem presented and applying these passages in a practical way.

4. **Memory reading** for memorization of significant passages. Many study programs include memory verses, and this is a popular way of teaching children. Some people have difficulty with rote memorization, including this writer. Let me

suggest something which has helped me. In addition to study and perhaps reading or saying a verse or verses out loud a number of times, try writing the passage and its scriptural reference repeatedly until you have it. Sometimes writing a verse in this way helps program it into your memory. Having certain key verses memorized will prove profitable when a question or problem confronts you suddenly.

There is a sense in which these purposes and methods may overlap, for discovery of truth in scripture may occur whenever and for whatever reason a person reads the Bible. Often a person will say, "I've read this passage many times and didn't catch that point before." This illustrates the thought that the application of a particular passage depends upon the question, the problem, or the fact-situation on the reader's mind as he or she reads scripture.

Bible Versions and Other Study Materials. I suggest that a person interested in pursuing the Bible further have at least two versions. For those whose language is English, consider the King James (Authorized) version and another version in more modern language. As I remarked in Chapter TWO, it's hard to surpass KJV in its rendition of the Psalms, Proverbs, and other poetic passages. A modern-language version, such as the New American Standard Bible (NASB), the Revised Standard version (RSV), the New International version (NIV), the Good News Bible, or the New American Bible (NAB: Catholic), provides the reader with the latest translation work of Bible scholars. Of course, Bibles are available in other languages, and the number of versions may vary. If price is a problem, one may look into Bibles available from the American Bible Society, P.O. Box 5601, Grand Central Station, New York, NY 10163. The society carries the Good News Bible, the KJV, the RSV, and the NIV, as well as Bibles in Spanish, French, German, Italian, and some Asian and American Indian languages. In addition to a Bible or Bibles, I would recommend a Bible dictionary or encyclopedia. Good ones may be obtained at book stores, and some come in paperback editions at a relatively low cost.

We have mentioned the interlinear New Testament before and would again mention that we have found the "Interlinear Greek-English New Testament" by George R. Berry to be very useful in finding literal translations of words and passages. You don't have to know Greek in order to use it, because the English meaning is under every Greek word. Instructions and footnotes help you to determine word order if you want to precise a sentence.

Another type of study help is the commentary. A commentary is a review and analysis of a book of the Bible, most often on a verse-by-verse basis. There are numerous commentaries available on each book of the Bible. Some are general in scope; others are of a more technical nature, many including studies of particular Hebrew or Greek words. One value of a commentary is that an author usually considers passages from other books of the Bible bearing on the subject under discussion. In using a commentary, it is well to keep in mind that the author is also giving the reader his or her opinion or point of view.

A concordance is another helpful book. It is a compilation of words used in the Bible arranged in alphabetical order. For each word it sets forth a portion of a verse containing the word and the name of the book and chapter and verse numbers. A concordance helps to locate a passage where one has only a part of it or even only one word. The best known of these is "Cruden's Concordance" for the KJV. "Strong's Concordance" is another for the KJV. Concordances are published for the NASB and several other Bible versions.

Another device which assists in the study of the four Gospels is a "harmony of the Gospels." In a harmony, the actual text of the Gospels is set out in side-by-side columns so that one may "harmonize" the action and the message as recorded in each Gospel. Those portions of a Gospel having no parallel in another Gospel are placed singly in a chronological sequence.

It is our hope that you will go on from this point with your own personal study of scripture and that this book has been a help in that direction.

Maranatha!

FBF Publications (located at 5695 McKinley Ave., P.O. Box 3296, San Bernardino, CA 92413) is a publishing effort to assist in the work of the FAMILY BIBLE FOUNDATION, INC., a non-profit religious corporation. The FOUNDATION's purpose is to promote greater understanding of the Bible and biblical principles. The profit margin for WHAT YOU SHOULD KNOW ABOUT THE BIBLE, which is kept as low as possible, will help to sustain publication of this book and the publication of other proposed study materials.

Additional copies of WHAT YOU SHOULD KNOW ABOUT THE BIBLE may be ordered by sending a check or money order for $12.50 per copy to FBF Publications at the address shown below. An order form is provided for your use. Perhaps you may wish to remove this page along the perforations on the left and pass it along to someone else. (Information on quantity rates is available on request.)

ORDER FORM

TO: FBF PUBLICATIONS,
    P.O. Box 3296, San Bernardino, CA 92413

Please send me _____ copies of WHAT YOU SHOULD KNOW ABOUT THE BIBLE. I am enclosing my check or money order for $12.50 per copy, which I understand includes shipping costs and any applicable sales tax.

NAME: _____

Number & Street _____Apt. No._____

P.O. Box No. _____

City & State _____

ZIP No. _____

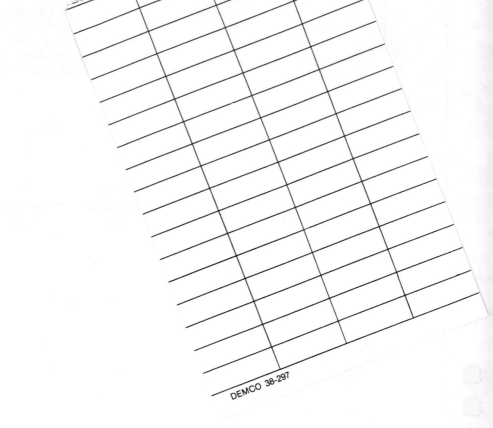

DATE DUE

DEMCO 38-297